CHANGE MYTHS

This page left intentionally blank

CHANGE MYTHS

The Professional's Guide to
Separating Sense from Nonsense

PAUL GIBBONS and TRICIA KENNEDY

ISBN 978-0-997-651287

Publisher: Phronesis Media | Denver, Colorado, USA
Senior developmental editor: Kelli Collins
Copy editor and proofreader: Tricia Kennedy
Diagrams: Andrés Goldstein and Tricia Kennedy
Cover design: Tricia Kennedy
Interior: Priya Paulraj and Tricia Kennedy

ALSO PUBLISHED BY PHRONESIS MEDIA

Leading Change in the Digital Age series

Book I: *The Science of Organizational Change: How Leaders Set Strategy, Change Behaviors, and Create Agile Cultures* (2nd edition, 2019)

Book II: *Impact: 21st-Century Change Management, Behavioral Science, and the Future of Work* (1st edition, 2019)

Book III: *Change Myths: The Professional's Guide to Separating Sense from Nonsense* (1st edition, 2023)

Humanizing Business series

Book I: *The Spirituality of Work and Leadership: Finding Joy, Meaning, and Purpose in What You Do* (1st edition, 2020)

Book II: *Culture, Capitalism, and Sustainability: A Guide for Purposeful, Ethical Businesses* (due 2023)

PRAISE FOR *CHANGE MYTHS*

Change Myths *exposes how many of the methods change leaders rely upon as truths are often handed down pseudoscience; the book shows why change experts have a responsibility to revisit the evidence behind what they recommend.*

MIKE ISKANDARYAN, WORKFORCE STRATEGIST AND AGILE CHANGE, MCKINSEY & CO.

Not afraid to revisit some urban myths about [how to] change? This book is superb at debunking some of the most accepted models. No one is safe, and I like it! Paul and Tricia have added to the field of change, bringing rigor to more scientific backing in management and leadership. While all great ideas might be great in their time and context, this book brings critical insights to upgrade your game in making change happen.

YVES VAN DURME, GLOBAL HEAD OF ORGANIZATIONAL TRANSFORMATION, DELOITTE

This book is brilliant. It challenged my thinking and beliefs, decades of organizational change practices, and how I interpreted my own experiences—a healthy reconsideration of the "truths" about change that will improve the field of organizational change.

WAYNE RESCHKE, FORMER SVP, CHRO ALLIANT ENERGY

Reading this book feels like the end of a bad relationship. You fall in love, embrace the highs, ignore the lows, then it all suddenly comes crashing down over Mexican takeout, tears, and some "Chad" driving her away in a black Mustang. Then, with a lot of real talk with your friends, you find a better you and maybe, just maybe, the love of your life. Paul and Tricia are your friends. They get it. The change models of yore—change curves, pseudoscience, and pithy axioms—are comfortable and feel good. But as you'll find out (if you haven't already), they can be destructive, gaslighting bullies. There's a better, more straightforward, and more positive way that refocuses on the people and narratives right in front of you.

SERGE ROMERO, FORMER HEAD OF M&A INTEGRATION AND BUSINESS TRANSFORMATION, FORTIS LIFE SCIENCES

PRAISE FOR EARLIER BOOKS IN THE LEADING CHANGE SERIES

Paul has the broadest, deepest, and most current knowledge and experience in change of any thought leader that I track, and I consider myself an avid learner. Paul has been "at the coal face" of change, doing the heavy lifting, and still managed to build and deliver real innovation that drives business value, which, for my money, is the real acid test of credibility. Paul has an uncanny ability to stretch across several adjacent domains to connect dots, spot incongruences, and showcase opportunities for moving forward. He breaks through old molds and offers new ways of thinking about and delivering change.

GAIL SEVERINI, PRINCIPAL, SYMPHINI CHANGE MANAGEMENT

Gibbons towers above business thinkers in the way that Drucker did in an earlier era. Even Drucker did not bring to business thinking the breadth of scholarship and originality of thought that Gibbons does.

ROBERT ENTENMANN, FORMER GLOBAL HEAD OF MARKETS, ABN AMRO

ABOUT THE AUTHORS

Paul Gibbons

Paul Gibbons is a partner at IBM Consulting—a thought leader and futurist on behavioral science, culture, leadership, and the future of work. He previously advised PricewaterhouseCoopers (PwC), KPMG, and Deloitte on talent, culture, and leadership.

From 2010-2020, he was on the keynote circuit across five continents, speaking on the future of business: Humanizing business, leading change, culture change, ethics, and the future of work. During that decade, he was also an adjunct professor of business ethics and leadership at several U.S. business schools.

He previously authored five books, most prominently *The Science of Organizational Change* and *Impact*, the first two books in the *Leading Change in the Digital Age* series. Those books birthed the conversation about change mythology. The first volume of his *Humanizing Business* series, *The Spirituality of Work and Leadership*, was published in 2021.

After "experimental careers" in computer science, derivatives trading, economics, and neuroscience, Paul spent eight years as a consultant at PwC before founding Future Considerations. That firm became Europe's top leadership consulting firm working with Shell, BP, PwC, KPMG, Barclays, and HSBC on leadership, strategy, and culture change.

Paul is a fellow of the Royal Society of Arts, a hyperpolyglot, ranked a "top-20 culture guru," and CEO "super coach" by CEO Magazine. In 2000, he was elected to the U.S. Academy of Management Council, and he is a member of the American Philosophical Association, the American Association for the Advancement of Science, and the Institute for Business Ethics.

He lives in the Denver area with his two sons and enjoys competing internationally at mind sports such as poker, bridge, MOBA, and chess. (You can catch him on television from time-to-time.)

Paul's favorite quotes

> *"True glory consists in doing what deserves to be written, in writing what deserves to be read, and in so living as to make the world happier and better for our living in it."*
> **PLINY THE ELDER**

> *"Extraordinary claims require extraordinary evidence."*
> **CARL SAGAN**

Tricia Kennedy (she/her)

Tricia is the founder and principal consultant at Kennedy Consulting Services, LLC (TriciaK.com), a boutique organizational change and leadership consulting firm that helps businesses excel through inclusive, human-centered, and evidence-based strategies and practices. She is known for her inclusive and collaborative style, inquisitive and reflective approach, and humble commitment to challenging the status quo in a quest for continuous improvement.

With over 15 years of experience, she is a seasoned enabler and facilitator of organizational change who specializes in a holistic change approach and a creative blend of art and science from multiple disciplines to deliver sustainable results. She has advised and worked with various clients over the years, including Microsoft, Medtronic, BNSF Railway, Lexus, Sony Pictures Entertainment, and Goldman Sachs.

Tricia's journey to a career in organizational change and leadership started with stints in graphic and web design, copywriting, and public relations for the entertainment industry. She then followed her lifelong fascination with and passion for the human condition to graduate school, where she discovered organizational change and evidence-based practice.

She is based in the Dallas-Fort Worth metroplex in North Texas, where she enjoys spending time with her partner, cats, and family, laughing and finding humor in this crazy journey called life. *Change Myths* is her first published work.

Tricia's favorite quotes

"Nobody has a monopoly on wisdom. Experts are sometimes wrong, and blowhards are sometimes right. Even in the internet age, the best response to a bad argument is a better one."

THE ECONOMIST (APRIL 2022)

"In the most devilishly wicked learning environments, the experience will reinforce the exact wrong reasons .... It doesn't take much to throw experienced pros off course."

DAVID EPSTEIN (*RANGE*, 2019)

ACKNOWLEDGMENTS

Alex Boulting. This book briefly began as a collaboration with Alex Boulting, one of the UK's most knowledgeable and experienced change management consultants—a leading voice in the future of organizational change. Alex has a passion for science and evidence-based management, and his blog series Mythbusters is a must-read on LinkedIn (find Alex at ebbnflow.co.uk).

Kelli Collins. In a fortuitous online encounter, Kelli and Paul met on LinkedIn. Paul had worked with editors at major publishing firms who were reputed to be the best in their fields, yet he found none were close to Kelli's grasp of how concepts should flow together and her eye for grammatical precision. Kelli devotedly edited Paul's book *The Spirituality of Work and Leadership*, which appeared in 2021. Kelli edited this book and helps manage its marketing and public relations while working full-time as an editor.

It takes a village. The chapters within were reviewed by dozens of change experts from around the world to whom we are deeply grateful: Paul Hughes, Koen Smets, Adam Gold, Wayne Reschke, Rob Briner, Alan Arnett, Paul Thoresen, Gail Severini, Gervase Bushe, Kelly Monahan, and Andrew Arora. Despite their generosity, the errors remain ours.

Paul's special thanks go to Dan Sweeney, a mentor and dear friend who passed away while this book was in its final stages. Dan was a senior executive at IBM and founder of several business ethics non-profits and is no doubt smiling that Paul now works at his cherished *alma mater*. Paul is thankful for the support of his colleagues at IBM who reviewed many drafts, particularly for the support of Amy Wright and the Enterprise Change community. His previous colleagues at Deloitte, Yves van Durme, Chris Norman, James Healy, and Lee Merovitz provided many insights from the coal face.

Paul's writing life would be less fun without his two sons, Conor and Luca; and his friends from the poker and crypto worlds, Dan Blum, Chris Moon, and Clayton Hamm.

Tricia's special shoutouts start with Peter R. Giulioni. It was Peter who first introduced her to the organizational change world almost 20 years ago. His guidance, support, and taking Tricia under his wing set her firmly onto a career path in change. She remains grateful for his early nudge into the deep end and ongoing support over the years.

There were and are many bumps in Tricia's road. She thanks those who both had her back and who held her up, especially her family and Vanessa Meier, Joseph Corri, Lauren Guido, Catherine Pasini, Will Goldberg (@IWillGoTravel), Justin Lew, Dianna Morrison, Maui Williams, Ken Perlman (CultureSync), Trish McManus, and Hiram Quinones (may he rest in peace).

Another shoutout goes to folks along the way who gave generously of their time when a stranger sought their experience and wisdom. Their readiness and willingness to not only listen and share, but also to challenge ideas with grace and kindness was a gift for which she is always grateful. Now, some of these strangers are friends. Paul is one of these folks, and Tricia is grateful to be his co-author, friend, and overall professional partner in crime. In this vein, special shoutouts are due to Daron K. Roberts (@CoachDKR #StayInTheDeepEnd),

David Wilkinson (*Oxford Review*), and Gordy Curphy (leadership is a team sport).

Lastly, Tricia thanks Steven Werther for bringing joy and laughter to her daily life and making her a better person.

TABLE OF CONTENTS

FIGURE LIST

FOREWORD

STEVEN TEN HAVE

Prof. dr., partner at TEN HAVE Change
Management, and supervisory board at
Center for Evidence-Based Management (CEBMa)

Change management is a discipline, scientific practice, and craft with both a mission and a moral obligation. Standing on the shoulders of leading thinkers like Kurt Lewin, James Q. Wilson, and Edgar H. Schein, change management scientists and practitioners must contribute to making this world a better place.

Science and the available evidence are essential ingredients—experiment and trial-and-error are sometimes a necessary, or even only, option. However, from a professional moral, societal, and human perspective carelessness, nonchalance, and lack of prudence are unacceptable.

Errors may be made, but they are unacceptable if they are the result of ignoring the best available evidence or the unwillingness to seek further evidence before acting. Workers have a vital interest and emotional vulnerability because of their dependence on leaders getting change right. Dedicated change professionals work in a respectful, responsible, and people-oriented way with the best evidence they can gather to deploy in their selection of interventions.

Therefore, busting change myths and separating sense from nonsense in a professional, evidence-based, and dedicated way is helpful and more than welcome, not simply necessary. In parallel, much economic, social, and emotional damage, as well as opportunity loss, is created by false prophets, would-be-professionals, and opportunistic and 'lazy' practitioners taking advantage of other people by selling their books, spreading their ideas, and being paid for bad consultancy. Every scientist and professional in the field must study the available evidence to treat organizations and people in change processes in the best possible way. They should take, as Noam Chomsky said, "a course in intellectual self-defense."

Change Myths takes and fuels the evidence-based perspective in a dedicated and contributing way. It would be a real asset in any intellectual self-defense course manual. *Change Myths* is critical and reflective, but also provides insights and guidelines that will help the practice of change management in a significant way.

PREFACE

KELLY MONAHAN, PH.D.
Future of Work director at Meta

Since Frederick Taylor introduced time-and-motion studies in the 1920s, using a scientific lens to inform management decision making has been a Sisyphean quest. The need to bring data and science into an otherwise subjective discipline persists today.

The unfortunate part of Taylor's legacy is that he lost sight of the humans driven by the complex interplay of emotions, intrinsic motivations, and need for affiliation—factors challenging to quantify.

While we have made tremendous progress in our technological tools and methods, we have done little to blend a humane **and** scientific approach to management—where data and science inform how we care for and lead people.

What authors Gibbons and Kennedy introduce is a means to combat the traps that arise when trying to bring a science-based approach to the human side of organizations, leadership, culture, change, and motivation. In an age marked with too much information and often riddled with pseudo-experts, it can be hard to discern what is true: *Whom do you trust? How can you recognize a reliable expert? How do you sort through the constant and conflicting information "inputs" received when making a decision?*

Answers to these questions hold tremendous consequences for leaders seeking to navigate turbulent conditions, often having to achieve more with fewer resources.

The authors call upon leaders to be **epistemically virtuous**—to take greater responsibility for updating their beliefs about how to act. The critical thinking tool they suggest, LIAR, helps leaders parse conflicting sources: *What do gurus say? What do academic experts say? What does their gut say? What does reason say?*

Armed with LIAR, and a half-dozen other critical thinking tools, the authors hope leaders can begin to discard management pseudoscience—the catchy, half-baked, often-false models that look good on a PowerPoint slide.

For those of us leading in the tech industry, a constant experimental mindset is demanded. At Meta, we use multiple avenues of data collection and empathic listening strategies to better paint a picture of the lived experiences of a diverse workforce.

The trap we are wary of is simply picking up where Mr. Taylor left off—replacing the stopwatch with something more advanced. Many companies do just that: Taking a naive approach to management metrics, such as measuring keystrokes or tracking employees' time on their computers. This misses the complexity and interactions of working within an ever-evolving system and often causes leaders to miss deeper root causes and effects.

As *Change Myths* points out, the complexity (or I would argue the reality) of work is hard to measure. It takes deep thought and puts emphasis on the often-invisible drivers of human behavior at work. It takes an outside-in view to learn how others have previously tackled the topic. And it takes great humility to recognize the greatness that comes when we can unlock the skillsets of people at work.

At Meta, we take the science **and** human complexity in our leadership decision making very seriously. We seek to advance our own methodologies to account for the many confounding effects that simply add noise to our knowledge. We are leaning heavily into experimental methodologies so we can move from a descriptive understanding of the world around us to a more causal view of the reality we operate within.

This is not for the faint of heart. It requires deep investment into people analytics and data infrastructure. Unearthing the complexity around us often requires us to re-examine deeply held assumptions and to tolerate cognitive dissonance as we embrace multiple sources of truth. But the reward for doing so results not just in better business outcomes, but a healthier and more efficient way to work.

Change Myths is an important resource for firms and their change advisors on the same journey.

CHAPTER I

Change curves: Is change like dying?

"The urge to compress the complexities of life into neat and tidy stages is irresistible."[1]

MICHAEL SHERMER (FOUNDING PUBLISHER OF SKEPTIC MAGAZINE)

About 30 years ago, Paul sat in PricewaterhouseCoopers' (PwC) London training complex, with an eagle's-eye view of the Thames River, attending their change-practitioner masterclass. Tricia took a similar course more recently. On different continents and in different years, the first model both learned was the "change curve" (see Figure I.1). That change curve depicts Elisabeth Kübler-Ross' work on the emotional **experience of dying** as a five-stage process and extrapolates this to how individuals experience change in organizations.

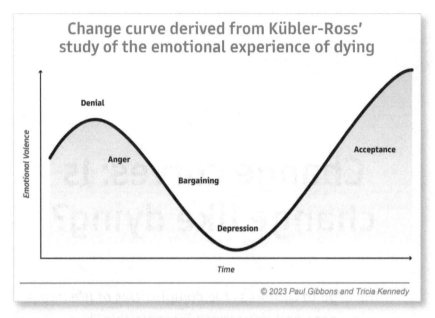

**Change curve derived from Kübler-Ross'
study of the emotional experience of dying**

Denial

Anger

Bargaining

Depression

Acceptance

Emotional Valence

Time

© 2023 Paul Gibbons and Tricia Kennedy

Figure I.1: Change curve derived from Kübler-Ross' study of the emotional experience of dying. The OG change curve takes Kübler-Ross' work theorizing the emotional experience of dying as a five-stage process and extrapolates this to how all individuals universally experience change in organizations.

This model, we two change newbies were told, was universal—a generalization of **how human beings experience change in organizations**.

We start here because the change curve is the lowest of low-hanging fruit and the myth-iest of change myths. With the benefit of 50 years' combined hindsight, it might seem absurd to compare the experience of dying with a new HR policy or software application at work, but The Force is strong with this one. Paul fell for it—hook, line, and sinker. It sent Tricia on a journey seeking evidence-based organizational change ideas.

Paul penned a short debunk of the change curve a decade ago in *The Science of Organizational Change*. Even before then, it had begun to fade from change methodologies at major consulting firms. Yet just a few years ago, it was still the logo and header of the most popular change-practitioner forum on LinkedIn. And still, at least once a week, some wannabe-guru posts a variation on LinkedIn to great applause. Despite robust debunking, the change curve has credible defenders—people who, in our view, ought to know better.

For readers who long ago disposed of the Kübler-Ross derived change curve and have long thought its application to organizational change misguided, read on. Critical thinking demands we have robust reasons for our beliefs, reasons which also equip us with the means to have the crucial debates that the change profession requires.

Claim

"Death is a delightful hiding place for weary men."

HERODOTUS (CIRCA 440 BCE)

Although philosophers, poets, and psychologists have described grief for centuries, the change curve (and its multiple variations) is derived from Kübler-Ross' research and writing during the 1960s. Although not the first, nor the last, stage model of dying, it remains the most well-known.

Kübler-Ross' original version is often abbreviated as DABDA and describes five stages: Denial, anger, bargaining, depression, and acceptance.

DABDA, in the minds of current adherents, asserts that no matter the context—death, transitions, family problems, growing older, or changes at work—change **always** involves a sequential, staged process with an emotional "dip" that then leads to eventual acceptance.

A central, recurring theme of *Change Myths* is how beliefs form, propagate, and become sticky. We first explore each myth's backstory: How it came into existence and when it started to be applied to change. Sometimes, that itself offers clues to its truth or usefulness. Did it, at birth, have solid foundations? And how, if purloined from other disciplines such as psychology or neuroscience, did it make the jump to organizational change?

What is the backstory of the change curve?

Backstory

"The reality is that you will grieve forever. You will not 'get over' the loss of a loved one; you will learn to live with it."

ELISABETH KÜBLER-ROSS

Elisabeth Kübler-Ross was a remarkable woman who features on every shortlist of the 20th-century's best-known psychologists. DABDA has passed into our language in almost the same way as the words "ego" (Freud) and "IQ" (Binet). In her day, she became a superhero. Time magazine named her one of the 20th-century's "Most Important Thinkers" and she received 19 honorary degrees.

On Death and Dying, her opus published in 1969, has been called one of the most influential books in the history of psychology. The goals of her life's work were grander than describing death's experience. The book's subtitle—*What the Dying Have to Teach Doctors,*

Nurses, Clergy, and Their Own Families—hints at her activist, not just academic, aspirations.

Kübler-Ross' contribution to humanity was giving a voice to the dying and forever altering how we treat, relate to, and care for people at the end of their lives. Before she opened eyes, the dying were shunted off to quiet corners of hospitals and called hopeless patients. Doctors of that era avoided discussing terminal diagnoses, even with the patients themselves. Her work laid the groundwork for ideas such as palliative care, living wills, and the hospice movement.

We take her legacy, centered around compassion for and engagement with the dying, for granted today—culture tends to work that way, our norms seem normal. It is hard to imagine a doctor lying to a patient or their family, or a world where we can't talk about death—but so it was.

Because of Kübler-Ross' star power, countless students in helping professions and social sciences—doctors, nurses, psychologists, social workers, sociologists, and more—went on to learn the DABDA model. Her acolytes, not Kübler-Ross herself, re-purposed DABDA from the experience of death to the grief of losing a loved one, and to broader use.

From her research on dying, a series of extraordinary extrapolations happened. First, her passionate followers extrapolated the model from the experience of dying to the experience of grieving. Second, scores of psychologists later extrapolated DADBA-as-grieving to the experience of loss generally. And third, the nascent organizational change world adopted the model to describe how people respond to change in organizations.

What did Kübler-Ross think?

When asked, she emphasized that her research focused on the experience of dying, not the grieving of surviving family and friends, nor how people generally experience loss. By some accounts, Kübler-Ross was horrified that her work had been extrapolated far beyond its original scope.

Sadly, and despite her warnings about misapplying her work to different contexts, DABDA's broad application was akin to locking the barn door once the horse was in the next county: It was already firmly ensconced in our collective psyche, culture, and in organizational change.

Regardless of the research quality undergirding DABDA or Kübler-Ross' own words and wishes, DABDA is used daily as a template for how people grieve, experience loss, and—remarkably—how they experience organizational change.

Kübler-Ross remains with us, a lift-and-shift of DABDA from the context of death to the context of organizational change.

The change world is replete with models, research, and gurus who make claims, offer insights, advance theories, and prescribe action to organizations. The same is true in life. We are inundated with medical advice, nutrition guidance, climate change stories, parenting suggestions, and political speeches. Given the quantity of such inputs, their conflicting nature, and variable quality, the citizen, voter, consumer, and change professional need a way to separate fact from fiction. LIAR is an essential tool for doing so.

Debunking change curves with LIAR

"For some people, a change curve might consist of excitement, enthusiasm, engagement, effort, and excellence."[2]

PAUL GIBBONS (*THE SCIENCE OF ORGANIZATIONAL CHANGE*, 2019)

Philosophers sometimes boil sources of knowledge down into four categories: Logic (L), intuition (I), authority (A), and research evidence (R) (see Figure I.2).[3]

LIAR suggests if you say you know something, you've reasoned it, intuited it, trusted that some expert got it right, and/or examined the research evidence. Though we talk more about LIAR and critical thinking later, it breaks down as follows:

- **Logic**—Does the claim use systematic, logical reasoning? Does the conclusion follow from its premises? Are there any logical fallacies?
- **Intuition**—Does the claim feel like it makes sense, subjectively or in your "gut"?
- **Authority**—Does the claim come from a credible and reliable source or authority?
- **Research evidence**—Is the claim supported by verifiable evidence and repeated, high quality scientific findings?

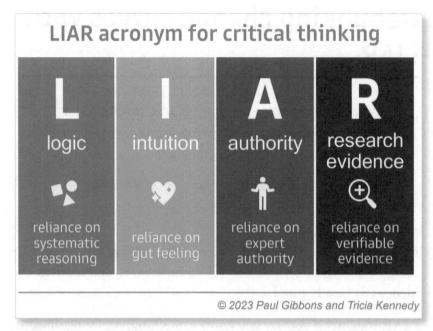

Figure I.2: LIAR acronym for critical thinking. Acronym corresponds to common epistemological questions based on the work of the philosopher Jenny Duke-Yonge at Macquarie University and provides a handy shortcut to aid critical thinking.

We invite you to conduct a thought experiment. Take a sample of things you know and "bucket" where they come from—say, on vaccination, diet, or economics. You may find that for some beliefs, the LIAR elements agree, but for other beliefs they conflict.

In this book we use LIAR to examine each myth, but you must decide for yourself how to weigh its four elements for different topics and claims. Even if we might like to be, we aren't sage enough to be a supreme court of change ideas and models.

Let's see how DABDA-based change curves stand up to the scrutiny of LIAR.

Logic (L)

"We are pattern-seeking, storytelling [beings] trying to make sense of an often chaotic and unpredictable world."

MICHAEL SHERMER (FOUNDING PUBLISHER OF SKEPTIC MAGAZINE)

Logic does two things for critical thinking. First, it helps weigh the sometimes-conflicting inputs of authorities, intuition, and research evidence (the IAR parts of LIAR). Many myths in this book make sense on a gut level and have some expert authorities behind them but fly in the face of research evidence.

The second role is to help the critical thinker reason between generalizations and specifics, and whether knowledge can be transferred from one domain to another—does an example from one context justify a claim in a different one (as in the case of dying and organizational change)?

Thinking about Kübler-Ross' DABDA, you might work through its premises as follows.

Premise A: DABDA stages accurately describe a dying person's emotional experience.

Premise B: Grieving follows a similar "death-grief" process, as does all loss. (Why should it?)

Premise C: Change entails some kind of loss. (Must it?)

Conclusion: Change, as a loss, mirrors the experience of dying.

In the research evidence section below, you may conclude that: a) DABDA isn't a general template for death, b) Kübler-Ross didn't view her work as a template for loss generally, and c) not all change entails loss.

Nobody doubts that **some** people experience **some** of the stages **some** of the time. But how helpful is that?

Logic helps us decide whether the somewhat trivial truth that some change can be emotionally difficult generalizes to **all** change is **always** difficult.

Intuition (I)—Simple, relatable, and sticky

DABDA accords with many people's intuitions. Its process is relatable, making sense on a gut level, because we have all experienced some of these emotions (and many of us have experienced all of them). Thus, DABDA might legitimize our feelings when we grieve (at least if our experience conforms). It gives us hope and comfort that no matter how dark the night, we will eventually reach stages of acceptance and peace.

DABDA is simple and memorable. By referencing it, legions of popular culture and media—from *Seinfeld* to *The Simpsons* and from countless TV dramas to daily TV news reports—perpetuate DABDA's intuitive stickiness.

Neuroscience suggests that more salient experiences are more memorable, especially when they are negative. So, our gut retrieves memories of work and life changes that sucked—where our response may have included (say) anger or bargaining. This is called

availability bias (more later). This intuitive relatability of change curves also extends to organizational change experiences. We retrieve more readily that awful re-organization, where we observed or felt (say) depression or denial.

Don't stop there.

With a little effort, it is also relatively easy to recall significant changes that were exhilarating and exciting, that even if hard, felt nothing like a considerable loss. And it may be possible to recall other emotions that aren't "primed" (another cognitive bias) by change curves—say uncertainty, emptiness, or confusion.

Authority (A)—DABDA and change-curve glue

Trust in authority and credibility of sources matters. Not just in change, but also in critical life choices (such as medical treatments, diet and exercise, and climate and environmental sustainability, among many others). For the change curve, that we can cite the eminent psychologist Kübler-Ross as its author lends credibility.

Kübler-Ross was a giant, and although she disavowed the extrapolations made from her research, many subsequent thinkers jumped on the bandwagon. Virginia Satir's work in family therapy brought us a modified version, losing the bargaining stage but gaining stages for shock, practice, and integration. Further variations have some combination of DABDA blended with either the unfreeze-change-refreeze model of Kurt Lewin fame or the transitions model of William Bridges fame.

A quick Google search for "change curve" yields a staggering 43-million hits, up there with Justin Bieber and PewDiePie. How many Google searches are there for "empirical validity of the change curve"? Probably not many.

Authority and credibility are important. Credentials and renown mean something, but not everything. Trust in experts is a useful and necessary shortcut—we don't have to look up and understand everything ourselves.

But popularity, as we see throughout *Change Myths*, can be a proxy for truth—a dangerous proxy. We can hide behind the popularity of our views rather than think for ourselves.

Research evidence (R)—Lots of talk, little-to-no action

"People have natural ways of adapting to loss, [but] everyone does it in their own way."[4]

THE CENTER FOR COMPLICATED GRIEF AT COLUMBIA UNIVERSITY

Earlier we noted three extrapolations, from the experience of dying to the experience of grieving, from the experience of grieving to loss of all kinds, and then from loss to organizational change. Let's take each in turn and examine the research evidence.

Has Kübler-Ross' DABDA, as a model for the emotional experience of dying, held up to scrutiny? She predicted a dip. Should that surprise us? Dips happen and we would expect dying to produce one.

But Kübler-Ross didn't just predict a dip, she also enumerated five sequential aspects of the dying experience. What about the panoply of other human emotions (say) sadness, emptiness, relief, or uncertainty? Are bargaining, anger, and depression more important than other emotions? What about dozens of other potential negative responses—are these wrong? Are these outliers?

Research evidence says no. The death experience is deeply individualized, and no shortlist of emotions is sufficient, especially not in prescribed order.

Has Kübler-Ross' DABDA, as a model for grieving the loss of a loved one, held up to scrutiny? If it had held up, we would expect it to explain and predict people's reactions **most of the time**—perhaps half of the time would be enough? One bereavement study, in contrast, found that it did so only 11-17% of the time.[5] This abysmal result indicates that only a few people go through some of the stages and only some of the time.

It seems we experience grief in our own way and do not follow prescriptive stages or any similar, universal template. Grief experts Stroebe, Schut, and Boerner put it this way:

> "Major concerns include the absence of sound empirical evidence, conceptual clarity, or explanatory potential. [DABDA] lacks practical utility for the design or allocation of treatment services, and it does not help identify those at risk or with complications in the grieving process. Most disturbingly, the expectation that bereaved persons will or even should go through defined stages of grieving can be harmful to those who do not."[6]

These findings are not the foundation on which we should build a model of anything, let alone one in a context as distant from death as organizational change. People are complex—dying, grief, and loss, as well as change, cannot be organized so simply and cleanly.

Now we know that DABDA as a model for stages of experiencing death—its original purpose—does not stand up to scrutiny. Could it still apply as stages of experiencing change in organizations?

It is easy to find dozens of online articles and blogs that exult the application of DABDA to organizational change. Even peer-reviewed journal articles sometimes rely on DABDA as an assumption and point to a source supposedly confirming it. What is impossible to find are high quality studies that quantitatively test the applicability and universality of the claim. Much of the research takes DABDA as a starting point, not the object of study.

David Wilkinson of the *Oxford Review*[7] has a blog post that declares the change curve real[8], tracing its journey from death to organizational change primarily through two journal articles (one in 1975[9] and a second in 1990[10]). Both studies report a pattern of reactions similar to DABDA among either newly deployed Peace Corps volunteers or healthcare workers, respectively, during an organizational change.

But if you venture into the weeds of the studies Wilkinson cites, you find a different story. In one, the researchers were examining the effect of stress (not change) on Peace Corps volunteers, and one of the stressors was food scarcity. The leap they require is to jump from severe hunger as a stressor to organizational change as a comparable stressor.

Organizational change researchers also point to dips in performance, learning, and productivity and use that dip to "confirm" change curves. One of the most comprehensive review of dips comes from Elrod and Tippet's 2002 journal article, which summarizes change curve research and compares a change curve to transition frameworks from multiple disciplines.[11]

The article makes a fascinating read, but the critical thinker notes **this isn't a test of change curve theory—instead, its validity is a premise**. The comparison with other theories reveals they all dip, which we find unremarkable. But Elrod and Tippet suggest that finding a performance dip in a single study and context equates to validating a "death valley" of grief and despair in organizational change. Quite a leap.

Another oft cited and so-called validation of change curves is the 2010 journal article by Nikula and colleagues, euphemistically titled "Empirical Validation of the Classic Change Curve on a Software Technology Change Project."[12] Perhaps written for IT experts venturing into the complex domain of organizational change, this case study makes a common rookie error: It is about project management, not change management. Its 16 pages cover extensive detail about the technologies involved, reasons for changing technologies, and the many obstacles faced by the project (including unrealistic planning and a rotating cast of project team members). There is barely any mention of the actual change recipients, the people affected by the project's outcomes.

Further, Nikula and colleagues take a curve for describing a human emotional experience and claim that it validates the change curve because financial indicators and profits over the 10 years covered by the case study appear to follow the curve's pattern. To conclude that a financial dip entails an emotional dip is specious.

Lastly, case studies are qualitative anecdotes of a single situation, not a research method designed to empirically test a hypothesis (more on this later).

So what?

It is easy to dismiss criticism and claim change curves are harmless, after all, not everything in life can be substantiated by science.

Few change practitioners have the time or patience to jump into the weeds, as we have done here. They are a practical bunch, and if they feel that change curves help them or their clients, who cares what the folks in the ivory tower think? Skilled change practitioners listen empathetically. It may not matter which models are in their head. Holding such templates for human emotion likely diminish empathy.

The tricky questions are: How do you know that DABDA is helping? How do you know something else would not work better? For instance, research evidence from psychology suggests that simply listening to people produces considerable therapeutic benefit—**almost irrespective of the therapist's approach** (e.g., cognitive-behavioral therapy, psychoanalysis, group therapy, experiential therapy).

Later, we discuss how practitioners can be self-deceived, persuading themselves that something which they are comfortable must also be useful and valid.

Not just dips, but humps, slumps, spikes, and plateaus

Elrod and Tippet, in their study of responses to change cherry pick their theories, only comparing **theories with a dip**.

Yet there are also change theories with a "hump." Two "cycle" theories, the fad cycle and diffusion of innovations, describe change and both have an **exaggerated rise and then tumble** as novelty wears off.

There are also change and learning theories that have a **plateau of rapid progress** followed by a flatline, and followed by more progress—an s-curve. (Our intuitions suspect this plateau effect is the more common shape of a learning experience.)

There are other possible change-curve shapes. Learning to ride a bike as a youngster usually requires sustained effort with no results for a while and skinned knees. Then poof, it happens. That change curve of long effort with slender results followed by a **spike** makes what was impossible now easy. That happens in change—complex projects may show no results for a long while, then they "go-live."

Sometimes, in personal change, we get prodigious results early (dieters for example). Progress often slows, motivation may then decline slowing progress further, and many of the initial gains (losses here) are given back—**a slump.**

The critical thinker is alert to such counterexamples before accepting as gospel such "curves" that generalize about learning and change (of which there are hundreds). Perhaps you are with us—the change curve is a poor generalization about individual change. But isn't it harmless? Might it help a few people?

The next section sets out potential harm from using change curves based upon DABDA.

Costs and consequences—Easy to remember, wildly popular, and intuitive? No doubt. Harmless? Not at all.

Our concerns are four-fold: Empathy, over-simplification, description versus prescription, and a weak foundation for organizational change management.

Does having a sequential shortlist of emotional responses help you empathize? How much does painting change as entailing predominantly negative emotions help the change practitioner effectively manage change? What about positive emotions, such as excitement, anticipation, and curiosity?

How much does reducing negative emotional experiences to a shortlist help people going through change? **Are we enabling curiosity and empathy or stymieing it?** Could believing there is a universal way to respond to change—despite "absence of sound empirical evidence, conceptual clarity, or explanatory potential"— blind us to individual differences and the lived experiences of its recipients? Could it impede the change expert's work instead of enabling it?

We share Shermer's concern that an "irresistible urge to compress life's complexities into neat and tidy stages" leads to mistakes. Do we, in making simplistic generalizations, serve the interests of our clients, ourselves, and/or the cause?

Yes, simplified models and mental shortcuts can be immensely useful, especially when explaining complex phenomena to potential clients. Simplification is seductive on both sides of the change professional's coin. Buyers of change services often want easy answers and simple, universal solutions (even when problems are not complicated or complex). Change professionals want to sell work, either internally or externally, and having a commonly accepted and tidy story tends to help.

Third, we **risk turning a description into a prescription**—a prescribed way people "should" respond to change. There is anecdotal evidence that murder trial jurors have convicted the accused because they did not display "the right" emotions as dictated by this imaginary grief script. In the blisteringly funny TV satire, *Six Feet Under*, a funeral director tries to persuade a deeply religious customer that their happiness about the bereaved having "gone to a better place" is denial—they should be angry or sad. Could adherence to prescribed stages of a change curve lock us into preconceived notions of what should happen over what is actually happening?

Finally, we worry that the study of organizational change is polluted. Linear, stage-based change models, from Lewin's unfreeze-change-refreeze to DABDA-based change curves and from Kotter's eight steps to ADKAR, are a shaky foundation on which to build future knowledge.

Alternatives and conclusions

"The notion of predictable life stages is toast.... 'passages' theories evaporated with changing social and economic conditions that blew the predictability of our lives to hell."

CAROL TAVRIS (AMERICAN PSYCHOLOGIST)

Change theory involves generalizing how change proceeds not only for groups and individuals in organizations, but also how change proceeds for organizations themselves. From these generalizations, the change professional or change leader delves into the context with the generalizations acting as a framework to guide practice.

If you expect DABDA, both what you see and how you intervene will likely be unhelpfully guided.

However, we wonder whether there are **any good general models of how people respond to change that go beyond the trivial.**

Remember, **some** difficult change can provoke **some** negative reactions, in **some** people, and only **some** of the time.

We maintain **specifics and context matter** in organizational change. Individuals differ, change types differ, change pace differs, change hierarchy differs (top down or otherwise), organizational culture and climate differ, and so on, seemingly, *ad nauseam*.

This lack of cookie-cutter generalizations is often troublesome for clients, who don't like to hear "it depends" when asking what a change professional plans to do. But it does depend.

Recall the other change and learning models without any dip (as change curves propose), which weave their way into dozens of DABDA's offspring. We saw **hump** models, where early enthusiasm wanes after initial hype. We pointed to **s-curves**, where change and learning plateau. We offered examples of spikes and slumps.

Rather than rely on DABDA or other templates for how people, by necessity, change, we favor the following alternatives, some of which are discussed in greater detail later.

Deep listening to change recipients, we believe, produces deeper empathy by connecting with recipients' lived experiences, not a preconceived template. This involves active listening and tools such as interviews, surveys, analytics, and focus groups to help better understand our stakeholders and meet them where they are. This is a future for organizational change where we no longer infantilize and misrepresent the very people we are supposed to help.

Diversity of change responses and interventions, not an average or prescribed response. Artful change practitioners know change affects different individuals and groups differently, and further differently by context. Our responses and interventions need to reflect that knowledge.

Change practices that are more inclusive of individual uniqueness and lived experience, as well as inclusive of additional change influences such as systemic factors, group dynamics, and social environments.

More evidence-based frameworks and models to guide decision making and intervention design for the many interdependent change components (e.g., leadership, communication, social environment, learning).

Greater use of complexity theory because organizations, groups, and people are complex systems.

These alternatives offer an opportunity for both the future of change (more generally); and the possibility for organizational change to evoke more positivity from its recipients, who experience change managed with appropriate early engagement and candor along with well-conceived and designed interventions to make the experience anything but hard.

We hope the reader gains three things.

1. Enough knowledge to decide for themselves the veracity and usefulness of change curves.
2. Insight into how myths form to guide further exploration of organizational change claims.
3. An epistemological tool for parsing claims in any knowledge area—from vaccines to climate science, from political claims to health product claims, and beyond.

What comes next?

This book started unusually. Many books start with an introduction, a roadmap of its contents, a conceptual overview, and a hint to the authors' motivation. We dove right in, realizing that some explaining is necessary to fill in some background and theory in later chapters.

Let's fill in some conceptual gaps and our motivation for writing this book.

CHAPTER II

Interlude: Why write this book?

"Be not the one who debunks but the one who assembles, not the one who lifts the rugs from under the feet of naïve believers but the one who offers arenas in which to gather."

BRUNO LATOUR (PHILOSOPHER OF SCIENCE)

What motivates a book such as this one? One likely to be pilloried in certain corners of the change profession.

We are motivated by four concerns.

1. The effect on human potential and worker misery when guided by the misguided (or change experts using bad ideas).
2. Whether change knowledge can be built upon faulty, outdated ideas and whether those old change models are equipped for 21st-century organizations.
3. How humans separate truth from falsehood. Particularly in organizational change, but also in life's big decisions (such as about health, politics, and how we raise children, to name just a few).
4. Potential economic and financial waste from choices made in the change field.

Parts of *Change Myths* are controversial. When a member of our network was shown a table from this book and sheepishly disagreed, your authors were jubilant—it sparked a useful discussion.

A book on a vast and important subject with no controversial content risks being both boring and useless. As Latour suggests, we look to stake out some territory and invite people to gather in our arena—perhaps even to pillory.

Why call them myths? Doesn't that alienate people?

"Extraordinary claims require extraordinary evidence."

CARL SAGAN (ASTROPHYSICIST)

You may agree that change needs to change, yet still wonder: **Why call them myths?** Why not build and create rather than tear down? Why not proceed positively and not dwell on what might be wrong, and instead build upon ideas of the past?

Your authors are sympathetic to the view voiced by philosopher and polymath Karl Popper: "Science must begin with myths, and with the criticism of myths." That is, progress starts by rooting out falsehoods.

Many of our friends in the change community endorse another meaning for myth: The timeless truth. This "timeless truths" interpretation of myths is found in the writings of Sigmund Freud, Carl Jung, Robert Bly, and Joseph Campbell. It positions myths as deeper, alternative forms of knowledge. Myths, in this scheme, get to grips with eternal archetypes and epic human stories in a way that rationalist approaches do not.

Some myths are cosmological, for example, the Nine Realms of Norse mythology. Myths make for great stories: The Ark, Valhalla, and Mount Olympus. Some of these myths, such as *The Hero's Journey*, are noble and inspiring (and make for good Marvel movies). Others are related to health, for example, spirits and humours cause illness.

But some myths are harmful because they are plain wrong. Medical myths don't cure illness, cosmological myths don't explain anything, and some myths better fit a worldview that includes authoritarianism, monarchy, and patriarchy rather than democracy.

Many myths even lionize violent and vengeful behavior. Some are hostile to women. Odysseus was forced to choose his fate between two evil female monsters—Scylla with six heads and Charybdis a sea monster. Harmful gendered myths, such as the difference between male and female abilities, and the supposedly natural role division between men and women, persist into the 21st century.

Herein lies the problem with a timeless-truth definition of myths: We must discard some—**and if you discard some, then not all myths are timeless**. Choosing between myths, good or harmful, means recruiting our moral faculties (say, against genocide) and Enlightenment values such as reason, freedom, and equality.

Myths as harmful falsehoods

We use the word "myth" differently: A persistent, widely-held but false idea—a misconception or fallacy.

Physics provides an example of how a myth can be useful during its time, but when science and time reveal them as falsehoods, they become harmful and impede learning. For millennia, Ptolemaic astronomy told us that the Sun revolved around the Earth. The ancient model was usable but absurdly wrong. However, it did allow humans to navigate by the stars and circumnavigate the globe. Pretty darn useful.

Today, a more correct model of the solar system often adorns children's walls. Had humans not debunked this geocentric myth during the 16th century our understanding of the universe today would be meager. Humankind could not have built a better understanding of the cosmos based on such a horribly incorrect premise. (Do galaxies and black holes revolve around the Earth, too?) Spacecrafts to other worlds would not have been launched. The James Webb Telescope would not have been sent 1.5-million kilometers from earth to "gaze back in time" at the universe's earliest moments, as it was in 2022.

Our view, albeit contested, is that the rigor of the human sciences lag behind the physical sciences. In the 19th century, when physicists were discovering the structure of the universe and matter, psychology favored phrenology (i.e., theory that bumps on the head revealed a person's personality). Even the early 20th century's most famous psychologist, J.B. Watson, warned parents of the dangers of parental affection ("too much mother love"). In other words, hugging and comforting their children's distress was injurious.

We need to ask whether myths such as unfreeze-change-refreeze and change curves fall into the timeless truths or harmless falsehoods category. Did Lewin unearth a timeless truth about change and social systems (only briefly and near the end of his 1947 "Frontiers in Group Dynamics" paper) in the same way Einstein's papers unearthed fundamental truths about the universe?

Human beings and human social systems (including organizations) are complex—there is still much to learn. Are our beliefs and myths impeding learning and knowledge progress in change?

Myths of organizational change

Organizational change is full of memorable, easy-to-understand stories with mythological stature. People continue to describe creativity as a "right-brain" preference and refer to themselves as "visual" learners. Every day, a change consultant posts some version of the change curve on LinkedIn to widespread applause in the form of likes and comments. Coaches and consultants sometimes place their Myers-Briggs (MBTI)® type on their social media-profile straplines. And some dating-site profiles even feature an MBTI type alongside an astrological sign to purportedly improve potential-partner matches.

The unhelpful metaphor is yet another form of change myth: People always "resist" change, organizations must be "unfrozen" to change, and to unfreeze them you need "burning platforms" because stress and fear are essential motivators for change.

Some organizational change myths have a science-y feel. For example, the notion that change produces the same physiological and neurological response as physical pain means change is pain, and often substantiated with a word salad of neuroscience concepts (i.e., neurobabble). Some of these myths also have a science-y history. Personality typing is among the most studied areas in applied psychology (and a $2-3 billion industry, as we see below). Because these myths take the form of memorable and easy-to-understand stories, they persist. They "stick" and become hard to dislodge, long after science has demonstrated their dubiousness.

A profession built on myths cannot progress

"Fables should be taught as fables, myths as myths, and miracles as poetic fantasies. To teach superstitions as truths is a more terrible thing. The child mind accepts and believes them, and only through great pain and perhaps tragedy can he be in after years relieved of them."

HYPATIA OF ALEXANDRIA (CIRCA 400 CE)

We are most concerned with the progression of knowledge in organizational change. Our collaborator and fellow mythbuster, Alex Boulting, says: **"Myths block curiosity and the search for further explanations."**

One view of the progression of knowledge is that new knowledge incrementally adds new truths to an existing stock of ideas. From this view, change is built on firm foundations of robust, timeless ideas that new ideas complement and enhance.

Karl Popper and Thomas Kuhn, two celebrated philosophers of science, upended this view of knowledge growth in the 20th century. A brief summary of their seminal ideas:

- **Knowledge progresses through trying to prove yourself wrong, not right**. In other words, if you were to test an idea such as ADKAR, aim first to falsify it, not prove it correct. For example, are all the stages essential? Is the sequence generally true? Is the framework sufficient for change? Answers: No, no, and no. Twenty-first century behavioral sciences suggest otherwise (as a later chapter examines).

- **Knowledge progresses through two stages**, a normal stage where new knowledge builds upon existing knowledge and a revolutionary stage where old paradigms are falsified and discarded. Organizational change, we believe, is firmly in the normal stage but is overdue a revolutionary stage.

For knowledge to grow incrementally, in a "normal" way (to use Kuhn's terminology) requires robust foundations. Organizational change is overdue a "revolutionary stage," we argue, because its foundations are not robust. What has been the cost to knowledge progression over the last 60 years with change curves and unfreeze-change-refreeze at its foundation?

In discussing myths, we frequently encounter the "so what?" argument. For example, even if the notion of learning styles is a myth, is it not harmless? No, that myth is harmful—as they all are in their own ways.

Wasted human and business potential

Readers have likely felt the effects of poorly managed organizational change—perhaps early in life when a school policy change was botched and almost certainly in their professional lives, regardless of tenure. They have likely seen stakeholders suffer mismanagement, coercion, role ambiguity, and/or lack of clarity and direction, and, thus, seen or felt suffering and struggle to reach their potential. They may, like us, have even seen mismanaged change result in labor unrest and/or industrial action.

The business community insists its workers keep up with technological advancements, constantly upskill, adapt when new technologies threaten livelihoods, work extended hours (often without extended compensation), and contribute to their organizations with passion and energy. In other words, organizations ask **a lot** of their workers. Change professionals owe these workers a **duty of stewardship** to manage organizational changes in ways that respect their dignity, emotional experiences, careers, and personhood.

In a new world, do old models work?

Organizational change management myths such as un-freeze-change-refreeze were birthed in the 1940s. Not everyone uses this one directly, but academics demonstrate that this model's structure (i.e., linear, n-step) informed and influenced most subsequent change models. DABDA comes from the 1960s. Kotter's eight steps, Hiatt's ADKAR, and Conner's commitment graph date from the 1980s and 1990s. Personality testing and learning style theories date from the mid-20th century. The idea that "change is hard" dates, at least, back to Machiavelli (15th century) and Hobbes (17th century), likely even back to Heraclitus (6th century BCE).

Do these models persist because they are so-called timeless truths or are they more like the QWERTY keyboard? This was an invention that was broadly criticized as a bad idea yet became the standard anyway. This is the MBTI story. Psychologists questioned its validity from the get-go, yet, 50 years later 90% of Fortune 100 companies use it (according to MBTI's website).

What other change ideas are too big to fail and too sticky to change?
Moreover, have change ideas kept up with the world's tumultuous changes during the last few decades? Consider some cultural and demographic upheavals in just the last decade shown in Figure II.1.

Business-context upheavals and related change challenges and/or opportunities

Upheaval	Challenge or Opportunity
Work from anywhere, personalized and flexible work arrangements, geographically-dispersed teams, and employee surveillance	Leading change for geographically-dispersed and heterogenous teams, custom change interventions, and trust vs. surveillance
Contingent workforces, gig economy, and growing employee power	Involving and engaging contingent workers in change, shorter-term tenure, and increased likelihood of resignation when displeased
Worker wellbeing, reasonable workloads, mental health, and pandemic safety versus 24/7, non-stop, and always-on culture	Change saturation, fatigue, and capacity demand higher prioritization and more consideration in change interventions
Corporate social responsibility, corporate ethics, employee activism, and sustainability versus increasing shareholder value	Corporate and brand values and perceived lip service versus action consistent with values becomes a factor in change efforts
Polarization, information overload, echo chambers, post-truth and fake news, science and expert distrust, and disinformation	Change leader authority diluted, credibility no longer assumed by position, and change narratives emerge from multiple sources
Personal privacy, data protection and ownership, cybersecurity, and data breaches	More regulatory and legal responsibility, also risk, on change professionals to protect stakeholder personal data and privacy
Big data, analytics and data-informed decision making, automation, artificial intelligence (AI), and machine learning	Change profession adds data and analytics to an already broad skillset; more sophisticated use of stakeholder data drive change actions
Populism, identity politics, tribal and in-out-group social dynamics, and socialized bias versus equity and inclusion	Heterogeneity of stakeholder populations demand more cognitive empathy and sophisticated segmentation practices
Customer centrism, shifting consumer expectations, brand values, and direct brand-consumer interaction	More sophisticated and strict alignment between change actions/practices and corresponding brand, values, and purpose
Digital transformation, enterprise agility, corporate pivots, and digital adoption	Current less-formal, ad-hoc, and slow-moving change practices incompatible with pace of business change and adaptation
Multi-media, multi-channel, asynchronous, and two-way communication versus attention competition and omnichannel saturation	Change profession has adapted more slowly than marketing and sales professions; more change experimentation and adaptability
Worker agency and autonomy, digital and asynchronous discourse versus supervisory control and in-person behavioral norms	More formal and methodical, marketing-like, change leadership and communications, and meeting stakeholders where they are

© 2023 Paul Gibbons and Tricia Kennedy

Figure II.1: Business-context upheavals and related change challenges and/or opportunities. Recent history is rife with cultural shifts, technological innovations, and other upheavals that not only affect business context, but also present challenges and opportunities to organizational change theory and practice.

This list of upheavals is far from exhaustive, and each one's change implications are many. We simply indicate a fast-changing world with consequences for how change is managed, presenting both challenges and opportunities for the field. Each upheaval merits a book on its own, depth out of this book's scope. We don't argue for or against any of them, nor for their relative importance, only maintain their relevance to change theory and practice.

With these culture and business changes, we invite you to ask whether decades-old change models are up to the task. Could thought leaders from the 1980s have anticipated contingent workforces, work-from-anywhere, the cloud, or AI-enabled businesses?

And while the world was busy changing, so was science.

Science has changed, has organizational change management?

What we call the "human" sciences are all about what makes humans "tick" (e.g., economics, sociology, anthropology, psychology, neuroscience). These sciences have progressed more in the first decades of the current century than they did in the last 50 years of the previous century. Consider just a few of those developments in Figure II.2.

Again, not an exhaustive list, but is organizational change theory and practice moving swiftly enough to advantage itself of these and other advances?

With evidence, we worry that current organizational change management thinking takes too few of these developments into consideration. Perhaps not all these developments affect change (and certainly not equally), but in our view, too many are overlooked or ignored.

We hope the change community will grow and adapt, perhaps because it must do so to keep up, but perhaps also because recent decades have taught us too much to ignore.

Scientific advances finding their way into organizational change theory and practice

Systems thinking and complexity theory applied to business	Evidence-based management (EBM) and practice (EBP)
Critical thinking as a key life skill	Psychological safety and inclusion
Distance and self-managed learning	Behavioral economics (e.g., choice architecture and nudges)
Learning technologies (e.g., MOOCs, OPMs)	Cognitive-affective neuroscience
Wellbeing, mental health, and resilience	Mindfulness and metacognition
Whole-systems change and Cynefin	Network effects, virality, and information disorder
Cognitive biases and de-biasing / bias minimization	Growth mindset and modern stoicism
Uncertainty and decision making	Purpose- and meaning-driven work
Managing polarities	Self-managed teams and holacracy

Figure II.2: Scientific advances finding their way into organizational change theory and practice. Some scientific advances in our knowledge and understanding of the human condition and social phenomenon are showing up in organizational change theory and practice.

Economic waste

Our final motivation is economic given the size of the organizational change market.

- Market for "digital transformation" (in 2022) is over $1-trillion and expected to grow at 20% for the next few years.
- The change management arm of one major consulting firm had $1 billion in 2021 revenues **in the U.S. alone**. (There are six consulting firms with similar-sized change practices.)
- Organizational-change **software market alone** (not services, just software) is expected to reach $3.9 billion by 2027 (e.g., digital adoption platforms, managing change tools).

Adjacent to the change market, with some overlap, are similarly huge commercial markets.

- Learning and development is a roughly $350-billion industry.
- Leadership development is a roughly $15-billion industry.
- Personality testing is a roughly $2-billion industry.

The question change professionals face is: Are we wasting clients' money? More than once, your authors were asked to facilitate team development using Insights® (a picturesque model that separates people into pretty colors based on their preferences). Insights® is far down the pecking order of empirical validity—perhaps alongside BuzzFeed's "Which *Game of Thrones* Character are You?" We'd like to say yes to these clients, but we also don't want to waste their money and time. What percentage of change dollars are misspent?

Estimates for organizational change failure rates range from the absurd, yet oft quoted, 70% to the optimistic 20%. Since it depends on what you call change and how you define change failure, we can't be exact, but most research evidence suggests nearer 30-40%.

Not all that failure lays at the change profession's door.

Indeed, some clients may ignore change professionals' counsel. Some changes fail because organizational change expertise is not recruited, is recruited too late, or is insufficiently resourced. Others fail because of poor strategic decision making, over-reaching ambition, and/or market forces. All true, but we suggest that at least some changes fail because of bad advice and practices based on dated and unsubstantiated change ideas. The "size of the prize" for getting change right is huge, and still, success rates hover at mediocrity.

How did we select the myths to cover?

All professions, including medicine, have a periphery of quacks, snake-oil salespersons, pretenders, pseuds, and self-declared experts or healers who are highly skilled at self-promotion. These aren't our target. In this book, we ignore the quack periphery. We won't discuss whether a team sweat lodge, drumming workshop, or labyrinth exercise is valuable (although, we have seen plenty of these). We pass over organization development (OD) shamanism even if the *Journal of Organizational Change Management* has published on the topic.[13]

We focus on the orthodox rather than periphery of organizational change management. Combining change myths from *The Science of Organizational Change* (first published in 2015) with Alex Boulting's list, removing duplicates, and taking Tricia's input, we landed on short list of eight. How did we choose these eight?

We asked the following questions:

- How much does the myth potentially cost organizations?
- How widely known and sticky is the myth?
- Could debunking the myth potentially alter standard change practice and make a difference (or are we wasting our breath)?
- Would debunking the myth be useful to change professionals and organizations alike?
- How surprising would the myth's challenge be to the change community?
- Does the myth's existence tell an interesting story and illuminate how some ideas (both good and bad) prosper while others do not?

This led to the list in Figure II.3.

Organizational change myths in *Change Myths*
Change curves derived from Elizabeth Kübler-Ross' study of dying
The Myers-Briggs Type Indicator (MBTI)® and personality typologies
Change resistance is unavoidable and must be mitigated
Accommodating learning styles improves learning outcomes
Urgency and burning platforms are necessary precursors for change
Change is always hard, fundamentally, emotionally, and physiologically
Information (via communication) changes behavior
Organizations are static and must be unfrozen

© 2023 Paul Gibbons and Tricia Kennedy

Figure II.3: Organizational change myths in *Change Myths*. There are many more organizational change myths than this book covers, and some myths it does cover could fill an entire book on their own; we tried to hit the more common and stickier ones.

We resist the temptation to offer hundreds of pages on theory before getting into the myths themselves. Instead, theory and myth chapters are interwoven.

Change professionals are often practical folks and we hope they find this structure engaging, or at least saves them from watery eyes and headaches. (See Figure II.4 for interspersed theory chapters.)

We take each myth in turn; add some theory and then explore another myth—rinse and repeat.

The principal goals, worth repeating, are not just to argue whether a myth is true or false using critical thinking, but also to:

- Generate new change insights,
- Counter misinformation (and provide tools to help you do the same),
- Pique curiosity,
- Advocate evidence-based practice (EBP) as the future for organizational change, and
- Promote critical thinking as an essential life skill.

The practitioner community should and will decide for themselves about each myth's veracity.

CHANGE MYTHS

Theory chapters in *Change Myths*
Applied critical thinking using LIAR acronym
(Human) sciences and organizational change
Evaluating evidence, just the basics
Spotting BS in change (and in life)
© 2023 Paul Gibbons and Tricia Kennedy

Figure II.4: Theory chapters in *Change Myths*. While this book is primarily about debunking change myths, theory and practice are inseparable because how we interpret theory (along with its premises, assumptions, and baggage) underpins and drives applied practice decisions.

What comes next?

In our discussion of DABDA-derived change curves, we applied the LIAR acronym to represent four sources of knowledge: Logic (L), intuition (I), authority (A), and research evidence (R). We didn't explain these sources much, such as where they come from and why we use them. The next chapter does that.

CHAPTER III

Applying critical thinking to organizational change

"The duty of the man who investigates the writings of scientists, if learning the truth is his goal, is to make himself an enemy of all that he reads and attack it from every side."

BIN AL-HAYTHAM (10TH-CENTURY PHYSICIST, MATHEMATICIAN, AND ASTRONOMER) [ALSO KNOWN AS ALHAZEN]

Goldilocks principle

Both professionals and their communities need to constantly challenge and update their beliefs about what works and what doesn't, or risk being left behind. The information age offers a glut of opinion daily; views cannot be revised with each and every news article, LinkedIn post, YouTube video, or TED Talk. To remain sane and "have a life," some of our thinking needs to be cordoned off, rejecting the impulse to constantly revisit certain beliefs. If every "input" required a trawl through academic literature and alternative sources, we wouldn't have time to "Netflix and chill."

In contrast, if every input that contradicts existing beliefs is summarily dismissed, then what we think becomes dated, wrong, or irrelevant. This is all more easily said than done.

Like Goldilocks, we need to strike a **"just right" balance** between these two extremes.

Cell membranes in your body are biological marvels. They also illustrate an example of such a balance. They have just the right amount of permeability, allowing nutrients and signaling molecules in; and just the right amount of impermeability, screening out toxins and micro-regulating the blood's pH, hormone, and ion concentrations. Cells die if their membranes are too permeable or too impermeable, letting in too much or keeping too much out.

Like cell membranes, change experts must maintain a delicate balance between permeability and impermeability—in other words, between what they ingest as true and discard as false.

Two caricatures illustrate the traps into which change experts easily fall. Let's call them Chad (too impermeable) and Sally (too permeable), both which can be found at every big organizational change conference.

Chad has been a change practitioner for nearly 30 years. Back in the day, he read all the books. He even wrote one. Chad has a suitcase full of certifications, all proudly displayed on his LinkedIn profile. His identity (and ego) is a "change expert." Chad speaks at all the conferences and has a very comfortable reputation and income.

Much of what Chad teaches is wrong and outdated, but he doesn't revise his beliefs because that would shatter his identity as an expert. So, he teaches what he has always taught. He sniffs at new models and ideas, rejecting anything that challenges his ways of seeing and operating from his lofty position in the change world.

On the opposite end of the spectrum, Sally has been a change practitioner for nearly 20 years. Unlike Chad, she reads everything she can get her hands on. Her identity is based on knowing and using the newest and hottest ideas from all the popular books, and she is magpie-like in her attraction to shiny, new ideas. Sally is the opposite of Chad. She doesn't question whether leaders should really eat last or whether a growth mindset is valid, nor does she question the (debunked) "marshmallow research" on emotional intelligence. She has certifications in "neuroleadership" but didn't stop to wonder if a cursory knowledge of oxytocin's role in the *nucleus accumbens* is truly useful to change leaders. She talks about constant disruption, and despite her voracious reading habits, she has never read Jill Lepore's robust obliteration of that concept.[14]

Returning to our cell-membrane metaphor, Chad's membranes keep everything out and Sally's let everything in. Chad's default setting is cynicism and Sally's is uncritical openness.

Don't be Chad or Sally.

A question guiding this book is: Does the change community have the appropriate permeability balance? If our community were a cell, would its membranes be open enough to novelty to learn and progress while still being critical enough to keep falsehoods out? Is it able to discard debunked (yet cherished) shibboleths that clutter our newsfeeds and bookshelves?

To develop such a balance between skepticism and openness, we use LIAR.

Critical thinking with LIAR

"If someone says, 'I saw Bigfoot the other day,' there are people who say, 'yeah, that's awesome!' And people who say, 'no, you're full of shit.' Both of those responses require no brain work, no critical thinking."

NEIL DE GRASSE TYSON (ASTROPHYSICIST)

Neil de Grasse Tyson worries about the absence of curiosity when people encounter new information. A more engaged, curious, and critical thinker would seek to learn more, such as asking where and when, how and why, and what other evidence was found.

Critical thinking and criticism shouldn't be confused. To freely call BS during disagreement is not critical thinking. It is the opposite of critical thinking. We can and should do better.

Systematically updating beliefs and separating fact from fiction is what philosophers call **"epistemic virtue"** (from epistemology, the study of knowledge). Epistemic virtue relies on critical thinking to guide belief and disbelief.

Epistemic virtue and the practice of critical thinking are the antivenom to fake news, management hype, conspiracy theories, fads, and junk science. They matter as much to organizational change as to other fields. Beliefs about people, organizations, and change guide practice and to paraphrase Voltaire, our garden of beliefs needs constant tending. The "gardening tool" we offer is LIAR—based on the work of philosopher Jenny Duke-Yonge. A handy tool for examining truth versus falsehood and for cultivating epistemic virtue. Try it on, test it out on your organizational change beliefs.

LIAR equips us with a framework to test beliefs and provides an invaluable tool for seeking that elusive permeability balance—allowing knowledge through the membrane while keeping toxins out. Individually, its elements prompt looking at our "truths" from four different perspectives. Collectively, it prompts parsing and weighting LIAR's elements to reconcile contradictions.

LIAR's four elements are shown in Figure III.1 and are summarized as follows.

Logic (L)

- Are the IAR tests aligned in what they suggest? Which LIAR element is most reliable for the claim?
- Does the logic of the idea stack up? Are there any logical fallacies to trip over?
- If a metaphor, is the metaphor apt?

Intuition (I)

- Does the idea "feel" right?
- Are intuition and gut feel the most accurate tests in the situation?
- Can I think of counterexamples?
- What cognitive biases might be skewing my thinking?

Authority (A)

- From where does this authority get their "authority"?
- How credible and reliable is the authority?
- Is the authority speaking on their topic of expertise?
- Has the authority done their homework? (How diligently have they pursued the truth?)
- Is there consensus or dissent among experts on the subject?

Research evidence (R)

- Does research evidence back or refute the claim?
- What is the quality of the available research evidence (see Chapter IX)?
- How much research evidence is there? Have the findings been replicated?
- Is there consistency between quantitative and qualitative research findings on the subject?

Figure III.1: LIAR acronym for critical thinking. Acronym corresponds to common epistemological questions based on the work of the philosopher Jenny Duke-Yonge at Macquarie University and provides a handy shortcut to aid critical thinking.

Logic (L)

*"When the facts change, I change my mind.
What do you do, sir?"*

ATTRIBUTED TO J.M. KEYNES [MORE LIKELY FROM ECONOMIST PAUL SAMUELSON]

We begin with logic, which is one method to evaluate truth and falsehood. An area where logic comes to the rescue is in the change profession's prevalent abuse of metaphor. Rather than the full suite of formal, symbolic logic taught in philosophy courses, we suggest using logic in five ways:

1. Parsing language use, particularly in metaphors;
2. Gauging generalization accuracy, such as "all change is like X;"
3. Evaluating reasoning, as when someone says "A is true, so B is true;"
4. Examining a claim's premises and assumptions; and
5. Arbitrating between other sources of knowledge (the IAR in LIAR).

Use of metaphor is a powerful influencing and sense-making tool, and leaders often use it to significant effect (e.g., "snowballing change" or "red thread"). There are entire issues of academic journals that praise metaphor's role in organizational communication. However, metaphors can be harmful, especially when abused, and can be hard to challenge because they aren't literal, thus never have empirical data to back up their truth or falsehood. Logic can step in to help parse these emotive and data-free uses of language.

For example, when anti-immigration campaigners refer to a "tsunami of immigrants," they are not literally talking about a flood. You cannot challenge or debunk the tsunami metaphor by asking how many kilograms of water are in a tsunami, or how many immigrants constitute a tsunami, or how much bigger a tsunami is than a trickle, or whether this year's tsunami is bigger than last year's typhoon.

Again, we can't test a metaphor's truth or falsehood with data, but we can apply logic to parse the speaker's use of language. Organizational change metaphors such as burning platforms, DABDA-derived change curves, and unfreeze-change-refreeze are similarly slippery. Clearly, nothing is actually alight, nobody has really died, and there is no ice. To debunk such change metaphors, logic drives the following questions: Is the metaphor apt? What is inferred by its word choice? What actions does it suggest? In what ways does change require something "burning"? How is it like someone dying? What are the intentions of the metaphor user? What are the consequences of its use?

Not only does logical reasoning help assess whether language is being used accurately, but it also helps navigate tradeoffs between the other three LIAR elements: Intuition, authority, and research evidence.

Take MBTI, the subject of our next chapter. The four-letter personality type MBTI assigns may feel intuitively right. You may also be inclined to trust MBTI because those who blog about it hold some social or institutional authority. But does research evidence validate your intuition and the views of bloggers?

When encountering such competing notions, logic guides a systematic examination of the strength and weakness of each source and allows them to be weighted comparatively. Through reason (that divinely human faculty) you can distill signal from noise, no matter how loud or tempting the noise may be.

Finally, formal logic helps assess whether knowledge can be transferred from one domain to another. We will see later that research in prison camps and electric shocks given to rodents are extrapolated to change. The chain of reasoning some writers ask us to buy is often of the form:

1. Electric shocks increased learning in rodents, so
2. Stressors, such as "creating a sense of urgency" or creating a "burning platform," help humans in complex social systems learn and change.

Again, the following questions warrant asking when using logic to distinguish between truth and falsehood.

- Are the IAR tests aligned in what they suggest? Which LIAR element is most reliable for the claim?
- Does the logic of the idea stack up? Are there any logical fallacies to trip over?
- If a metaphor, is the metaphor apt?

Intuition (I)

"Most people feel they understand the world with far greater detail, coherence, and depth than they really do. The illusion for explanatory knowledge—knowledge that involves complex causal patterns—is separate from, and additive with, people's general overconfidence about their knowledge and skills."[15]

ROSENBLIT AND KEIL (THE MISUNDERSTOOD LIMITS OF FOLK SCIENCE, 2002)

Fellow change experts may fear we are trying to crush the life out of the intuitive judgments change experts make all the time—to "scientize" the art and craft of organizational change management.

That is not the case. An expert will observe patterns in a complex system that a non-expert misses: A car mechanic or doctor will "see" things that a layperson will not. In change, an expert's intuitive pattern recognition may lead to a course of action, like correcting insufficient engagement with a particular stakeholder group, even if no strong evidence is available to demonstrate that the engagement level was insufficient.

Intuition is a valuable source of knowledge, but on its own there are four primary traps to avoid.

First, avoid the trap of attaching more certainty to your intuition than it merits. One famous political leader said, "my gut tells me more than expert brains do." Few people likely have the chutzpah to say something that stupid out loud, but this idea that we have almost-magical intuitive insight that works better than reason is seductive yet delusional (according to famed psychologist Daniel Kahneman). Even a close read of Gladwell's best seller *Blink* reveals his thesis is not to trust your gut above all else and in all situations, but that hard-earned expertise improves gut-level pattern recognition.

Second is the trap of not updating your gut with observable results from the world around us. In the change example above, humble examination of whether our hunch about the insufficiently engaged stakeholder group was correct and led us toward a useful intervention. Cognitive biases, such as **confirmation bias** and **self-serving bias**, tell us the easiest person to fool is ourselves. If you don't find a way to triple-check your confirmation and self-serving biases, and get past your ego, your gut floats out of touch with reality.

The third trap is individual intuition in a team setting, which is prone to let us down when it comes to social learning. It is hard to reconcile your own gut feelings with the rest of a team's gut feelings. You may trust your own intuition, but why should anyone else? Why is one team members' gut feeling better than any of the others? The other LIAR knowledge sources are necessary to make such a determination.

Fourth, is the trap that intuition is too vague a term. The kind of intuition that comes from years of practice, study, and experience sometimes allows experts to make more accurate and insightful (but not rational) decisions than the less practiced and studied. Then there is unlearned intuition, the untutored sense of truth or falsehood the first time we encounter something (perhaps instinct is the better word here). Society, rightly or wrongly, uses the same word to refer to both kinds.

We aren't "intuition trolls," but we do believe—as Daniel Kahneman proposed in *Thinking, Fast and Slow*[16]—that we need to apply both "System I" reasoning (i.e., fast, frugal, intuitive) and "System II" reasoning (i.e., analytical, painstaking, reflective) to strike a balance that leads to more careful and discerning decision making.

The following questions, again, help strive for balance between System I and System II reasoning:

- It may "feel" right, but are intuition and gut the most accurate tests in this situation?
- Can I think of counterexamples?
- What cognitive biases might be skewing my thinking?

Authority (A)

In a world of algorithms, filter bubbles, and non-linear effects such as virality, the war for our attention and "truth" (in change and more widely) is often won by gurus—individuals who are masterful marketers but less thorough thinkers. Once established, the "truths" of gurudom are reinforced by $50,000 speaking fees and TED conferences. Credibility is gained from popularity, and legitimacy is drawn from expensive platform branding. If a multi-billion-dollar industry backs a tool or idea like the MBTI it looks credible, even as professional psychologists clutch their pearls.

As Kahneman puts it in *Thinking, Fast and Slow*, "a reliable way to make people believe in falsehoods is frequent repetition because **familiarity is not easily distinguished from truth**. Authoritarian institutions and marketers have always known this fact."

This problem leads to two recurring and troubling themes of the information age (visited in each chapter):

1. Popularity becomes a proxy for expertise and
2. Commercial success becomes a proxy for validity.

Authorities are fallible because they are human, everyone makes mistakes. But the change world is particularly guilty of committing the "appeal to authority" logical fallacy as an epistemic trump card. Amusingly, physicist Richard Feynman said, "I always quote Einstein because nobody ever argues when you quote Einstein." There appears a fondness in our profession for quoting Alphabet's CEO or Apple's practices, or any Ivy League professor (dead or alive), likely because they get the least pushback.

One of the most widespread myths in the change world is that 70% of organizational changes fail. This claim originated from offhand remarks by gurus such as Kotter, Nohria, and Hammer, which then spread like wildfire, even finding its way into peer-reviewed journals as a premise.

This myth spent nearly 30 years as fact until being comprehensively debunked by Paul in *The Science of Organizational Change* and corroborated by others.[17] Still, as recently as 2022, the claim appears in *Harvard Business Review* (HBR) marketing materials received by Paul and Tricia (see Figure VIII.2 on page 127 in chapter 8).

This failure claim might have been shorter lived if the epistemically virtuous change expert, hearing it in 1996, used their intuition to challenge it (e.g., "whoa, my intuition tells me that percentage is way too high, what evidence do they have?"). Had more practitioners in the mid-1990s trusted their guts rather than swallowing it uncritically from Harvard's gurus, perhaps this myth would have been stillborn, possibly saving us about 30 years of nonsense. In this case, intuition would have brought us closer to truth than authority alone.

Epistemically virtuous learners realize they have a responsibility to make sure the "somebody else" they rely upon is robust. Again, asking the following questions:

- From where does this authority get their "authority"?
- How credible and reliable is the authority?
- Is the authority speaking on their topic of expertise?
- Has the authority done their "homework?"
- Is there consensus or dissent among experts on the subject?

It would help if more gurus and authorities were transparent about their sources of knowledge. And while sifting through academic papers can be tedious, the best academics and researchers painstakingly cite both their sources and the reasoning used to arrive at their claims. In the change world we should at least strive for a happy medium between arduously citing sources, impulsively trusting our intuition, and blindly adhering to claims made by authorities.

Research evidence (R)

"Just stamping out anti-science and bad science would eliminate an enormous amount of business waste."

PAUL GIBBONS (*THE SCIENCE OF ORGANIZATIONAL CHANGE*, 2019)

Researchers systematically gather evidence to explain phenomena. Done well, research is a beautiful thing. Einstein's mathematics hypothesized that gravity would bend light. Other scientists doubted him, and it wasn't until 15 years later that evidence gathered during a solar eclipse settled the argument. Einstein was right. Einstein was also proven wrong by research evidence during his lifetime. He was skeptical about certain aspects of quantum mechanics (popularized as "God does not play dice"), while that is exactly what the universe appears to do. (The nature of subatomic reality is probabilistic.) This illustrates the superiority of cumulative knowledge progression via the scientific method and a scientific mindset over authority, popularity, and fame.

Chapter IX goes deeper into some common research designs used to systematically gather evidence (e.g., lab experiments, field experiments, surveys, cohort studies, case studies) along with their varying strengths and weaknesses. The change field makes extensive use of case studies, and some of change's most well-known books (and the models in them) are based on either case studies or field observations, then generalized to all organizational change separate from any context (including Kotter, Conner, and Hiatt).

Such broad generalizations from one context to another are **qualitative overreach** since qualitative research designs like these are descriptive. There is nothing in a case study or field observation study methodology, by design, to indicate generalization beyond its specific context because they do not mathematically control for confounding variables; they are designed for in-depth understanding.

They make fabulous theories and generate many exciting hypotheses, which then warrant further quantitative (i.e., the predictive end of the research method spectrum) exploration to determine if similar findings exist outside of the original context (see Figure IX.5 in a later chapter for more on this complementary role between quantitative and qualitative research designs).

Take an organizational change case study at Google, for example. There is likely rich detail and nuance available in its results, but only at Google. What worked or didn't work there is unlikely to translate to a non-profit environment such as Habitat for Humanity. Similarly, a case study from China's People's Liberation Army won't likely provide much insight for a Bay Area tech startup.

Change professionals', executives', and managers' lives would be much easier if change theory's 40-plus-year quest for universal, easy-to-understand models of how individuals behave during change were not a fool's errand. We repeatedly visit the tension between how **general, accurate, and useful** any given model is. Few survive all three tests.

Healthy skepticism versus dogmatic certainty

"To be a skeptic is not merely to doubt everything simply because one can, nor to be rendered catatonic by fear of the unknown; skepticism requires giving trust when the evidence is unexceptionable, even if we may end up being wrong."[18]

LEE MCINTYRE (PHILOSOPHER OF SCIENCE)

Knowledge is a human enterprise and humans are fallible—as we've seen, each of the four claim testers has its own kryptonite, they work best collectively.

Although a correlation coefficient or a survey result looks science-y, it too, is fallible. Even the strongest-looking systematic research relies upon many factors (e.g., sound methodology, sampling procedures, verification, and the usual tradeoffs from selecting a research design). To debunk myths, you have to get into the weeds—far below a paper's first-paragraph abstract.

To illustrate, a famous anti-vaccination study, known as the Mawson study[19], purportedly showed that unvaccinated children were less likely, by a considerable margin, to develop chronic illnesses, allergies, and developmental disorders. (A scientific victory for anti-vaxxers the world over.) Not until well into the study's third page, under "research methods," does it fall apart. Essentially, the method was to ask anti-vax parents whether they thought their kids were healthier. We wonder what they said: No, my kids have suffered because of my anti-vax choices. Doubtful.

A second illustration is Purdue Pharma's now infamous claim that less than 1% of pain patients treated with opiates become addicted. Attempting to justify this as an acceptable level of risk (and despite centuries of knowledge that opium and other narcotics have strong addictive qualities), Purdue cited a *New England Journal of Medicine* study. Upon closer examination, there was no study, let alone a high-quality quantitative experiment, but only a short letter to the editor.[20] This misrepresentation helped fuel the opioid epidemic. Sometimes the weeds matter.

Similarly, logic depends on an argument's premises; its chains of reasoning, even if robust, rely upon sound premises about the world somewhere up the line. Sometimes thinking things through logically requires getting into the weeds of those up-the-line premises (or down the line, depending on your perspective).

Authority depends on whom we trust. **Most of our knowledge about the world comes from somebody else**. An epistemically virtuous learner realizes they have a responsibility to make sure the "somebody else" they trust are themselves rigorous in how they pursue knowledge.

Also, authorities with deep expertise in their field sometimes **veer off-topic**—for example, the famous Jungian scholar Jordan Peterson opines on an array of topics about which he knows very little. Even famed chemist-polymath Linus Pauling, winner of two (!) Nobel Prizes opined obsessively about vitamin mega-dosing and thought vitamin-C cured cancer. (We are all still human.)

Do we blindly trust big, popular, and famous names (say Simon Sinek or Malcolm Gladwell) or do we go further and question both their sources of knowledge and the limits of their expertise? Gladwell, for instance, is frequently disdained by professional psychologists for sins such as cherry picking evidence (among others) yet appears widely admired by the change profession. (Gladwell probably earns more in one afternoon than psychologists do in months, so he may enjoy the last laugh.)

On its own, intuition is the most fallible of the four claim testers, yet it provides invaluable input, especially when considering complex systems that appear, initially, to defy logical analysis. The most effective coaches and facilitators use intuition all the time.

Moreover, all science starts with an intuitive judgment about the world, a hypothesis not yet explored, or a hunch to try something new and see if it works. Intuition is a form of evidence, just not the most reliable.

The four LIAR claim testers are most valuable in combination. They frequently conflict—a feature, not a bug—prompting the critical thinker to arbitrate across them, parsing and weighting to reconcile contradictions (e.g., my gut says A, while research evidence says B, and Simon Sinek says C). The beauty is: Place your epistemic chips where you like and believe as you wish. That is a great freedom, but to paraphrase Spiderman and Voltaire, with great freedom comes great responsibility.

We believe the change community, in its current state, broadly relies too heavily on intuition and popular authorities and too little on logic and research evidence.

People are better served recognizing limits we all have to our interpretations and understanding, or being more skeptical—it isn't about other people, it is about all people (you and me, too).

What comes next?

The Myers-Briggs Type Indicator (MBTI)® is the 800-pound gorilla in the psychometrics world. People love it. Some describe it as life changing. However, is it valid? Is it useful or harmful? How do we square its popularity with research that suggests it is neither useful nor valid?

CHAPTER IV

Myers-Briggs Type Indicator (MBTI)®: A multi-billion-dollar fraud?

[THE AUTHORS ARE GRATEFUL TO ALEX BOULTING FOR HIS CONTRIBUTIONS TO AN EARLY DRAFT OF THIS CHAPTER.]

Although there are hundreds of personality-typing instruments—DiSC®, Insights®, Keirsey Temperament Sorter®, Herrmann Brain Dominance Instrument (HBDI)®, Hogan Personality Inventory (HPI)®, The Enneagram Institute's RHETI®, and more—we focus on the Myers-Briggs Type Indicator (MBTI)® due to its sheer reach and recognizability. One estimate puts the personality testing-and-consulting industry at $2-3 billion annually. Each claims to be science backed and each claims better science than the alternatives. Altogether, is the industry a multi-billion-dollar scam?

Claim

The Change Managers Handbook claims that personality categories are a "helpful way to think about the differences between people" used to "inform the content, styles, and channels of communication that we choose, enabling us to connect effectively with as many people as possible."[21]

The Myers-Briggs Type Indicator (MBTI)® website claims: "With these insights you can make more informed decisions, better communicate with others, and build stronger relationships, all based on the **science** of your personality."[22] [emphasis ours]

Insights® categorizes people into colors (fiery red, sunshine yellow, earth green, and cool blue) to help "people understand themselves and their colleagues so that they can have more respectful, productive, and positive working relationships, even across virtual boundaries."[23]

Backstory

"Without evidence to support its theory or its findings, the type indicator was, in the eyes of psychometricians, little better than a horoscope; she [Isabel Briggs] was nothing more than an old, unrelenting charlatan."[24]

MERVE EMRE (*THE PERSONALITY BROKERS*, 2018)

Humankind has attempted to understand itself by drawing boxes around people for millennia. Personality typing goes back at least

2,500 years to the Greek physician Hippocrates and later to Greek physician Galen. They conceptualized four "types" resulting from imbalances in "humours": Sanguine, choleric, melancholic, and phlegmatic (see Figure IV.1). As with later attempts, the Greeks made use of the best science of the day, and imbalances in humours (long discarded in Western medicine) are still found in traditional Chinese and Ayurvedic medicine.

The hot science of the 1800s was heredity, where personality theory takes a sinister turn. Francis Galton's 1869 book *Hereditary Genius*[25] categorizes people by supposedly inherited traits such as feeble-mindedness and criminality. This insight, thought Galton, would allow society to breed "fitter" population members by encouraging those with desirable traits to have more children. Others took this idea further, suggesting that preventing the feeble-minded from breeding through sterilization would enhance our species' prospects. Eugenics was born and its tentacles extend into the 21st-century. It attempts to blame poverty and crime on racial and other inherited traits rather than socio-economic causes, systemic factors, and institutional failures. Eugenics theory was one Nazi justification for its "Final Solution."

The 21st-century's dominant personality type instruments, including the MBTI, trace their roots back to Freud's student, Carl Jung. Through his engagement with psychiatric patients and readings in human history and culture, Jung developed a comprehensive view of human nature, notably his "archetypes" on which MBTI is based. He also developed a family of concepts which, although not taken seriously by academics, are the foundation of some New Age thought, such as "synchronicity," "shadow," "collective unconscious," and "psychic energy."

Jung blended his metaphysical ideas with his psychoanalytic (i.e., Freudian) conceptualization of people. For example, he saw extraversion as an outward flow and introversion as an inward flow of "psychic energy." Today's psychological definitions of these terms are more precise and no longer rely on Jung's spooky psychic energy.

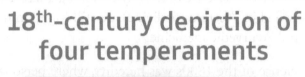

© 2023 Paul Gibbons and Tricia Kennedy

Figure IV.1: 18th-century depiction of four temperaments. Do you think these dudes would get many hits on Bumble today? (Retrieved from Wikipedia.)

Not only did Jung believe in far-fetched mystical ideas, but he also held extreme views on race. In the *Zentralblatt für Psychotherapie*, he wrote: "The Aryan unconscious has a greater potential than the

Jewish unconscious" and "the Jew, who is something of a nomad, has never yet created a cultural form of his own and as far as we can see never will."[26]

Altogether, Jung was more mystic than psychologist, more speculator than researcher, and someone whose ruminations on humankind took on a misanthropic, racist taint (which, tragically, was common at the time). This trifold combination of woo, racism, and guesswork finds a home in Jung's intellectual descendants, such as the eponymous Jungian scholar Jordan Peterson (author of the self-help best seller *12 Rules for Life*), whose regressive and authoritarian ideas on race, culture, women, and hate speech have made him a darling of the "intellectual" dark web.

However, turning Jung's funky ideas into a 21st-century, multi-billion-dollar money machine took American commercial savvy—a mother-daughter pair. The mother, Katharine Briggs (b. 1875) developed a passion for psychology and despite her lack of any formal training, speculated that there were four mutually exclusive types of people—mediative, critical, sociable, and spontaneous. Katharine ditched her own four types in 1923 when she read Jung's book *Psychological Types*. She adopted Jung's archetype-typology wholesale, the book becoming her new "bible" for which she jettisoned her own classification. Katherine Briggs passed this passion for personality onto her daughter, Isabel Briggs Myers (b.1897), who was similarly untrained. Isabel then developed the Myers-Briggs Type Indicator (MBTI)® questionnaire and first published it in 1962.

Despite academia's frosty reception and harsh critique of MBTI in the 1960s and 1970s, it persists 60 years later. Consulting Psychologists Press bought the franchise in 1975 and their marketing skill made it (still) the world's most widely used personality assessment. Ignoring its dubious intellectual heritage and empirical debunking, the current owners continue to claim it is "based on sound psychological theory and backed by more than 70 years of research."

Critical thinking with LIAR

How does MBTI hold up against the scrutiny of LIAR? Let's advance it through our claim testers and see what surfaces.

Intuition (I)

"We listen to views that make us feel good, instead of ideas that make us think hard."

ADAM GRANT (ORGANIZATIONAL PSYCHOLOGIST)

Simply believing a personality description is tailored specifically for us (and its contents are vague enough to allow broad interpretation), we feel a satisfying "click" and are more likely to rate it as accurate; whether or not the description actually is tailored to our own personality. It does not matter if it comes from BuzzFeed, astrology, a fortune teller, MBTI, or a credentialed personality psychologist. This is called the **Barnum-Forer effect**.

Two psychologists, Ross Stanger in 1947 and Bertram Forer in 1948, administered science-y looking personality assessments to an unwitting audience (Stanger to personnel managers and Forer to his students). Both men ignored the respondents' actual responses and instead gave them made-up results. Stanger gave his respondents random, generalized results unrelated to their actual answers; more than 50% reported highly accurate results (and not a single respondent claimed inaccuracy). Forer gave all his students the exact same vague, made-up vignette (also unrelated to their actual answers); the students rated the vignette's accuracy, on average, as 4.24 on a scale from very poor (0) to excellent (5). That is exceptionally accurate for something pulled straight out of the two psychologists' backsides.

The Barnum-Forer effect helps explain why many pseudosciences prosper. Think fortune telling, astrology, Enneagram, Strengths-Finder, and MBTI. It feels good to be told nice things about ourselves and we are more willing to hear criticism if we believe it is individualized, just for us. Personality tests rely on this psychological phenomenon and its feel-good click.

When Paul tells BuzzFeed he likes reading, it parrots back that he is like Tyrion Lannister and not Joffrey Baratheon, like Hermione Granger rather than Draco Malfoy. Amazing! BuzzFeed tells Tricia she is most like Jon Snow among the Stark siblings (based on her sword pick and Nymeria as her favorite dire wolf). She, too, is like Hermione Granger (based selections such as an invisibility cloak, loving cheese, tea, and Eminem).

The "personality assessment" nicely reinforces our self-concept.

Back in MBTI-land, Paul is an ENTP, who supposedly "tend to be bold and creative, deconstructing and rebuilding ideas with great mental agility. They pursue their goals vigorously despite any resistance they might encounter." (If only!)

Tricia is an INTJ, who "tend to be forward-thinking and future focused. They're often visionaries with large, far-reaching goals—but they operate mostly under the radar." (What does this even mean?)

Other personality tests and quizzes (as do con artists[27]) rely on this phenomenon and its associated feel-good reaction. **It should not surprise anyone that what we say about ourselves in a questionnaire will sync with what its results feed back to us about ourselves**.

But do any of these things make Paul or Tricia any wiser, more self-aware, or better leaders? (In fact, our leadership coaching work, to be useful, frequently must challenge the gap between a leader's self-concept and their behaviors.)

Authority (A)

"Psychological pseudoscience dies hard, especially when there are commercial interests at stake."

PAUL GIBBONS

MBTI got its intellectual chops from Jung, one of the 20th century's most well-known psychologists. If you challenge MBTI, you are likely to hear Jung's name trotted out as its authority. Although your authors do not find much salvageable in Jung's work, his ideas were foundational to early organization development (OD) professionals, informing the work of both Wilfred Bion of The Tavistock Institute® and Lewin's National Training Laboratories Institute for Applied Behavioral Science (encounter groups and sensitivity training). Questionably, Jung remains one of psychology's giants, and (disturbingly) the OD community still has connections with his ideas.

Adam Grant disparagingly calls Jung's research method "me-search" (as opposed to research) because of Jung's reliance on intuition, gut feel, and personal experience to create knowledge. Me-search is largely a solitary process, not a robust exchange in the ideas marketplace among scientists, and not dispassionate empirical study. The me-search method is endemic in consulting and the change profession. For example, Paul recently systematically reviewed dozens of "change readiness" models used by the profession, and none of them were based upon academic models of change (in other words, they were made-up me-search).

We might ask why Jung's ideas on personality retain such authority despite their flimsy intellectual history? There are two principal reasons: **Commercial success and complexity theory.** Part of the "authority" of MBTI comes from 1.5-million individuals and 89 Fortune 100 companies who take the MBTI personality test every year. Look out once a marketing machine gets hold of an idea that makes people feel good and supposedly helps them understand themselves (that is, if you don't think too hard)—and no matter what professional psychologists think about it. In other words, **MBTI's popularity and commercial success have become a proxy for the expertise that otherwise debunks it**.

The other reason MBTI and similar instruments persist comes from complexity theory, where we encounter phenomena such as lock-in, increasing returns, path-dependence, and switching costs. These phenomena, recall, help explain the widespread use of a QWERTY keyboard. Not because it is the most efficient, but early typewriters used it. Once you learn QWERTY, the **switching costs** of learning a different keyboard layout are too high.

Similarly, personality tests and other commercial psychometrics benefit from **increasing returns**; in other words, the more people that use it the more useful the instrument becomes. This combination of increasing returns and switching costs lead to another complexity phenomenon called "lock-in."

Since MBTI dominates the personality psychometric scene, many organizations are **"locked into"** the MBTI language. Were a business to attempt a switch to (say) the Five-Factor Model (FFM or Big Five), those users would be speaking a foreign language, there would be fewer people with whom to easily converse about personality—a claimed benefit of MBTI. This is analogous to iOS versus Android. Once all your family photos, text messages, files, and more are on an Apple platform, not only is it effortful to switch to an Android platform, but it is also easier to interact and engage among other iOS users (e.g., the blue chat boxes show up across Apple devices, but the green ones are device specific).

Despite the high switching costs and lock-in popularity of MBTI, two top scholars in the field of applied psychology, Rob Briner[28] and Adam Grant[29], have written debunks that are both entertaining and thought-provoking.

Logic (L)

"I don't believe in astrology; I'm a Sagittarius and we're skeptical."

ARTHUR C. CLARKE (BRITISH SCIENCE-FICTION WRITER)

Psychologists debate whether there is any such thing as a personality "type." Professor Rob Briner wisely asks:

> "[Is] personality something that actually fits tidily into types or categories? Or is it something that has relatively independent dimensions or traits along which people vary? I may, for example, be a bit more extrovert than you and you are a bit more conscientious than me. But that does not mean we have different personality types as such. If we incorrectly put anything into categories that don't exist, then what have we achieved? It may look neat. It may 'make sense.' We may like it. But it is wrong, misleading, practically unhelpful, and even harmful."

About 30 years ago, a group of psychologists around the world began a massive effort—a multi-decade, cross-cultural series of research studies[30] to better identify and understand personality traits, and to do so empirically and statistically—and with "a careful conceptual analysis of what most personality tests were trying assess"[31]—instead of relying on an archetype premise and mesearch (i.e., less woo, more science).

The results of these groundbreaking studies, and the personality trait taxonomy psychologists and other scientists prefer today, is called the Five-Factor Model (FFM) or the Big Five. The research effort and its results also spurred many new and ongoing studies, as good science should, so we continue to learn even more about personality trait dimensions using this model.

The Five-Factor Model dimensions (sometimes abbreviated for memorability as OCEAN) are:

- **Openness to experience (O)**—Inventive and curious versus consistent and cautious.
- **Conscientiousness (C)**—Efficient and organized versus extravagant and careless.
- **Extraversion (E)**—Outgoing and energetic versus solitary and reserved.
- **Agreeableness (A)**—Friendly and compassionate versus critical and rational.
- **Neuroticism (N)**—Sensitive and nervous versus resilient and confident.

We find overlap with Jung's ideas for only one dimension—extraversion. Notably absent from Jungian archetypes is neuroticism—a tendency toward anxiety, depression, and self-doubt. He missed that one, which is fascinating given that he saw real patients and presumably encountered real neurosis (to use a dated term). As Adam Grant wittily puts it, MBTI is like, "a physical exam that ignores your torso and one of your arms."

Finally, we should wonder whether a trait concentrates people into extremes or whether a trait, say extraversion, is distributed evenly, with most people a little introverted and extraverted (and depending on context or mood). Formally, the question is whether a trait is distributed unimodally (e.g., standard distribution) or bimodally, as shown in Figure IV.2. If we took 100 people and measured their height, there would be a spike at around 5' 8" (152 cm) and a familiar bell-shaped curve around that mean (i.e., average). However, if my sample took gender into account, it would be bimodal with a peak for average male and female height. According to psychologist David Pittenger, "because the MBTI is a typology, we would expect that its scores would be distributed bimodally, not normally."[32] However, MBTI shows a normal distribution, meaning there is a concentration of people in the middle and fewer at each extreme, which flies in the face of reality for typologies.

Perhaps we have persuaded you that the idea of a personality type based on Jungian archetypes is bunk. But what of claims that personality tests such as MBTI "work"—that is, they help solve organizational problems?

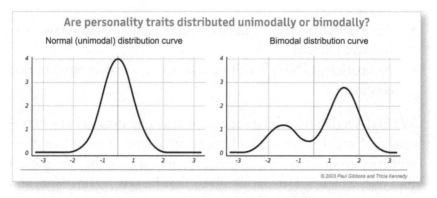

Figure IV.2: Are personality traits distributed unimodally (e.g., standard distribution) or bimodally? The latter, but MBTI proposes the former.

Research evidence (R)—Do types predict anything useful about people's role and performance?

"I like the scientific spirit—the holding off, the being sure but not too sure, the willingness to surrender ideas when the evidence is against them."

WALT WHITMAN (AMERICAN POET AND ESSAYIST)

A personality trait is distinguished by its relative stability over time as a genetic behavioral predisposition, which is distinct from other learned and situation-dependent attributes of human behavior (such as skills and self-regulation behaviors). It is in this context that we examine MBTI, as a personality inventory, and one of the most widely recognized and used. **Often overlooked is that traits are tendencies, so while these are shown to be relatively stable and persistent over time, they are not immutable**. A person can act contrary to an innate preference, both deliberately and through learned behavior.

If I took a personality test on Monday that said I was outgoing and deliberate and then on Tuesday took the same test that said I was shy and impulsive, it would not be much of a test. Psychologists call this **test-retest reliability**. MBTI performs poorly compared to other personality tests. Its website claims a test-retest reliability of 75-90%, whereas external evaluators find it in the region of 50%.[33]

More important than its statistical properties is whether psychometric personality measures **predict** how we will behave and interact with the world (i.e., that they are predictive of behavior and how people will perform in certain roles). Personality test vendors claim that organizations can use them to recruit, structure teams, shape communication and learning, reduce conflict, and that individuals can use them to manage their time and guide their decision making and career choices.

Is MBTI stable and accurate enough to help employers select staff for certain jobs?

It seems not. The seminal work on this was a meta-analysis of 85 years of research published in 1998 by uber-psychologist Frank Schmidt.[34] He found that personality tests were among the poorest predictors of job performance. The best predictor was general-mental ability (i.e., smarts or intelligence). Of the personality traits Schmidt reviewed, the trait conscientiousness had the most predictive validity. Notably, MBTI does not measure conscientiousness.

Other researchers have evaluated the relationship between MBTI and factors such as risk tolerance, problem solving, information systems design, conflict management, and leadership. The researchers found "few consistent relationships."[35]

Not only is it hard to demonstrate any benefit to MBTI other than its feel-good nature, but could there also be costs and consequences to using it? Might it be harmful?

Costs and consequences

"For it is one's psychological type which from the outset determines and limits a person's judgment."

CARL JUNG (SWISS PSYCHOTHERAPIST)

Jung seemed to believe that psychological type **"determines and limits"** a person's judgment due to its inherited nature. What might be the costs to a narrow, misplaced, fixed, and misleading view of personality that informs people's views of themselves and others? While researchers have failed to find benefits, we are unaware of any who have studied possible harms. Here, we will speculate.

First, personality assessments may **reinforce a faulty self-concept**. They use notoriously unreliable self-reports that "playback" what you think about yourself and thus depend on pre-existing levels of self-awareness. For example, Tricia may view herself as someone who cares deeply about others and who likes to share information, work on teams, and collaborate. Behaviorally, it is **possible that none of those self-perceptions are accurate**. Consider fictional character Michael Scott (David Brent in the original UK show) of Dunder Mifflin (see Figure IV.3)—a hilariously dysfunctional leader who is also spectacularly self-unaware. He would doubtlessly tell a questionnaire that he is democratic, collaborative, communicative, empathetic, and fair. How useful is a test that feeds his narcissistic self-reflections back to him?

Lead character from TV show *The Office*, both UK and U.S. versions

© 2023 Paul Gibbons and Tricia Kennedy

Figure IV.3: Lead character from TV show *The Office*, both UK and U.S. versions. Would either David Brent's or Michael Scott's MBTI results reflect their personalities and/or help make them better leaders?

Second, typing has consequences. The **boxes we draw around things determine how we judge and interact with them**. If we consider people as types, either casually (as we communicate or think about our careers) or formally (using types to shape decisions about people's livelihoods), there is an ethical imperative to get things right.

Recall that firms may use personality psychometrics to select staff for certain roles, but they do a bad job of that and are therefore not only unhelpful but also unfair, denying opportunities to some who might otherwise merit them and vice versa. This might unfairly lead to fewer leadership opportunities because candidates aren't "the right type" and bias toward selecting leaders based on faulty and imagined links between MBTI and performance.

Third, the "type" view of personality covers up people's ability to flex their style according to circumstances and (worse) their ability to learn and grow. Lore is attached to certain traits, for example, that extraverts make better salespeople or public speakers. If you buy into the lore, you may deny yourself opportunities to lead, sell, or speak. Adam Grant fulsomely debunked that lore in his article, "Five Myths about Introverts and Extroverts."

There is research that personality traits account for approximately 30% of leadership ability (the other 70% attributed to learned behavior). For instance, one 2002 meta-analysis by Judge and colleagues using the Five-Factor Model looked at 222 correlations from 73 different samples and found a relationship between leadership effectiveness and both extroversion and openness to experience.[36] Recall, also, that correlation is not causation. Once again, traits not types appear to be a more useful, robust, and predictive indicator of the organizational outcomes we care about.

Fourth, personality assessments (paradoxically) **might make us less self-aware**. Psychologists distinguish between "type-awareness" and "state-awareness." We require the latter to be aware in the moment whether more introverted or extraverted behaviors would be most context appropriate. Is now the time to speak up or should I listen? We need to be constantly aware of whether F-behavior (feeling) would be more useful than T-behavior (analytical). A fixed view, such as "I'm an ENTP," might impair **dynamic state-awareness**.

Lastly, if these costs are real, the benefits meagre, and the science bunk, billions of dollars are wasted that might be spent more beneficially toward supporting people's professional growth. When a tool has no predictive validity and there is no connection between that tool and workplace outcomes, should we then use other tools with no predictive validity (e.g., BuzzFeed, astrology, and tarot cards), as some organizations do, to assign roles to people? Would you use those tools to stimulate team discussions about collaboration? As psychologist-blogger Michael Timms says, "the introduction and influence of pseudoscience into workforce planning, policy, and management is bizarre and dangerous."

Alternatives and conclusions

"The key to making a good forecast is weighing quantitative and qualitative information appropriately."

NATE SILVER (AMERICAN STATISTICIAN AND AUTHOR)

People seem to love personality tests. Some people claim that personality testing insights were life changing. Some say it sparks conversations about productivity between different "types." But long before Jung and Briggs, humans built the Pyramids, Notre

Dame, the Panama Canal, IBM, and the world's parliaments. As a species, we are already pretty good at communicating and collaborating. Has MBTI made us better? Does it make it easier to talk about differences, conflicts, interests, and preferences?

When using MBTI to form teams, people report that it provides valuable guidance. However, to adequately study whether MBTI helps teams "form, storm, norm, and perform,"[37] one would need to compare the performance of many teams formed with MBTI compared with a control group of teams that used other methods. Such a study does not exist.

There are alternatives to "type" questionnaires, such as MBTI. One we saw is the Five-Factor Model (FFM) or Big Five trait questionnaire, which was created using robust research methods (not me-search) and has been put through the academic wringer, testing its internal and predictive validity for organizational use.

A further trait-based personality test is HEXACO: Honesty and humility (H), emotionality (E), extraversion (X), agreeableness (A), conscientiousness (C), and openness (O). Your authors don't have a dog in this fight and encourage readers who want to continue using personality psychometrics to look hard at the alternatives that researchers endorse (preferably researchers without a company to run or a product to sell).

We could even use BuzzFeed's questionnaires with a team—"typing" people and using that to stimulate conversation about how Han Solo types work alongside Leia and C3PO types. However, **it is the conversation that adds value, not the questionnaire**. And if you pick the right pop-culture icon—*Game of Thrones* or *The Sopranos*—the conversations might be more fun. Personality and individual differences are real, but artificial categories are not necessary to reap the benefits of a healthy respect for individual differences and conversations to better understand these differences.

We arrive at a pessimistic view of MBTI. Much of its authority comes from its popularity, it fails many tests of logical assessment, has a checkered intellectual history, misses many critical categories, and attempts to validate its claimed benefits have failed miserably.

What comes next?

Before diving into the next change myth, we offer a conceptual examination of scientific themes particularly relevant to organizational change.

CHAPTER V

The (human) science of organizational change

"The fundamental cause of the trouble in the modern world today is that the stupid are cocksure while the intelligent are full of doubt."

BERTRAND RUSSELL (20TH-CENTURY PHILOSOPHER)

Many myths explored herein are in widespread use—it would be no fun at all exploring something nobody has heard of. Moreover, many are in use by experts, even if patchily. The teaching community remains firmly committed to learning styles, academic experts refer to Lewin's "unfreeze" as fundamental, and MBTI, according to their website, is administered 2-million times a year.

If we are right that those three myths teeter between useless and harmful, then how? Partly this happens because humans are predictably fallible (or as Dan Ariely says in his famed book, *Predictably Irrational*[38]). This fallibility, combined with the complexity of organizations (and the people in them) means that a traditional feedback loop which would allow self-correction of errors doesn't work. For example, if you use Kübler-Ross' DABDA in your work as a change practitioner, how do you know it is beneficial? If you use MBTI, how do you know it produces the outcome you want?

This chapter reminds us that we need healthy skepticism (even about things we feel sure of), continuous curiosity, and greater use of evidence-based practice to inform how we intervene as change experts.

People, social systems, and organizations as complex systems

"Most beliefs are formed within a social context (and not based solely on facts), so shouldn't social context matter in changing them?"

LEE MCINTYRE (PHILOSOPHER OF SCIENCE)

Complexity is misunderstood, and the word is frequently mis-used—it does not just mean complicated. A microchip is complicated—the processor in your computer has in the region of a billion transistors. Yet, you can predict the output of a complicated processor (otherwise, it would not be of much use).

In contrast, complex systems have multiple interdependent elements that interact non-linearly. (There is way more to say, other features are teleology, adaptiveness, self-organization, and spontaneity, but those are beyond this treatment.) Systems such as these—the brain, the immune system, or the climate—all display behaviors that its parts alone cannot explain—a phenomenon called **emergence**. Prediction in a complex system (e.g., weather) requires experimentation and supercomputers that crunch tera-bytes of data. Even with this computing power, weather can be unpredictable, even on very short timescales, such as a few hours. (See Figure V.1 for example characteristics of complex systems.)

The theme of emergence is essential when talking about neuroscience (as we do later), and whether neurotransmitters or neuroanatomy help change experts act upon macro-level phenomena such as adoption and engagement.

In human systems, we have the additional complication of human agency and unpredictability. Say we intervene to increase the productivity of a contact center. Thousands of factors and perhaps hundreds of human agents determine the system's outputs. Understanding cause and effect precisely is impossible—in plain terms, there is just too much going on. As much as we may wish otherwise, it is harder to prove that whatever we did "worked." That is, demonstrate it was better than doing something else or even doing nothing at all.

People and companies (say, the personality psychometric industry) need to be cautious in their claims because causality cannot be definitively established in complex systems. They aren't.

Recall using MBTI to develop teams—was it MBTI (and the questionable science behind it) that helped the team or was it that they talked to each other for half a day? When various talk therapies (e.g., psychodynamic, humanistic) are compared empirically, there is a non-specific positive effect unrelated to the type of therapy. In other words, talking works. (Who knew?)

Could another, better explanation be that the team leader is taking their team's development seriously (and doing many things in addition to MBTI, such as coaching, emphasizing expectations around teamwork, or holding weekly team standups)? We can't easily know what actually caused the benefits in team performance. Even if we measure them, which we rarely do. (Alas, people just saying it feels valuable is insufficient, as the Barnum-Forer effect inclines us to like nice, science-y looking things about ourselves.)

Sadly, organizational change work is, by necessity and nature, uncertain.

Sample characteristics of complex systems

Whole is greater than sum of its parts
The system cannot be fully explained by disassembly of its component parts, the combination and intertwined nature of its parts results in emergent phenomena and properties above and beyond the simple sum or difference of its parts.

Parts are interdependent and interrelated
When parts of a complex systems are changed, altered, or intervened upon, other changes occur throughout the system and/or to the system as a whole.

Continuous motion and evolution
Complex systems are continually in motion and evolving over time, displaying adaptive characteristics, based on variation both inside and outside the system. There is not a knowable end point or equilibrium, it is constantly changing.

Nonlinearity and limited predictability
Change of inputs is not proportional to output—small changes in conditions can lead to different dynamics over time. These properties prevent its description by mathematical systems based on linearity and, thus, limit predictability.

Inter -disciplinary and cross -disciplinary
Behavior and phenomena of a complex system is related to the type and context of the system itself, and thus, crosses perceived boundaries among disciplines (similar to organizational change's cross-disciplinary nature).

Figure V.1: Sample characteristics of complex systems. Systems theory differentiates between simple, complicated, and complex systems; where complex systems display certain characteristics not found in simple and complicated systems.

Measurement is hard, do it anyway

"Not all that can be counted counts, and not all that counts can be counted."

W.B. CAMERON (SOCIOLOGIST)

Despite the ridiculous Druckerism (which he may or may not have said, "if you can't measure it, you can't manage it," we don't measure everything in change—we can't. And if you accept what we say about complex systems, even if we did measure, we still cannot be entirely certain.

That doesn't lead straight to nihilism, such as "if we can't measure it nor predict it, then we need to rely only on our gut or trust the guru." However, our intuitions are particularly fallible when evaluating ourselves, and if we are to trust expert authority, we must also consider expert fallibility.

What we can do is discussed more fully in Chapter XII about spotting BS. To foreshadow, even though certainty is elusive, we know some people perform better than others in the same job. Retention has been researched extensively for decades—why people quit and why they stay. The statistical predictors of retention are summarized in a recent high-quality meta-analysis.[39] Twenty-six factors are summarized, ranging from external factors (e.g., the unemployment rate) to work-related factors (e.g., pay and role clarity) and personal factors (e.g., age and job tenure).

In the red-hot talent market of 2021-2022, some storied companies (such as Meta and JPMorgan Chase) offered six-figure, mid-year retention bonuses in hopes of clinging onto its top talent. We speculate that in many cases this was a knee-jerk rather than a fully considered reaction. It is easy-peasy to cut people a fat check. It is more taxing to think carefully about and intervene on drivers of worker satisfaction, including culture, climate, and leadership behaviors. Furthermore, such strategies risk appearing unfair—what does the worker at the next desk think about their colleague getting a $150,000 bonus? (And those are only the bumps we know about—at investment banks, that may be a fraction of the scratch offered to a high-performing trader.)

As a sweeping generalization, change practitioners rarely use empirical research such as the retention example—in our experience, mostly not at all. Although evidence-based practice has begun to seep into organizational change online forums and academic literature, we fear that it has not yet touched the corpus of practice.

While there is a solid trend in business toward using people analytics to measure results, never have we seen the effects of communication, team development, leadership development, and workshops measured in rigorous ways that would pass muster methodologically. Rarely have we worked with a diligent HR practitioner who, to use our example, looks hard at the research on retention before acting.

Human fallibility and cognitive biases

"Experts who acknowledge the full extent of their ignorance may expect to be replaced by more confident competitors, who are better able to gain the trust of clients. An unbiased appreciation of uncertainty is a cornerstone of rationality—but it is not what people and organizations want."

DANIEL KAHNEMAN (NOBEL PRIZE WINNER IN ECONOMICS)

Kahneman warns that "appreciation of uncertainty" and skepticism about our knowledge are hallmarks of rationality, and yet "it is not what people and organizations want." There are few CEOs, politicians, or public figures known for the deep humility that the uncertainty of the world demands. And for good reason, research evidence on power and first impressions consistently indicates we crave certainty whether merited or not.[40]

Even school children today are taught about **confirmation bias**, but too few change experts account for it in how they evaluate their practices. Confirmation bias works hard to justify our beliefs about the world and works harder still to avoid cognitive dissonance associated with being wrong. Moreover, confirmation bias is just one of hundreds of biases that distort our evaluations, judgments, and interpretations of the world.

The most damning cognitive biases concern ourselves and our own effectiveness in the world—such as **illusory superiority**. Over 90% of Americans believe they are above-average kissers and car drivers!

And the worse you are (i.e., the more unaware you are of your ignorance), the better (i.e., more informed) you think you are. This is the **Dunning-Kruger effect**[41] (shown in Figure V.2)—an inverse relationship between how much someone knows about a topic or field and their confidence in their opinions and knowledge. We see examples of Dunning-Kruger in climate science and vaccine research: People with 40 years of experience express their views **cautiously**, whereas keyboard warriors tend to express theirs with **dogmatic certainty**.

In our own travels, we often come across leaders who view themselves as "excellent with people" and "skillful at navigating change," whether or not they truly are. Fellow change experts can likely relate to having spent a good chunk of their careers trying to justify the need for their expertise—persuading organizational leaders they are not as gifted with deep insight into how change works in organizations as they think they are.

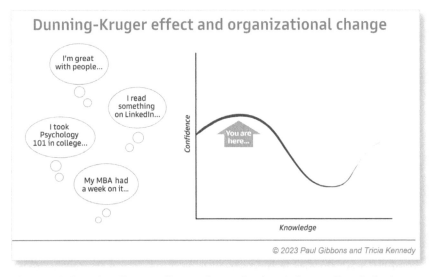

Figure V.2: Dunning-Kruger effect and organizational change. People feel overly confident about subjects which they actually know very little; and most people incorrectly believe they have stellar people skills.

Current research finds more than 100 cognitive biases, whereas here we focus on three lesser-known ones that affect our relationship with change knowledge (e.g., models, paradigms, tools):

- **Endowment effect,**
- **Status-quo bias, and**
- **Familiarity bias.**

The **endowment effect** tells us that when we own something, we value it more. When students were given a chocolate bar or a coffee mug at the beginning of a class, they were much less likely to want to trade at the end of the class, regardless of their preferences before the experiment. Because the mug became "my mug," participants valued it more.

Change practitioners feel a sense ownership for the models they use, so value them more. This leads to some of the stickiness that we see in the profession. Once you adopt something, the endowment effect makes you less likely to give it up. People crow at length about their certifications, say, in MBTI, neuroleadership, or Prosci. Once certified, they become attached—and disinclined to question what they believe they "know."

Status-quo bias is similar, it is a preference for the current state of affairs. Relevantly, this bias surrounds our beliefs because we want our beliefs to cohere—to form a consistent narrative. Changing a single belief (e.g., in a favored theory) might precipitate an unraveling of our other beliefs. If, during the course of this book, you come to the conclusion one of your current beliefs (e.g., AD-KAR) is rubbish, it likely provokes discomfort (i.e., cognitive dissonance)—OMG! What else in my repertoire of beliefs about organizational change is suspect?

Finally, **familiarity bias** leads us to prefer "name recognition" when selecting ideas. Once we have heard of something, especially over and over, we are more likely to invest in it. For instance, investors are more likely to buy stocks in companies they work for, companies of brands they consume, or simply companies they have heard of due to brand awareness.

These three biases predispose us to hang onto existing knowledge—small-c conservatism—that then further impairs our ability to revise what we believe in the face of contrary evidence. Even experts (because they are, after all, still human) fall into this trap—the effect likely even stronger than for non-experts because their "expert" identity might be threatened.

Experts as great pretenders

"The premise of [Thinking, Fast and Slow] is that it is easier to recognize other people's mistakes than our own."

DANIEL KAHNEMAN (NOBEL PRIZE WINNER IN ECONOMICS)

In late 1799, a vigorous George Washington went for a ride and returned feeling feverish. He was dead within a day. Over those 24 hours, doctors drained 40% of his blood, treated him with a salve of dried beetles, and gave him an enema. Medical historians think his doctors killed Washington, but they weren't quacks. They were the best in the country and they used the best knowledge of the day.

During the next century, Hungarian doctor Ignaz Semmelweis discovered that women giving birth in a clinic staffed by doctors died at five times the rate of those giving birth in a midwife-staffed clinic. By not washing their hands, the doctors were unknowingly killing women by spreading streptococcus bacteria throughout the maternity ward. Midwives were women and midwifery was seen as close to witchcraft by the doctors. Imagine trying to persuade a community of 19th-century male doctors, even with solid evidence, that their practices were inferior to those of "mere women."

Doctors ridiculed Semmelweis—perhaps saying, "I'm a highly trained doctor, of course I don't spread disease more than those midwife witches." He became a pariah, dying in an asylum before history redeemed his contributions to the germ theory of disease. That theory, though radical at the time, would go on to save billions of lives with its antiseptic and sanitary practices (e.g., washing hands)—more than any other medical protocol except vaccination.

Those examples were so long ago, surely doctors and medical professionals today could not be so self-deceived.

The numbers are not good. In one British Medical Journal survey, only 14.2% of respondents said they used evidence-based medicine in their daily practice, and 15.6% said they used it occasionally.[42] How could that be? Because doctors, like change practitioners, are **humans, who are inclined toward doing what they are comfortable or familiar with, or learned during formal education, rather than what new evidence suggests.**

Expert fallibility also depends on whom one deems an expert. Social media are full of famous change experts who are full of baloney; conversely, some strong thinkers lack the will, time, or temperament to market their ideas actively and persistently. Social media, problematically, tends to skew ideas towards the simplistic—or ideas that fit tidily on a slide or infographic. It is a question worthy of attention by the change community—who are our thought leaders and what makes them so?

Science, pseudoscience, and non-science

One theme of this book is the role science and evidence play in organizational change, visible not only in each myth chapter's research evidence section but also in theory chapters about evidence and spotting BS (see Chapters IX and XII).

This raises some questions:

- Is the "science of organizational change" even a worthwhile goal?
- Or, by its very nature, is organizational change an art, craft-like and unsuited to scientific foundations?
- Do scientific approaches to change risk reductionism, positivism, and/or scientism?
- How scientific is the field already?
- What are the origins of change ideas, how have they evolved, and how have they been tested?
- How might change practice improve by applying abstract notions of evidence and science?

Why is astronomy a science and astrology a pseudoscience? It is an important question, and an entire branch of philosophy (philosophy of science) is dedicated to what science is and how it works.

Whether the Large Hadron Collider, vaccines, or organization science, science provides a **systematic, progressive learning process** to help us understand the world. (At the risk of oversimplifying, Figure V.3 shows some hallmarks of science.)

Quick-and-dirty checklist: is it science?

☐ Hypotheses developed that seek explanation for natural phenomena

☐ Results of tests can be (and are) replicated by other researchers

☐ Hypotheses generate predictions that are testable and falsifiable

☐ Testing and replication happen in a community (research not me-search)

☐ Hypotheses are tested by weighing evidence gathered systematically

☐ Conclusions are not presented with false certainty (warrant not proof)

© 2023 Paul Gibbons and Tricia Kennedy

Figure V.3: Quick-and-dirty checklist: is it science? A few questions to help quickly determine if a claim emerges from the rigor of the scientific method or, otherwise, is likely flimsy.

The first thing an organizational change professional likely notes is that not every model we use, nor every practice we adopt, is scientific by these tests. McKinsey's 7S model is somewhat useful but isn't testable. Likewise, an experiment to test unfreeze-change-refreeze can't be designed because it is a metaphor. Inability to test core change concepts leads to a free-for-all—for example, the number of change readiness models dreamed up by consulting firms that bear no resemblance to tested ideas about human motivation and learning.

That is not to say that everything we do, every model we use, or every practice and intervention we make must pass all the above tests. The misguided stance that **only** science answers the important questions about the world is (pejoratively) called **scientism**.

However, this scientism riposte does not provide a get-out-of-jail-free card or a methodological free-for-all. In our view, change professionals are closer to a "methodological free-for-all" than to an overly scientistic approach to knowledge.

There is a form of **knowledge nihilism** in the change community, it goes something like this: "Sure, myth X isn't true, but I find it useful," or "all models are false, but some I find useful." Yet a map of Westeros won't get you to Tulsa anytime soon. A practitioner "finding something useful" is subject to the litany of biases we have articulated—and, harshly, seems code for "I'm comfortable using it." (So what?)

Just because all models are imperfect representations of reality, like images on the wall of Plato's cave, does not absolve the model user of responsibility to ensure that theirs track to reality and are also not harmful.

As a community, we must further ask: If your experience using a model is the sole test of its usefulness, how can you possibly **know** it is useful? What evidence do you have? How do you know you aren't guilty of self-deception or self-justification?

These are hard questions. And as Paul offered in *The Science of Organizational Change*, "no client, in nearly 30 years of consulting, has ever asked whether I have evidence to justify my choice of approaches." Given that clients don't—who are likely relying on change professionals' authority and expertise—we need the courage to shine the spotlight on ourselves.

What comes next?

Next, we venture into change resistance, a topic so embedded into organizational change practice that introducing doubt to its truth and usefulness risks ridicule.

CHAPTER VI

Vive la résistance? A harmful metaphor?

"Hence it is that, whenever the opponents of the new order of things have the opportunity to attack it, they will do it with the zeal of partisans, whilst the others defend it but feebly, so that it is dangerous to rely upon the latter."

NICCOLÓ MACHIAVELLI

If change were easy, bookstore self-help sections might be empty and change consultants out of a job. The notion of resistance is paradigmatic in organizational change. There isn't a book, certification, or training course that does not at least mention change resistance.

But is resistance a good, general way to look at facilitating change and removing its obstacles?

This chapter suggests that the resistance to change notion, while intuitively attractive, is naïve and even harmful.

Claim

People always resist change and the change professional's primary job is to overcome that resistance (or so we were taught early in our careers).

In this view, resistance is a natural, universal, and automatic reaction to change. Some writers, as we see in another chapter, view resistance as part of the brain's neurobiology (i.e., it is "hardwired").

The logic goes: No matter the type of change—large or small, transformative or trivial, complicated or simple—resistance will rear its ugly head and threaten success and value creation. This threat, then, requires both early bud-nipping and ongoing vigilance to identify and quickly tamp down, sometimes through inspiration and persuasion and sometimes through coercion and dominance. Overcoming change resistance is like a never-ending game of whack-a-mole.

The resistance-to-change myth is tricky to tackle because change is sometimes hard. Our riposte can't be that there is never opposition to change—that resistance doesn't exist. Our argument is more nuanced, **that resistance is a bad metaphor used naïvely** that leads to destructive ways of tackling change obstacles.

Backstory

"Trust is the resistance antivenom. If people trust leaders, difficult change is much easier. If they don't trust leaders, even easy things become hard."

PAUL GIBBONS (*THE SCIENCE OF ORGANIZATIONAL CHANGE*, 2019)

Change resistance first appears in the academic literature in a 1948 seminal paper by Coch and French.[43] From them we get today's notion that resistance is an opposition to change that is **maladaptive**. For these early thinkers, the aim of "overcoming resistance" was to make stakeholders get with the program.

Kurt Lewin, the great thinker and change pioneer, was fond of linking social science concepts to physics and his works can be read as lending importance to the concept of resistance. His unfreeze-change-refreeze model and force-field analysis try to map systemic forces that oppose change as part of what he called "the field." Lewin was informed by Gestalt psychology and the growing scientific interest in emergence, which both posit that the sum of a system's parts cannot fully explain its outputs. In this spirit, he theorized that as external stimuli interact with a person or group, they create a dynamic "social space." The various elements (fields) that make up this social space enable movement-toward (driving) or movement-against (resistant) each other.

Lewin saw resistance as a feature of social systems and a balance between change and stasis—not as a binary, maladaptive response, nor purely a psychological phenomenon.

Though Lewin's view of resistance was both sophisticated and systemic, **today's usage focuses on the psychological, not the systemic (i.e., people resist change, not systems)**.

Resistance through the LIAR lens

"People who appear to be resisting change may simply be the victim of bad habits. Habit, like gravity, never takes a day off."

PAUL GIBBONS (*THE SCIENCE OF ORGANIZATIONAL CHANGE*, 2019)

Logic (L)

We saw that metaphors cannot be wholly true or false, thus, cannot be proven or disproven with evidence. This makes them slippery to challenge and a favorite tool of political demagogues, and also makes logic a particularly useful evaluation tool.

When considering a metaphor, a critical thinker asks: Is it apt? What kind of thinking follows from the metaphor? What are the speaker's intentions in using it? What kind of actions does it suggest? To use our earlier example, if someone refers to a tsunami of immigrants, we can ask: What attitudes toward immigrants are inferred and what kind of actions does reference to a tsunami suggest taking?

The word "resistance" comes from the Latin *resistere*—to make a stand against. Early meanings in English were moral, political, military, or armed physical opposition. In 20th-century France, the term *la résistance* described the French citizenry's anti-Nazi activities. In 21st-century U.S. politics, #resistance was a hashtag and movement birthed to oppose what many viewed as a return to mid-20th-century authoritarian leadership.

Implicit in these meanings of resistance is a challenge to authority, which logically begs: From where does an authority get its authority (power)? Some organizational changes indeed resemble this question. In 1970s and 1980s Britain, changes to working conditions (notably elimination of worker tea breaks) led to industrial action and strikes. In more recent U.S. history, Evangelical Christian pharmacists resisted healthcare doctrines requiring them to provide patients with birth control.

In these examples, the "resistance" metaphor seems apt. But how many organizational changes conflict with people's deep-seated beliefs (e.g., contraception) or cultural beliefs (e.g., tea breaks)? The idea that "people resist change" is a **general statement about all change**, not just a statement about change of an ideological nature.

To foreshadow the costs-and-consequences section, if you are leading change and encounter opposition, the mental association of resistance with "us versus them" political resistance may tempt you to frame resistance as something to be squashed.

Other meanings of resistance may be at the root of this usage. Clinical psychology borrowed the term resistance to characterize "abnormal" (sometimes called maladaptive or disordered) responses to the external world. For psychoanalysts (i.e., Freudian psychologists), resistance suggests suppressed thoughts or memories that with surfacing resolve mental disorders (i.e., a psychological defense mechanism but one that impairs therapeutic progress).

In physics, resistance is opposition to the flow of current in an electrical circuit. Resistance is high in insulators and low in conductive materials. Early thinkers who began to use the term in social systems and later organizational change may have had this analogy in mind.

From both the political and the psychological points of view, resistance is cast in a negative light. The thought of resistance to change as a maladaptive response is commonplace in organizational change—less among experts in the field but certainly among the general business community and its leaders.

Intuition (I)

As a concept, resistance to change resonates intuitively because people (generally) value autonomy and rarely like being told what to do. To decry the concept of resistance to change is not to deny that humans can sometimes be mule-like in their stubbornness.

But does the concept of resistance help us align resisters? A significant portion of U.S. citizenry opposes vaccination. Does characterizing their perspective as resistance help change their minds? Not at all. Labeling critics and opposition as resistant is more likely to cause them to dig in their heels even deeper. (Social psychology has terms for this including the **backfire effect** and **reactance**.)

The term resistance also resonates in a social sense. Psychology research evidence reveals a human tendency to divide people into "in-groups" and "out-groups." Those resistant to in-group norms are generally considered as belonging to out-groups; in-groups are superior to out-groups in the minds of the "inners." Though natural, and perhaps linked to our tribal evolutionary history, this too, is an unhelpful mindset. Characterizing a group as "out" is more likely to strengthen its internal cohesion and resolve to defy the "others." Recall the negative connotation associated with "resistance to change," which in caricature means: Those of us in power know what is right, and you (the resisters) need to get with the program.

Authority (A)

"There is nothing more difficult to take in hand, more perilous to conduct, or more uncertain in its success, than to take the lead in the introduction of a new order of things. For the innovator has enemies in all those who profit by the old order, and only lukewarm defenders in all those who would profit by the new order, this lukewarmness arising partly from fear of their adversaries ... and partly from the incredulity of mankind, who do not truly believe in anything new until they have had actual experience of it."

NICCOLÓ MACHIAVELLI (*THE PRINCE*, 1513)

Although the resistance-to-change idea reaches back at least as far as Machiavelli and then to great mid-20th century social scientists, we think Lewin might be appalled at how the term is used today.

As we saw, Lewin was influenced by an interest in emergence, through Gestalt thinking and perhaps through exposure to Warren Weaver's writings on the topic in the 1940s (viewed as complexity theory's birth as a broad area of scientific interest[44]). He also understood feedback loops from his interest in the emerging science of cybernetics. He saw social-system behavior as the product of multiple variables that interact and feed back on one another. He was conscious of the effect of power dynamics on who were the resisters and who were "the good guys." In sum, **Lewin's terminology found its way into popular change literature, but his thinking did not**.

Nonetheless, most of the authority behind using the term "resistance" comes from its widespread, unreflective, and harmful use.

Research evidence (R)

Despite the term's popularity today, **many organizational science researchers reject it**. In a 1999 review of scholarship on the matter, authors Dent and Goldberg say the following:

> "[Resistance] is taken as a fact of life by those people who have not had the opportunity to study the question of how people change. In spite of our best intentions and efforts, the conventional wisdom concerning resistance to change has not been significantly altered by academic work in the past 30 years."[45]

The research evidence on change resistance is fragmented and weak. In a 2017 academic book that systematically reviews change management evidence, *Reconsidering Change Management*, the authors found scholarly disagreement on what change resistance means, how to define it, and whether resistance exists.

However, where change resistance is measured—perhaps using the Resistance to Change (RC-B) scale—weak correlations are found with creativity, goal accomplishment, satisfaction, commitment, and trust.[46] From a practitioner's point of view, this is a useless finding. The correlations found are weak, and correlations don't tell us about causation, only that a weak relationship exists. Moreover, we might misconstrue the direction of causality when assuming causation from correlation. For example, it may be that people who score lowly on measures of job satisfaction are more likely to resist or that low trust causes resistance to change rather than vice versa. It may be that lower goal accomplishment makes resistance more likely, or even some combination thereof.

Often practitioners don't care much about the nuances of correlation, measurement scales, sampling error, and research methods. Resistance is still a useful concept, they might say. The problem with that line of reasoning (i.e., who cares about the statistics, it works) is that it is hard to know whether something works unless you can evaluate your results objectively (as we see in Chapter IX). In the case of change resistance, you can't.

Costs and consequences

"People don't resist change;
they resist being changed."[47]

PETER SENGE (*THE FIFTH DISCIPLINE*, 1990)

Organizations are complex and sometimes having a single word or tidy narrative can be helpful for sense-making. But the term "resistance" does more harm than good. Here are some practical reasons to further supplement the more theoretical explanations above.

Resistance is polarizing and unleaderlike

When we recruit a single word (and further assume it is a binary, yes-or-no phenomenon) to describe something complex, we risk lumping together things that shouldn't be so lumped. In organizational development (OD), almost everything that looks like a lack of alignment gets called resistance. And as we saw, the word resistance carries negative linguistic baggage, both psychologically and politically.

When leaders use the word "resistance," they abdicate responsibility—why aren't they doing what we want them to do and what we told them to do? When encountering opposition in organizational change, we should first ask ourselves: How clear were our intentions? How much support was offered? What in the system could have been in the way? Leaders playing the resistance card are **pointing the telescope the wrong way—at their followers instead of at themselves and their leadership.**

In our view, good facilitators of organizational change develop an intense sense of curiosity as to why reactions are unexpected or suboptimal and examine their own effectiveness first.

Resistance ignores reasons

When we talk about resistance, we describe a symptom, not its underlying root causes. Good doctors don't do that—fevers have different causes which range from mild to severe (e.g., infection, sunburn, blood clots, colds, flu, and stomach bugs). Focusing on symptoms rather than causes leads to error—doctors do not want to treat sunburn as they treat appendicitis.

Better understanding root causes of organizational problems help us intervene more effectively. Only by understanding, in some depth, why people differ and oppose can we make progress without coercion and force. If we fail to empathize and shift resistant behavior, we often fall back on coercion and brute force, which likely further strengthens any resistance, notwithstanding ethical concerns.

Traditional treatments change practitioners are taught early in their careers (at least in our own) ignore the complexity of human reactions to change, focusing only on the rational (e.g., it is a bad idea) and the emotional (e.g., it triggers fear or anger). This, again, is the responsibility of leadership. However, change recipients may not know **how to change—that is, what steps to take**. They may have hard-to-change habits or may think a change is unfair or impairs autonomy. Finally, the "resistors" might simply disagree with the course of action—and they might not be wrong to do so.

Ignoring this nuance risks failure.

To understand, get curious. Figure VI.1 shows some of the broader social and psychological sources of resistance—different causes require different thinking about what to do.

Reasons to resist change

Source	Why Resist?
Social (Group)	Disruptions to power, status, access, and/or information, as well as important relationships, in existing social groupings
Cultural (Group)	Group norms and expectations, both espoused and unspoken, reinforced though rituals, mimicry, language, iconography, and more
Political (Group)	Think and act in 'tribes', or inline with groups which we feel affiliation, also value loyalty to and inferred status from affiliation
Rational (Individual)	Posses insufficient or wrong facts and/or disagree with reasoning on which facts are based (ie., agree with premises, dispute conclusions)
Habitual (Individual)	Habits and routines produce lack of adoption and/or relapse, even if desire to change exists
Emotional (Individual)	Feel anger or fear about uncertainty (ie., Can I do this? How dare they! Will I lose my job?)
Pragmatic (Individual)	Needs to know not only 'what' and 'how' but also 'why', and skills and tools to do what is asked
Identity (Individual)	Threats to sense of self and/or identity, or how we see ourselves and our place in the world
Fairness (Individual)	Violations to norms of justice and fairness, in terms of both equitable results and fair processes
Ideology (Individual)	Violations to values, philosophical stance, and/or moral and ethical beliefs
Agency (Individual)	Need to feel in control of personal choices and actions, as well as their consequences on our lives
Liberty (Individual)	Expect self-determination, freedom, and opportunity to self - actualize

Figure VI.1: Reasons to resist change. People might resist change for any number of reasons, even any combination of reasons, of which some are observable, and some are not; and some people might not resist change at all.

Resistance ignores perspective

Change is not always about workers who resist management "from the bottom up." The 1990s ushered in a sea of change in working practices with the introduction of laptops and email, first into banks, tech, and professional services firms. Resistance to such change did not come from these firms' 20- and 30-something consultants but from their 40- and 50-something partners and vice presidents. Many senior leaders flatly refused. Even today, some senior business and political leaders proudly eschew modern workplace technologies such as Slack, Teams, Trello, and Jira.

Organizational change looks different from the bottom of an organization than from the top, or from the middle. The benefits may be unevenly spread and the costs may be concentrated on just a few people. The unipolar idea of resistance—there is the change (righteous) and the resistance (wrong)—ignores the many different perspectives across an organization.

Resistance divides

This brings us to the notion of power. In organizations of the past, people were expected to simply do as they were told. While that expectation has faded somewhat over the centuries, it lives on today when it comes to decisions such as company direction and resource allocation, policies that dictate reward and punishment, good versus bad conduct, and what constitutes success or failure.

When it comes to change resistance, those assigned power within an organization make value judgments between what is "buy-in" (good) and what is "resistance" (bad), who is resisting and who is "on the team," what is wrong and what is right, and what is good for the company and beneficial for its people.

Organizational structures already create an us-versus-them dichotomy, a decider-doer binary, and a subject-object relationship. You are either in or you are out, like membership in a Greek fraternity or sorority. When "the top" talks about resistance, they are talking about people not complying with their directives and conforming to their expectations. They are gently flexing their power muscles. The term is never neutral, the people who resist are never equals and are never "on the team." When we treat people as outsiders, it breeds negativity and may generate an unintended cycle of mistrust.

Power often decides the difference in opinion between normative and non-normative responses to events in the world. For instance, power played a part in the historical vilification of homosexuality, which maintained its classification as a mental disorder until 1973. Political elites and the all-powerful psychiatric profession said it was so, so it was. Power also vilifies protestors unless they are from the power holder's "team." They are shot at Kent State, in Tiananmen Square, in Gaza, and in Northern Ireland on Bloody Sunday.

An overcoming-resistance mindset makes things worse

Resistance, as used by Lewin, connoted a complex, systemic, social, and psychological phenomenon. Today, in organizations and in a psychological sense, the word is used principally to refer to people not doing what authorities want them to do.

The problem with ignoring the complex, systemic, and social is that it leads you to **focus attention and blame on people whose agency is limited**. In a major, failed finance re-organization at British Airways, the change team ran an influencing and training campaign to "overcome resistance." This intervention made staff more cynical, as the main reasons for change resistance were cultural, structural, and systemic. Finance functional leadership was ambivalent, and their internal stakeholders were dead set against the re-organization. Further, HR policies reinforced the old structure. By pointing fingers at staff for something they had no real control over, these well-intentioned, well-designed change interventions made things worse. Pointing the finger at staff wasted time, money, and resources, and it also jeopardized the project goals as staff morale tumbled.

When gardeners design flower beds but ignore factors like climate, soil, sunlight, and plant interactions, they are bound to fail in obtaining the flower bed they envision. Like this, a change professional faces the costs of almost-certain failure if they design resistance interventions based upon personal factors while ignoring complex social and systemic factors. With this ignorance comes a costly mess of counterproductive, unintended consequences that are likely to cause more harm than help.

Alternatives and conclusions

"Trust is the antivenom for resistance to change."
PAUL GIBBONS (*THE SCIENCE OF ORGANIZATIONAL CHANGE*, 2019)

To offer a how-to guide on the "overcoming resistance" mindset is to risk writing a book within a book. To be more concise, here are a few suggested alternatives.

Welcome resistance

People rarely discuss resistance as having a protective function, but it may. While resistance is most often viewed as "a bad thing," it may protect firms by moderating or balancing leadership excesses and poor decisions. Employees at Alphabet (Google) formed an organized resistance to the military use of its AI. When WeWork's leadership decided not to serve meat or reimburse employee expense claims for carnivory, their workforce resisted a move they saw as paternalistic overreach. Without weighing in on the right or wrong, we see such opposition (avoiding the term resistance) as a counterweight to (possible) management error.

Think in systems

Start with the systemic layer. Assess and seek to understand relevant processes, practices, and performance indicators (along with organizational structure and design) with an eye for both potential consistencies and inconsistencies between the current and desired future state. For instance, perhaps an objective is to decrease silos and increase cross-functional collaboration. To achieve this, first examine existing social and cultural norms around hierarchy and if any current performance indicators encourage competition among the groups which you hope to increase collaboration. Failing to consider systemic factors, of which the above is a simple instance, can stop a change effort in its tracks before you even get to social and personal layers.

Dig into the social layer

Assess and seek to understand social dynamics such as perceived group memberships, common collaboration practices, power dynamics, hierarchal influences on behavior, cultural values, symbols, and unspoken norms. Perhaps an objective is to cultivate more open and honest dialogue between the top and bottom tiers of an organization. If the current culture and climate are strongly hierarchal, we need to consider that before even getting to the personal level. Are your espoused values consistent with more openness? Perhaps you can link espoused values to both systemic modifications and interventions designed to minimize expected hierarchal behavior. As social beings, factors like unspoken cultural norms and trust are stronger predictors of human behavior than personal feelings, experiences, and perspectives.

Be curious about people

Don't seek to identify resistors only to corral and call them out. Instead, seek a deeper understanding of individual perspectives, lived experiences, and how roles and responsibilities inform perspectives and expectations. Utilize the power of **perspective-taking and cognitive empathy** skills to obtain a bigger picture of who-is-who and how their lived experience might have shaped their perspectives.

Consistent with the oft-heard cliché that feedback is a gift, resistance meets a double standard. Why would you aggressively tamp down the gift of feedback from your stakeholders if it encourages positive change outcomes? This looks like curiosity and empathy first and trying to change behavior second.

Change expert Wendy Hirsch puts it this way: "Instead of thinking of change recipients' reactions as binary, either good (acceptance) or bad (resistance), we can be more curious, look for more varied responses, learn more, and engage more deeply."

Engage

Most importantly, engage your stakeholders in the process of understanding across all three layers—systemic, social, and personal. Obtain inputs and suggestions from those affected, engage them in co-creation, include them in continuous feedback loops, and learn from them.

Assume positive intent instead of sidelining, approach with curiosity instead of judgment, and diligently seek a clearer understanding of the system and its inter-related parts. Systemic, social, and personal misalignment are part of the exploration, but confronting them doesn't have to be adversarial and antagonistic.

In other words, **broaden your perspective from individual change resistance to understanding and facilitating an environment** conducive to the desired change. Instead of looking for pockets of resistance among individuals to vigorously attack, dig deeper to examine the systemic, social, and personal layers and how they interact to create the current state.

What comes next?

Resistance received a somewhat philosophical treatment because, as a construct, it is less amenable to empirical testing.

Next, we turn to learning styles and their effect on learning outcomes—a topic on which there is an abundance of empirical research, all of which is unsupportive of effectiveness.

CHAPTER VII

Learning styles: Do they improve learning outcomes?

"Spoon feeding in the long run teaches us nothing but the shape of the spoon."

E.M. FORSTER (ENGLISH NOVELIST)

Although MBTI is the 800-pound gorilla in the personality psychometric world, "learning styles" is perhaps even more widely accepted. Ninety-three percent of science teachers believe in them, and 32% would still use them when teaching regardless of what evidence indicates.[48] Science teachers! Because the teaching profession and corporate learning departments use learning styles so much, they have found their way into parenting and the public consciousness.

Many change practitioners, coaches, and industrial and organizational (I-O) psychologists use learning styles to this day. They may use them when designing training and coaching or when tailoring communications and other interventions. In our view, learning and change are so intertwined that we need robust ideas on learning to catalyze change in both people and organizations.

Claim

Learning styles is a century-old psychological concept, composed of three related claims:

1. People prefer to learn in certain ways—for example, VARK (visual, aural, reading, and kinesthetic)—a **descriptive** claim.
2. When information is presented to people in a manner aligned with their learning-style preferences, they learn faster or better. This is called the **"matching" or "meshing" hypothesis**—a **prescriptive** claim.
3. Presenting information according to learning preferences is in the interests of learning and the learner—an **ethical and practical** claim.

Below we see that learning styles are wasteful and, likely, harmful. Even for professionals who don't use learning styles, there is value in understanding their popularity, as it sheds light on how ideas that were never robust and have been thoroughly debunked still come to pass for psychological truths—how the learning, growth, and change knowledge base was corrupted by this pseudoscientific idea.

Backstory

"Education is not the filling of a pot but the lighting of a fire."

W.B. YEATS (IRISH POET AND PLAYWRIGHT)

Psychology's history is replete with attempts to categorize people, some of which have been malign, such as to justify discrimination. Learning styles are not malign in their intent; they are supposed to serve both learning and the learner. Their guiding philosophy is attractive—that we are neither good nor bad learners, but rather have style preferences not innate smarts or intelligence.

Parents particularly like this.

The Onion, a satirical newspaper, lampooned learning styles with a 2000 headline: "Parents of Nasal Learners Demand Odor-Based Curriculum." The article parodies, "my [nasal learner] child is not stupid…. [t]here simply was no way for him to thrive in a school that only caters to traditional students who absorb educational concepts by hearing, reading, seeing, discussing, drawing, building, or acting out."

By implication, these style preferences (like personality traits) are hereditary and "hardwired" into our brains, so we can do little to change them. The less attractive truth is there are substantial differences between **how quickly** and **how well** different people learn. While it is comforting to think that we aren't less smart than Einstein, just learn differently, it is bunk.

Learning style ideas, historically, extend as far back as Aristotle. But in the 20th century, Ernst Meumann's 1913 book *The Psychology of Learning* began to formalize these ideas. The first learning-style inventory was born in 1975 through the work of psychologists Rita and Kenneth Dunn. Now, there are nearly a hundred learning style inventories, about 30 popular ones, and the production and marketing of learning-style inventories is a multi-billion-dollar industry.

Different learning-style models do not overlap a great deal. In addition to VARK, there is Sternberg's triarchy (analytic, creative, and practical), and a school (Kolb, Honey, and Mumford) that propose concrete, active, abstract, and reflective styles. And that is just getting started.

This instantly raises questions for a critical thinker: Why are there so many? Why is there so little overlap? Have they been evaluated side by side, and are all, some, or none of them right?

Critical thinking with LIAR

"The acceptance of psychological myths can impede our critical thinking in other areas."[49]

SCOTT LILIENFELD ET AL. (*50 GREAT MYTHS OF POPULAR PSYCHOLOGY*, 2010)

Intuition (I)

According to dodgy urban legend, stodgy-old Boomers and Gen-Xers prefer newspapers and books, while Millennials and Gen-Zers disparage paper and prefer audio and video. Some people like pictures and others like words, some prefer working with their hands and movement and others prefer solitary reflection, and the list goes on— which can extend into how they prefer to learn.

Learning styles' first claim—we have preferred ways of taking in information—is true, but only trivially so.

Does a jump from "I like to learn this way" to "I learn better this way" make sense? The first is a subjective preference, the second a statement of fact that can be assessed empirically. Do "visual learners," in fact, learn better visually? A review of research evidence, below, says the answer is no.

111

Recall the Barnum-Forer effect—how science-y looking tests claiming to give us personalized insights feed a fascination with ourselves and our uniqueness. This same fascination feeds astrology, multiple-intelligence theories, BuzzFeed quizzes, MBTI, and, yes, also the learning styles industry. The learning style idea, like the notion of multiple intelligences, "makes room" for non-traditional ways of consuming information.

Authority (A)

Psychologists who pioneered development of learning styles are well-regarded by the profession. Kolb, Sternberg, Dunn, and Mumford made significant contributions to the field in other areas. However, as we've seen, deep and specific expertise does not confer validity on every utterance or idea. We will see later how even deep expertise in neuroscience can persuade neuroscientists to wade into macro-psychological and sociological territory in which they have little to offer.

Popularizers tend to be popular. Less popular are the buzz-killers, the researchers who painstakingly investigate a hypothesis and try to alert the world to its falseness. Imagine yourself at a dinner party conversation where someone claims: "I'm an A (auditory) learner and learn best with auditory material."

How well does the conversation proceed if you assert that no relationship exists between learning preference and its speed or effectiveness?

One central, recurring theme of this book is that popular, intuitively-attractive psychological ideas tend to triumph in the lay-psychology media, while researchers doing the arduous work of falsifying and testing hypotheses get no airtime. Can you name a single meta-analytic study author on personality traits, multiple intelligences, or learning styles?

Another recurring theme is the power of an "installed base" of users backed by a commercially viable industry to propagate falsehoods. Hundreds of websites with (mostly paid) learning style tests rake in cash, and teachers continue to talk with students and parents about learning styles—how will the idea ever die?

Sadly, **popularity and power remain proxies for truth**. Non-experts, such as Betsy DeVos (former U.S. Secretary of Education) referred to herself as a visual learner during her U.S. Senate confirmation hearing and promised she would "ensure all children have access to education that fits their learning style."

Research evidence (R)

"Man's mind, once stretched by a new idea, never regains its original dimensions."

OLIVER WENDELL HOLMES SR. (19TH-CENTURY AMERICAN POET)

Given that people have a strong preference for their learning style (sometimes with fierce pride), then they ought to learn quicker and better using their style—called the matching or meshing hypothesis. We might expect results to be self-fulfilling and find a **strong relationship between learner preference and how effectively they learn**. After all, learners should more enthusiastically devour material delivered in a preferred modality, right?

Study after study has shown this to be false. There is a vast difference between how someone reports they learn and how they actually learn. In a 2008 exhaustive study of the literature, Paschler and colleagues found:

"Although the literature on learning styles is enormous, very few studies have even used an experimental methodology capable of testing the validity of learning styles applied to education. Moreover, of those that did use an appropriate method, several found results that flatly contradict the popular meshing (matching) hypothesis."[50]

To show how inaccurate people's insights are into how they learn, students were given "smartpens" that tracked when they did homework. Smartpen behaviors measured behaviorally how much homework students did; those behaviors **were correlated** with test success (R=0.44). However, there was an **inverse correlation** (R=-0.16) between test results and self-reported homework time.[51] This reveals something **important to note about self-perception and self-reports**—they measure what people think they do, which is very different from what they actually do. Homework behaviors predict test performance—no surprise there. But self-report of homework behavior is inversely correlated, a distressing surprise. Furthermore, the few students who did behave as they reported performed no better or worse for knowing or not knowing their learning-style preference.

That **70% of respondents do not behave as they report**, even after completing a learning-style inventory, tells a fascinating story: Do self-report data reliably reflect behavioral reality?

Researchers also study what is called "**construct validity**"—an accumulation of evidence to support that a test indeed measures what it says it measures. In an evaluation of learning-style assessments, only one (Allinson and Hayes' Cognitive Style Index) met all four scientific criteria for validity and reliability—predictive validity, construct validity, test-retest reliability, and internal consistency.[52]

More succinctly, the very notion that matching learning styles improves learning outcomes is nonsense.

Lastly, one of many meta-analyses that showed the learning styles emperor was butt-naked claims:

> "Learning style instruments have not been shown to be valid and reliable, and there is no evidence that understanding one's learning style improves learning and its related outcomes."[53]

Nonetheless, much ink has been spilled defending learning styles. One researcher summarizes these defense attempts as:

> "Some learning style theorists have conducted repeated small studies that tend to validate the hypotheses derived from their own conceptualizations. However, in general, these studies have not been designed to disconfirm hypotheses, are open to expectation and participation effects, and do not involve wide enough samples to constitute valid tests in educational settings. **Even with these built-in biases, no single learner preference pattern unambiguously indicates a specific instructional design.**"[54] [emphasis ours]

Logic (L)

"[To] be good at anything worth learning (the cello or Call of Duty), you are going to suck for a long time. If you get used to sucking and persevering, you can get good at anything."

PAUL GIBBONS

There is a logical, untested premise underlying learning styles research—that people learn when they are "comfortable" and according to preferences. This idea is not easy to defend philosophically (besides having been debunked empirically). Indeed, the essence of both the "growth mindset" idea and the now-popular "grit" idea is that learning proceeds when people are "comfortable being uncomfortable" or outside of their comfort zone. We do not attempt to either defend or debunk growth mindset and grit (science will do its thing over time to make a determination), simply highlight these ideas as antithetical to the notion that comfort and learning are "paired" in any meaningful way.

Learning how to learn appears to involve extracting the learning nectar from wherever it may be found, however comfortable or uncomfortable it may feel.

Again, the logical flaw is leaping from "I like visual learning" to "I learn better visually" and then further to "teachers ought to present me with information visually." In yet another study, Hussman and colleagues found that, "most students' study strategies did not match their professed 'learning style,' and even when the two aligned, it didn't correlate with higher course achievements."[55]

Costs and consequences

"Live as if you were to die tomorrow. Learn as if you were to live forever."
MAHATMA GANDHI

Learning style philosophy makes a third, **prescriptive** claim that teachers (or communicators) **should** match learning modalities to learners' preferred style.

Scott Lilienfeld, the late psychologist, introduced an additional learning styles problem with a sports analogy when interviewed on Paul's *Think Bigger, Think Better* podcast.[56] Young soccer players have strong leg dominance like we all have hand dominance (i.e., most right-handed kids are better with their right foot). The way to develop young wannabe Ronaldos is not to have them avoid left-foot drills; the path to mastery is learning to use their left foot to almost the same capability as their right. **In other words, focusing on learner preferences might be injurious to learning and achievement.**

In our complex world, learning how to learn is critical. We need to take in information, assimilate it, and think critically about it, but information today comes to us in multitudinous ways. Most enjoy YouTube (well, at least those under 40 seem to), but a YouTube preference that potentially marginalizes other learning modalities means a learner ill-equipped for the 21st century—**when learners must be agile and able to handle diverse sources of knowledge (not just those they prefer).**

All teaching-related professions (including coaching, organizational change, and learning and development) need to have these conversations. For instance, one CEO client tried weekly one-on-one coaching sessions with her team for a month, only to conclude they were not time well spent. Paul had to remind her, gently, that a month is not long enough to "not suck" at coaching nor to cultivate vital business results from coaching. Paul also recalls, amusingly, a VP client who took a yoga class for stress saying, "I tried it once and I wasn't any good."

Most things worth learning are not easy to learn—hence, the "sucking and persevering" notion we endorse.

Alternatives and conclusions

"Smooth seas do not make skillful sailors."

AFRICAN PROVERB

More important than matching learning modalities to learning styles is matching learning modalities to **content type**. If you want to learn to skate, YouTube will only get you so far—you need to lace up those skates and get in the rink. To learn math, you need to learn to manipulate abstract symbols using paper or screens. Math videos and podcasts may help, but there is no substitute for grinding through equations and diagrams. If you want to learn to play piano, you need to read music, but also the more time you spend touching the keys, the better.

This alternatively suggests teaching **modalities that adapt to the content**, as opposed to learners' self-described, preferred styles.

Focus on learner experience is understandable, even noble. If a half-century of debating learning styles has a silver lining, it is the attention paid to individual differences in the classroom.

Teachers do more than just pour information into students' heads. Developing a hunger and appetite for learning is possibly the most important attitudinal meta-skill. In that regard, thinking about learner experience opens a door to conversations about the joys of learning.

When a student struggles, the application of bad ideas like learning styles and fixed mindset might catalyze a shift in learning modalities. However, with compassion teachers can work to exterminate the idea that learning ought to be easy and teach more perseverance.

Nonsense is peddled daily about how people learn and society is filled with harmful ideas about what appears to be the single-most crucial meta-skill: Learning to learn.

Learning styles are an idea bad for children, bad for businesses, and bad for a world where the learning imperative becomes stronger yearly.

What comes next?

Learning styles show the risks of taking something subjectively "obvious" and extrapolating it to a causal relationship and prescription for professionals.

Next, we encounter a myth more difficult to test—the notion of a burning platform or sense of urgency.

CHAPTER VIII

Burning platforms and benzodiazepines: Is urgency helpful or harmful?

"Many of the big problems we encounter in organizations and society don't require burning platforms. To solve bigger, more complex, and ambiguous problems, we need open minds, creativity, and hope."[57]

CHIP AND DAN HEATH (*SWITCH*, 2010)

"Creating a sense of urgency" is the first of John Kotter's eponymous eight steps from his 1996 book *Leading Change*[58]—frequently cited as the best-selling organizational change book of all time. Kotter doubled down on the concept in 2008 with a sequel titled *Sense of Urgency*.[59]

Some more critical change professionals have rightfully abandoned the idea, yet urgency pops up again and again. Many executives and change leaders still live by it and some change gurus still teach it as canonical truth (having read the popular books from 30 years ago).

Sense of urgency as an idea appears based on faulty assumptions about people, organizations, change, and leadership. At best, it is rarely applicable, and at worst, it is harmful—both to individual change projects and longer-term drivers of organizational performance, such as culture and climate.

Claim

For Kotter, creating a sense of urgency means: "Urgency is unbelievably important when you're talking about, not little changes, but big changes." It is foundational not just to his ideas but also to many of his 1980s and 1990s contemporaries, who laid the foundations of organizational change management practice.

When we talk about urgency, we lump its "sibling concepts" together in our critique, including:

- Create a burning platform,
- Hold feet to the fire,
- Give a short, sharp shock,
- Orchestrate pain,
- Wield a big stick, and
- Change or die.

When evaluating generalizations such as the above, we want them to be **mostly true** and the **assumptions** on which they are based to be **generally valid**. Moreover, when applying such a generalization to our practice, we would like it to be **beneficial**.

Is this the case with "sense of urgency" and parallel ideas? Are they generally more accurate than false? Are they based upon sound assumptions? Are they useful to change practitioners and beneficial to change initiatives?

Backstory

How to motivate, how to galvanize action, and how to initiate change are questions leaders have grappled with throughout time. In war, the leader's job was to get the sullen masses to fight for their cause. In the battle of Thermopylae, Leonidas tells his troops, "the barbarian is come near, while we are wasting time." Shakespeare's Mark Anthony intoned, "Cry havoc! And let slip the dogs of war!"

Margaret Thatcher favored treating youthful offenders to "short, sharp shocks."

Thus, creating a sense of urgency is an ancient idea where it is assumed the **authority figure saw clearly what is needed, their job then was to motivate, and urgency was a primary tool (cultivated through pain and fear)**. Your authors are both just old enough to remember when corporal punishment was the norm at home and school—behavioral change was delivered to children through a red bottom—and was deemed essential to character development. In the 1980s and 1990s workplace, similarly, leaders thought "putting the fear of God" into staff was central to good leadership practice.

Was this ancient motivational tactic ever sound? Does it apply in today's organizations? Does research evidence back it up?

Critical thinking with LIAR

What does critical thinking using LIAR suggest about the notion of urgency and its underlying assumptions?

Intuition (I)

At first blush, urgency is yet another myth that clicks with intuitive, historical, and cultural ideas about change. Unreflectively, the idea of a sluggish or static organization or indolent workers in denial who need a burning platform, seems reasonable.

Do today's businesses need to pick up the pace? Or is an alternative maxim "go slow to go fast" more apt? Perhaps more urgent conversations at RIM (Blackberry) or Kodak could have saved those companies from disruption. But that is management lore, do we know it for sure? And even if we are sure, is that a sound general maxim?

When testing ideas against our intuition, we must be careful of **priming effects** (e.g., when we are told a word or a number, our perception leans toward similar and related words and numbers). For instance, when primed with the word "doctor" subjects will recall the word "nurse" more readily than an unrelated word, such as "cat."

Critical thinkers double-check: Are there counter examples?

Counter-intuitively, today's workers might live in a constant state of urgency, agitation, stress, and pressure—expected to tirelessly adapt, upskill, and embrace workplace changes without complaint. Does introducing a change as urgent against this frenetic backdrop make sense? The leader's confusing message would seem to be, "yes, everything is urgent, but this one is REALLY URGENT."

A second counter-intuitive example is what change professionals call "change fatigue," or the idea that all workers (including senior leaders) are exhausted from a constant barrage of change initiatives, which are frequently conflicting and/or incoherent—all of which are expected to be received and embraced gracefully.

Yet a third counter-intuitive example comes from the Theory Y half of Douglas McGregor's Theory X and Theory Y from the 1950s and 1960s. Theory Y posits that people are inherently and naturally committed, motivated and creative, requiring little-to-no supervision to be productive. Here, the leader's change role is to tap into that wellspring of positive energy, ambition, and passion.

Theory Y's counter intuitions better describe 21st-century organizational zeitgeist than do Theory X's (which posits the opposite of Theory Y, or that people are inherently lazy, lack ambition, and only care about themselves).

Logic (L)

Some organizational changes seem to demand a "sense of urgency." If the movie theater is on fire, leaders need to get people to put down the popcorn.

However, is this idea of urgency applicable to change problems businesses face today? Is it not only mandatory, but also the first step leaders should take in organizational change?

Before accepting a notion as true, ponder its assumptions. When someone says, "create a sense of urgency," they are making specific assumptions about people and motivation, organizational dynamics, and positional leadership (see Figure VIII.1).

Burning platform and urgency assumptions

Category	Assumption
People and motivation	People are lazy, complacent, and resistant, thus, are motivated by carrots and sticks
Organization dynamics	Organizations prefer the status quo, thus, are in denial, stuck, and/or sluggish
Positional leadership	Leaders rose to the top by merit and have the answers, thus, are not the problem

© 2023 Paul Gibbons and Tricia Kennedy

Figure VIII.1: Burning platform and urgency assumptions. Claims about the importance of urgency and burning platforms to behavioral change are based upon assumptions, or premises, about human behavior that simply don't hold water (neither individually nor in combination).

These assumptions logically appear more false than true.

People who claim a sense of urgency is necessary for change are making an illogical leap from **some change** requires urgency to **all change requires urgency**. Intuition makes the first premise seem plausible, but critical thinking leads us to wonder about that leap from "some" to "all." If **generalizations** ignore context and diversity, they can be **stereotypes or over-generalizations**—a risk that all the canonical change models run, from Lewin's unfreezing to change curves.

Conceptually, something is urgent only in comparison to other things. In other words, if everything is urgent, then nothing is urgent. **If all change efforts require a fabricated sense of urgency, then no change efforts are genuinely urgent.**

A management technique found even in today's companies is to keep the emotional temperature warm or hot, maintaining a constant state of urgency. Paul and Tricia have heard many a senior leader, over the years, repeatedly and confidently predict impending doom, recession, disruption, or downsizing. These leaders were intentionally exaggerating (and frequently incorrect) about the impending doom, it was their go-to method for goading followers into action.

Authority (A)

No greater authorities exist in organizational change history than Lewin, Kotter, Conner, and Schein.

Conner, a pioneer and founder of the field, beat Kotter to the punch by a couple of years with his **burning platform** metaphor, coined in his 1992 book *Managing at the Speed of Change*.[60] He suggests that "**orchestrating pain messages** throughout an institution is the first step in developing organizational commitment to change." [emphasis ours]

Kotter (another pioneer and founder) follows shortly thereafter with his change bestseller *Leading Change*, where his eight-step model has "a sense of urgency" in pole position. He went as far as to claim: "Real leaders often create these sorts of **artificial crises** rather than waiting for something to happen." [emphasis ours]

"Artificial crises" is a remarkable thing to say; it sounds as if this esteemed Harvard professor emeritus is advocating intentionally and knowingly misleading others. This Kotter and Harvard malarky continues to this day—see a recent marketing email from the *Harvard Business Review* in Figure VIII.2.

Harvard Business Review (HBR) marketing email (2022)

Master Change Management

Learn how to best establish a sense of urgency, win support, and silence naysayers to achieve buy-in and increase your odds of success.

Tapped to lead a change initiative — and afraid it will fail like so many others? You have reason to worry: 70% of change efforts do fail.

Beat the odds with this premium, customizable Accelerating Change PowerPoint™ presentation with detailed leader's notes. Take advantage of the opportunity to bring John Kotter's proven 8-step process to life, and use it to get buy-in for your change initiative. Plus, eliminate weeks of slide deck creation.

ACCELERATING CHANGE
Based on the work of JOHN P. KOTTER

Join the elite 30% who succeed with this customizable vehicle for driving change in your organization.

$99.95

BUY NOW   VIEW PREVIEW

© 2023 Paul Gibbons and Tricia Kennedy

Figure VIII.2: *Harvard Business Review* (HBR) marketing email (2022). Even the uber-prestigious, supposed research publication HBR seemingly still believes in urgency, or perhaps they don't mind turning a blind eye to make a buck on behalf of one of their business school's most famous professors emeritus.

Note the absurdities: For a measly $100 and with a single Pow-erPoint deck, you too can "learn how to best establish a sense of urgency," "silence naysayers," and "join the elite 30% who succeed." Neither creating a sense of urgency nor silencing naysayers strikes us as good leadership—and the "70% of change fails" myth is among the most puerile and pervasive change rubbish.

Research evidence (R)

"Support for ideas have to be undermined and destroyed if change is to take place."[61]

EDGAR SCHEIN (SWISS-AMERICAN PSYCHOLOGIST)

People who defend using negative stimuli to goad performance or initiate change frequently cite Yerkes and Dodson's 1908 finding that rodents who received moderate electric shocks increased learning and performance. (Rodents!) This finding only reinforced Behaviorist Psychology beliefs that punishment (even as far as incarceration and corporal punishment) is an effective and ethical way of changing behavior.

Lewin extrapolated these rodent findings to human social settings postulating, "to break open the shell of complacency and self-righteousness it is sometimes necessary to bring about an emotional stir up."[62] Can you think of a personal or business change example where "breaking open a shell" has worked?

During the 1950s and based on research performed in Communist Chinese prisoner-of-war camps, Schein describes change processes, "in which the prisoner's physical resistance, social and emotional support, self-image and sense of integrity, and basic values and personality were undermined, thereby creating a state of readiness to be influenced and changing."[63]

Again, one must worry about whether a POW's readiness to change by "undermining" their physical, social, and emotional wellbeing usefully and ethically translates into how best to influence the 3rd-floor IT department during the 21st century.

These notable change authorities, all pioneers and founders in the field, are lined up against us here. To reject this urgency notion, we Davids of today must slay Goliaths from the past.

It is arguable, incorrectly in our view, that those were different times, not just different contexts (such as prison camps). Lewin, Kotter, Conner, and Schein might have been right at the time. Or perhaps their findings only apply to rodents and brainwashing prisoners? For example, in the 1980s, nearly 90% of Americans approved of corporal punishment of children. In 1989 the UN Convention on the Rights of the Child codified its prohibition, and at the turn of the millennium most European countries banned it. That may explain the change founders' errors. Brilliant as they may be, their values reflected the times, organizations were different and cultural norms were different.

We prefer to think that these change founders were never right. Organizations and cultural norms today have made such harsh leadership behavior unacceptable. And scientific research over the last 60 years has progressively shown such ideas false in human psychology, organizations, and change.

Humans tend to change with the times (eventually), and one of these foundational thinkers appears to have changed tack. In his later work, Schein seems to stand back from his earlier view that negative stimuli are necessary to motivate action. His **process consulting** philosophy is a "philosophy of helping," basing change on more humanistic methods: Inquiry, deep listening, positive regard, and person-centered counseling—along the lines of psychologist Carl Rogers' legacy, who is a founder of Humanistic Psychology.

Schein's apparent sea change followed the zeitgeist, or the cognitive revolution in psychology, that shifted theories of motivation theory away from external-stimulus behaviorist views to multidimensional views that recognize concepts such as meaning, intrinsic motivation, and human flourishing.

Today in business, formal change theories focus mostly on the positive, but the behaviorist mindset (caricatured by "carrots and sticks") lives on simultaneously with some of the trend towards more positivity.

The result of these legacy ideologies is companies with both cuddly rhetoric (mandatory today) and coercive mindsets and actions.

For example: Performance-improvement plan (PIP) policies shed light on the persistence of 20th-century theories of motivation and behavior change. In one behemoth, global firm a PIP results from a poor performance review and stipulates automatic termination if targets documented in the PIP are not met within 30 days, no matter which factors may have contributed to a missed target. Use of this shock tactic does change behavior—smart employees immediately start talking to headhunters and recruiters. The mind-numbing part of these PIP policies is the employee subject to the PIP rarely has any power or influence over target achievement. In the short term, performance in this "fulfilment" role depends almost entirely on supervisor and senior leader effectiveness.

In our own experience, PIP policies such as this one is not a solitary example, they are quite common. Furthermore, in our own interviews with folks who have experienced a PIP process report suffering extreme distress and wellbeing issues. (In short, they look for another job, and if they remain may be miserable and anxious.)

Dutch academics ten Have and colleagues, in a 2017 systematic review of the urgency literature, conclude, "**the scientific research**

literature does not support the claim that a sense of urgency is crucial to successful organizational change."[64] [emphasis ours] Indeed, in the absence of high-quality research about urgency, ten Have and colleagues relied on studies examining proxy concepts, fear appeal and time pressure. While they found that time pressure increased cooperative behaviors in a laboratory setting, the attendant fear became counterproductive because it elicited short-term thinking and only temporary behavior changes. (We see more about this 2017 work by ten Have and colleagues in a future chapter because it is the only broad-based, in-depth, and systematic review of change axioms we have found.)

Urgency and burning platforms come from some of the most authoritative names in the change world and may feel intuitive, at first glance, but the competing claim testers of logic and research evidence point us in the opposite direction and ultimately refute them.

Costs and consequences

"All things are subject to interpretation. Whichever interpretation prevails at a given time is a function of power and not truth."

FRIEDRICH NIETZSCHE (GERMAN PHILOSOPHER)

Above, we asked whether "sense of urgency" was broadly true, an over-generalization, or grounded in inaccurate assumptions about humans, change, organizations, and leaders. Now, we explore whether the urgency mindset has deleterious consequences.

Some possible consequences, set out below, include that the urgency myth creates an undue emphasis on haste, a crisis mentality (toxic culture), an unhelpful attitude toward dissent, and reinforces a dysfunctional view of leadership.

Haste makes waste

Businesses sometimes fail because they don't act urgently enough, but other times they fail because they **act too urgently**. Swiftness comes with a price, as does slowness, there are tradeoffs to both. We have seen many ill-conceived projects fail because of **too little** deliberation and too much haste: The knee-jerk reorganization, near-sighted downsizing, impulsive acquisition, and non-aligned initiative. Business leaders often do things that are **familiar and easy to do** rather than thinking through what is **right to do**.

Crisis, what crisis? The emotional tax

Urgency and its siblings (e.g., burning platform, holding feet to fire) are designed to encourage fear, which we now know is destructive to creativity, decision making, and emotional safety in the workplace. It insinuates that people in organizations need Yerkes-Dobson-inspired stimuli for optimal performance. But attention and higher-order thinking are stymied during any short-lived burst of energy and strength triggered by a fight-or-flight response. For example, urgency is a common tactic in phishing and other similar scams because it effectively preys on a quick burst of fear to prevent thinking (i.e., act now, think later)—Pay right now on this phone call or risk arrest, the police are on their way; or click on this link now and log into your account or risk identity theft, your account has already been hacked.

Organizations today demand higher order thinking (sometimes called the knowledge economy), whereas with the harsh manual labor of a century ago (when Yerkes-Dobson did their research) it is arguable (albeit, unethically) that creative and higher-order thinking were of dubious merit.

Living with constant anxiety entails health risks associated with prolonged stimulation of the adrenal cortex and cortisol production, which diminishes immune response. Additionally, prolonged states of hyper-vigilance, or spending excessive amounts of time in this hyper-aroused survival mode, are known to cause heart damage, obesity, and increase risk of both depression and post-traumatic stress disorder.

We don't dispute that emotional arousal is essential; there are other, less harmful, aroused emotional states that are more conducive to cognitive performance: Inspiration, excitement, determination, or passion.

Creating toxic cultures and other unintended, long-term consequences

Urgency can become sewn into an organization's culture. We speculate that urgency cultures may produce multiple unintended effects.

Exxon, for example, is among the most profitable companies in the world but is also infamous for its toxic culture. A 2022 *Bloomberg Businessweek* article suggests that Exxon's high-pressure culture began in the 1990s, when its CEO Lee Raymond's management style earned him the nickname "Iron Ass." Today, Exxon has the highest attrition rate among the oil majors and the report suggests that while pay and benefits are above average, innovation, collaboration, and psychological safety continue to suffer.[65] An insider opined that the remuneration does not compensate for a toxic culture.

In the U.S. at Wells Fargo, legal authorities found enough evidence of a relationship between senior leadership pressure and salespeople criminal activity (opening false customer accounts) to impose legal settlements that cost Wells Fargo $3 billion between 2002 and 2016.[66] On the other side of the Atlantic, three France Telecom executives were convicted of "creating a corporate culture so toxic [during the 2000s] that 35 of their employees were driven to suicide."[67]

This is not to suggest causality between urgency or burning platforms and such extreme events, simply to highlight real-life potential extremes of toxic culture. Instead, we ask the reader to wonder with us whether an urgency mindset contributed to the problem.

Silencing naysayers and great-man leadership theories

Figure VIII.2 shows *Harvard Business Review* still actively promotes urgency as a guiding change principle. Note the casual assumption that leaders are entitled to "silence" people and (worryingly) that they always have a clear and correct view of company direction.

This is allied to what are called great-man leadership theories— that select visionary and powerful men alone have the insight and authority and are born to lead. Such great-man stories are more exciting than the patient, mindful, and compassionate servant leader who, through thoughtful stewardship, served their company for 30 years. Yawn. Who wants to hear about that? (See sidebar on great-man leadership.)

Great-man leadership theories and urgency

Many ideas about leadership and management are grounded in early conceptualizations of leadership, or great-man theories.

History is full of well-documented examples of great-man leaders gone wrong that illustrate the dark side of power and dominance at the root of these theories, yet we still find political and organizational models today that follow a traditional great-man script: Strong, powerful, and elite men who are born to lead. They alone know what best and right, and stereotypical masculine traits like aggression and hyper-competitiveness are prized to "whip the troops" into shape.

Even if this leadership idea sounds like a caricature or God complex, easily poked fun or demonized, it is no mere historical artifact. Beliefs consistent with great-man leadership scripts are alive and well in the 21st century.

Sheer persistence of the great-man leadership script speaks volumes about how deeply it resonates intuitively. Especially in political and business scenarios, countless big names in positions of power feel their position gives them the right to coerce, manipulate, inflict pain, and harshly wield their dominance in the name of motivation and progress in what they imagine is the right direction.

Alternatives and conclusions

To ask if change requires a sense of urgency suggests the follow-on question, what do you mean by urgency? Urgency means **importance requiring swift action**. "Exigency" is a reasonable synonym.

Urgency, it follows, implies that change fails because of a lack of **importance** or **swiftness**. We accept, without argument, that for change to happen, some importance must be attached. The organizational leaders with whom your authors have worked wield long lists of things they would like to change. It is a sign of leadership maturity to realize not all of them can happen, at least not all at the same time. Leaders must prioritize by deciding what matters most and what deserves their focus and attention. This applies to leaders at every level—even the newly minted—in both personal and professional realms. For executive leaders (likely Kotter's target audience), their list of organizational priorities (e.g., strategy, operations, talent, and technology) becomes weighty. They must choose which to make more important than others and in what order.

But swiftness is a different matter altogether. Steven Covey popularized a distinction between urgency and importance that suggests not everything that is important must also be urgent and vice versa. In his conception, an **important** change is consequential, mission-aligned, and of enduring value.[68] An **urgent** change may be none of those, but urgent changes do require immediate attention. Urgent changes may be reactive, like a fire to put out. It is urgent for consultants to complete their timesheets on time, for instance, but is it also important? Some business change focuses on long-term value, like creating a brand, changing culture, researching new products, or developing relationships—these are important, but are they also urgent? These questions (and more) should form the basis of our thinking as leaders hone their ability to prioritize effectively.

Covey's insight seems to be that if one pays sufficient attention to long-term (important) value, there are then fewer fires to put out (urgent). If you tend to diet and exercise (important), you are less likely to require immediate medical care (urgent). If you nurture high-trust customer relationships (important), it is less likely that an upset customer will call demanding to see you the next day at 6 a.m. (urgent).

This nit-picky pedantry about word choice in a book written over three-decades ago may be irritating—but "sense of urgency" and "burning platforms" have become canonical truth. If people only remember one of Kotter's eight steps, the first (urgency) is usually the one.

Urgency and burning platforms further imply there are clear beginning and ending points for organizational changes. And while many change efforts might be practically structured in such a linear fashion, change is constant and evolves. Leaders should wonder whether a change should be kicked off with a crisis, and then crisis piled upon crisis, leading to change fatigue and low levels of workforce engagement and wellness.

Eustress is the idea that there is a beneficial amount of pressure that challenges and inspires, but eustress is subjective. One person's eustress is another's harmful stress. There is also a larger question of whether stress imposed from above is ever the "eu" type of stress. **Psychological safety** research evidence suggests the opposite: Desirable outcomes, such as innovation, collaboration, team performance, and retention are more likely in a "safe" climate rather than those with high levels of negative emotional arousal.

Pain, fear, coercion, and manipulation have no place in the ethical professional's toolbox. Successful, ethical, and human-centered organizational change does not require urgency. Moreover, urgency as a leadership maxim or mindset is likely harmful.

There are alternatives. Leaders ought to be taught and held accountable for trusting, supporting, and engaging, as well as removing obstacles and creating high-performing teams, instead of cracking the urgency whip. Agile organizations, growth cultures, psychological safety, and dynamic organization structures are further possible examples (see Paul's *Science of Organizational Change* for further discussion).

What comes next?

We have talked about the R in LIAR, or research evidence, without guidance into different kinds of evidence, their different uses, their built-in strengths and weaknesses, and without cautions against misuse.

Next, we offer a basic guide to different kinds of evidence.

CHAPTER IX

Evaluating evidence: Just the basics

"A balanced argument doesn't weigh two sides equally. It weighs the strongest evidence more heavily. Critical thinking isn't about representing every view. It's about recognizing your own biases and giving serious consideration to the facts that contradict your hopes and beliefs."

ADAM GRANT (ORGANIZATIONAL PSYCHOLOGIST)

A central, recurring theme of *Change Myths* is the role of science and evidence in choosing which theories, methods, and models are most effective in professional change work. In organizational change, we encounter many forms of evidence (e.g., cohort studies, case studies, consulting firm benchmarking, randomly controlled experiments, meta-analyses, and attitude surveys). Change practitioners need to know which of these to trust and when.

There are year-long and semester-long courses that **merely introduce** research methods. This chapter isn't a comprehensive treatment but rather a guide for the practitioner to parsing different kinds of change evidence they likely encounter daily.

Informal evidence

"We don't see the world as it is; we see it as we are."
ANAÏS NIN (FRENCH-BORN AMERICAN AUTHOR)

At risk of introducing a too-simplistic treatment, there is evidence gathered formally, and there is evidence gathered informally. Daily, humans gather informal evidence and draw conclusions from it.

Imagine taking a new route from work and arriving home ten minutes later than usual. We may conclude that our usual route is better and that the new route is a dud. However, we don't have access to any counterfactuals. What would have happened if we had taken our usual route? Perhaps there was a local sporting event affecting traffic on both routes?

A friend is a fan of some of the wilder extremes in alternative medicine, including shamanism and homeopathy. If we dare broach the subject, our friend claims to have first-hand empirical evidence "proving" those treatments **caused** health and wellbeing breakthroughs. We might reply asking—but if you do yoga, meditate, walk 30-minutes a day, eat vegan food, go to the gym, lead a purposeful life, and have warm and supportive friends—could it not be those practices rather than the homeopathy or shamanic rituals that lead to health and wellbeing? Our friend's reasoning follows the **post-hoc ergo propter-hoc fallacy**—it preceded it, so it caused it.

Therein lies the trouble with informal evidence—a viper's nest of logical fallacies and cognitive biases await us. Humans are inclined to **see what they believe** rather than believe what they see. That is, humans mostly decide what to believe and then seek out evidence to justify those beliefs, whether consciously or subconsciously, as our friend above does. This is the trap of informal evidence gathering, especially in a complex system: We create tidy explanatory narratives; the real story is not so tidy. The brilliant mathematician Nassim Taleb calls this the **narrative fallacy**.

As a community, change practitioners share and create social agreement on change models such as ADKAR, change curves, and Kotter—tidy narratives about what is true and what works. We build these shared narratives around informally gathered and anecdotal evidence from which change narratives emerge.

However, as nerds are prone to say, "the plural of anecdote isn't data." A collection of narratives, not collected systematically, is better than a single story, but perhaps not by much.

Post-hoc ergo propter-hoc and narrative fallacies undergird entire industries—such as the dietary supplement industry. According to one industry whistleblower, Dr. Stephen Barrett, "almost all supplements, in people with adequate diets, give you nothing more than expensive pee."[69] (There are exceptions, of course, for deficiencies due to aging, pregnancy, and so forth.) The supplement industry is a $60-billion behemoth that hides behind lax regulatory requirements and narrative fallacies—yet another example of **commercial success lending "authority" to something largely refuted by science**.

Social evidence for narratives is also shaped by filter bubbles and algorithms because humans tend to form communities around shared interests and beliefs, and social algorithms playback content in which we have expressed interest—both creating bubbles and echo chambers. For example, conspiracy theorists tend to gather in the same online communities, so from their point of view, the social evidence for their points of view is overwhelming, everyone they are close to believes just as they do. (In information science, this network phenomenon is called the **majority illusion**—the idea that if our beliefs are widely held, then they *must* be correct.)

And so it is with organizational change—our community has self-formed filter bubbles and echo chambers, and because of those, we are more likely to see ideas with which we agree (rather than disagree) in the fora where change ideas are discussed.

While there is a lot to be said for informal evidence gathered by the experienced practitioner, the informality of that evidence gathering, coupled with the very human desire to see oneself as knowledgeable and effective, usually means sloppy evidence evaluation. In turn, that sloppiness can easily spill over into practitioners' change beliefs.

The practitioner's expert tacit knowledge and intuition, calibrated and refined by scientific research evidence, is both necessary and important. This is consistent with definitions of evidence-based practice (EBP).[70] It helps the expert professional evade the trap identified by famed physicist Richard Feynman: "The first principle is that you must not fool yourself, and you are the easiest person to fool." When both tacit and formal evidence accumulate in tandem, confidence increases and knowledge progresses. (See Figure IX.1: CEBMa's evidence-based practice model for the elements of EBP.)

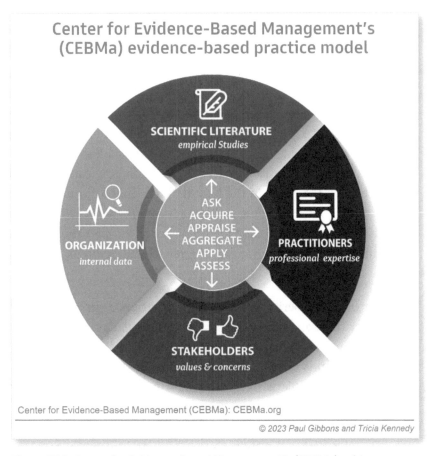

Figure IX.1: Center for Evidence-Based Management's (CEBMa) evidence-based practice model. A common misconception of evidence-based practice is that it only entails scientific research evidence (R in LIAR), whereas it combines R with three other elements and is context specific.

Community science

Another variety of informal evidence is the collective knowledge that emerges from the informal, field-based experimentation of daily life, experience, and expertise over generations. This variety of evidence gathering and knowledge-making evolves over long periods in professional communities. Examples range from farming to big business.

Humans have been farming for about 10,000 years. Over time, they slowly got better through experimentation and knowledge sharing (particularly after the advent of trade, which allowed the exchange of knowledge from the East to Eurasia and vice versa). For example, crop rotation and letting fields fallow can be traced back as far as 6,000 years in the Middle East. That informal science led to farming improvements, which allowed the world to grow its population from 300 million at the dawn of the first millennium to a billion by the time agricultural science emerged (e.g., genetics and the nitrogen cycle).

Such informal experimentation and experience, in millions of fields, over thousands of years, produced knowledge. For example, crop rotation, irrigation, and the plough preceded agricultural science by thousands of years. However, some of that knowledge was suspect. One example is that religious rituals, such as rain dances and human sacrifice, influence weather conditions and crop flourishing. Once agricultural science emerged, we could begin to separate the wheat from the chaff amidst ancient, informally gathered evidence that had produced agricultural breakthroughs but also agricultural myths.

Business is similar. The world economy is about $100 trillion, much of which is made up of business activity. Businesses have been innovating and changing effectively for millennia. Though change experts, organizational psychologists, consultants, and organization development (OD) experts have joined the fray recently, businesses have been changing without our help for a long time. What emerged over extended periods in millions of enterprises (large and small) was informal management science. As with farming, community science improved business practice over centuries, but

144

not until the establishment of formal, evidence-based management science (less than 100 years ago) could science be separated from pseudoscience, or breakthroughs from myths.

Management science, like agriculture, inherited many myths because entering the Industrial Era, the only templates that existed for large, complex organizations were churches and armies. As management science became more formal in the 20th century, we began to dispel myths inherited from those institutions—for example, that good leadership is command and control.

Non-systematic, day-to-day field experiments have generated a body of knowledge in the change community. Still, those practitioner narrative-derived insights need to be verified, insofar as possible, by formal evidence gathering—a hallmark of science.

Formal evidence

*"[E]verything in science is open to dissent. There is **always an alternative hypothesis that could be true**, but this doesn't undermine warrant....This is why science cannot offer proof but must instead rely on the **idea that belief is warranted when a theory has sufficient credible evidence and has survived rigorous testing**." [emphasis ours]*

LEE MCINTYRE (PHILOSOPHER OF SCIENCE)

"[A]ny single method is biased and that only **by thinking critically about the strengths and weaknesses** *of various methods, and using multiple methods to overcome single-methods biases, can rigorous results be achieved."* *[emphasis ours]*

MICHAEL PATTON (QUALITATIVE AND APPLIED RESEARCH EXPERT)

Formal evidence, as we use the term, emerges from research designed and performed according to the rigors of the scientific method, whether quantitative, qualitative, or mixed methods. It also adheres to certain quality criteria and displays certain scientific hallmarks, which include:

- Systematic data gathering procedures with an intention to follow the evidence where it leads,
- Hypothesis development that attempts falsification not verification,
- Open and transparent assumptions, procedures, and reasoning to support replication attempts, and
- Adhere to language that reflects degrees of certainty and uncertainty with an eye toward warrant (not proof).

There are thousands of books on formal research methods and designs. Underpinning these research methods are (or ought to be) principles from philosophy, especially philosophy of science. In what sense are social science constructs such as "intelligence" real? What does it mean to say two things have a causal relationship compared to a correlational relationship? What are the strengths and weaknesses, or limitations, of different designs? The intellectual rabbit hole burrows deep, so we resign ourselves to covering only some of the basics.

Essentially, research designs can be conceptualized on a spectrum, where the quantitative end is more prescriptive and the qualitative end more descriptive. Collectively, and along with mixed methods designs, these research designs produce knowledge and research evidence at varying levels of breadth and depth. Figure IX.2 shows a sampling of quantitative and qualitative research methods as they appear on a spectrum.

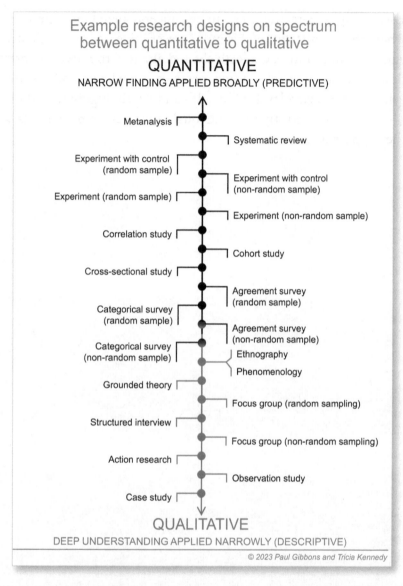

Figure IX.2: Example research designs on spectrum between quantitative and qualitative. All research designs involve trade-off decisions, putting them on a spectrum between quantitative and qualitative. The experienced critical thinker understands these tradeoffs and weighs the evidence accordingly.

Although Figure IX.2 is arranged vertically, this is more a function of how we hold books—with the long side vertical and the short side horizontal— and is not to imply that "top is better." However, there are hierarchical features to research designs depending on the researcher's purpose and intent.

Where the **quantitative** end of the spectrum aspires to prediction and generalizability of findings, or exploring if a relationship exists between two things (either causally or correlationally), **by design their findings are not descriptive of meaning**—studies in this tradition **tell you a lot about a little** or produce a narrow finding that applies broadly.

Conversely, where the **qualitative** end of the spectrum aspires to description and meaning, seeking in-depth and contextual understanding of phenomena, **by design their findings are not predictive or generalizable**—studies in this tradition **tell you a little about a lot**, or produce deeper understanding that applies narrowly.

Professional researchers make complicated and difficult choices when designing a research study, weighing both the tradeoffs and strengths and weaknesses of different methods, and making decisions about which one is best suited to answer their research question. Since researchers are human, sometimes their choices are poor, may appear irrational, or aren't well suited to their question. Moreover, certain specialties might lean toward a set of methods more than others. For instance, I-O psychologists tend to favor the more empirical, OD professionals tend to favor qualitative inquiry, and consultant researchers tend to favor benchmarking and surveys. We look briefly at each of these designs below.

Quantitative research methods

"Because qualitative and quantitative methods involve differing strengths and weaknesses, they constitute alternative, but not mutually exclusive, strategies for research."[71]

MICHAEL PATTON (QUALITATIVE AND APPLIED RESEARCH EXPERT)

Quantitative research designs are used to identify statistical relationships between variables. Some designs seek cause-and-effect relationships—for example, increased goal setting causes increased task persistence, or increased psychological safety causes team performance improvement. From a practitioner's point of view, these are ideal because causal findings provide clearer direction for what to do. (As in, if I can increase psychological safety then my team's creativity will also increase.) Some designs seek only to uncover relationships (i.e., correlation, either positive or negative), but not causality. For example, as goal setting increases task persistence increases but we don't know if one causes the other (or something else), only that they move together (a positive correlation).Or as psychological safety decreases employee stress levels increase but we don't know if one causes the other (or something else), only that they move together (in this case a negative correlation). It turns out that verifying causation is much more difficult.

Confidence in relationship findings from quantitative designs are high (when performed well) because such designs utilize experimental techniques, quantitative data collection, and mathematics, but also hopefully such tactics as random sampling, sufficient sample sizes, control groups with randomized assignment, and multiple trials of the same experiment.

The "gold standard" for quantitative research designs is the meta-analysis, especially when evaluating high-quality randomized-controlled experiments. Meta-analyses aggregate groups of other quantitative studies and apply mathematics to determine if the findings are consistent across the studies it aggregates—this aggregation and resulting analyses increase confidence beyond a confidence level that can be attributed to a single study (i.e., an accumulation of evidence pointing to the same conclusion). One caveat with meta-analyses: Their findings are only as good as the quality of the studies they aggregate. Meta-analyses are instrumental in medicine; for example, a meta-analysis of vaccination research might aggregate hundreds of studies on millions of patients over many decades.

Systematic reviews resemble meta-analyses in that they aggregate large groups of other research studies to evaluate consistency of findings (leveraging accumulation of evidence), but they are not limited to only quantitative studies, and they do so without the mathematical techniques of a meta-analysis. The organizational change field is lucky that a team of Dutch organizational scientists, Steven ten Have and colleagues, apply the systematic review method to some of the more popular change axioms in the in their 2017 book *Reconsidering Change Management: Applying Evidence-Based Insights in Change Management Practice.*

A systematic review of change management evidence—*Reconsidering Change Management*

An axiom is a self-evident claim that requires no proof. Axioms are often the premises that serve to logically prove other statements on which they are based. From the axioms of Euclidean geometry, for instance, an entire geometrical system is built to enable the fields of architecture, cartography, and engineering.

What passes for knowledge in organizational change management is similarly built upon foundational axioms. Change axioms are the core of orthodoxy, shibboleths if you will, for example that certain leadership styles (e.g., transformational) are better than others during organizational change, that culture drives performance, that people resist change, and/or that trust matters.

If we believe the axiom that participation is essential to successful organizational change, the practitioner can build a case for specific participation interventions (e.g., workshops or feedback loops) without having to defend the need for participation at every turn (although it is a belief worth questioning, or at least needing more research, according to ten Have and colleagues' findings).

As such self-evident claims based on shared understandings, axioms are useful starting places—**if (and only if) they are correct**. If they are not correct, you risk wasted effort (at best) or potential harm.

The authors of *Reconsidering Change Management* have done a great deal of valuable heavy lifting for the organizational change field in their systematic review, which examines not only what are change's taken-for-granted axioms but also how these axioms stack up to the available research evidence.

Figure IX.3 lists **18 axioms of change** identified by ten Have and colleagues and summarizes their systematic review findings. To attempt this analysis from scratch on our own might have taken years. Fortunately, *Reconsidering Change Management* lays much of the groundwork.

Organizational change axioms from the book *Reconsidering Change Management* (2017)

#	Axiom	Conclusion	Evidence Quality
1	70% of all change interventions fail	very unlikely	none
2	A clear vision is essential for successful change	likely	low
3	People will not change if there is no sense of urgency	somewhat likely	low
4	Trust in the leader is needed for successful change	likely	moderate
5	When managing change, transformational leadership style is more effective than transactional one	very unlikely	moderate
6	Organizational change requires leaders with strong emotional intelligence (i.e., EQ)	unlikely	moderate
7	Supervisory support is critical for the success of change	very likely	moderate
8	To realize change in organizations, a powerful guiding coalition is needed	likely	negligible
9	Employees' capabilities to change determine the organization's capacity to change	somewhat likely	low
10	Participation is key for successful change	unlikely	moderate
11	Resistance to change should be defused early on in the change process	somewhat likely	low
12	A fair change process is important in achieving successful change	likely	low*
13	Organizational culture is difficult and time-consuming to change	minimal support[†]	very low
14	Organizational culture is related to performance	minimal support[†]	very low[§]
15	Goal setting combined with feedback is a powerful tool for change leaders	very likely	moderate to low
16	Commitment to change is an essential component of a successful change initiative	somewhat likely	moderate
17	Financial incentives are an effective way to encourage change and improve performance	very likely	moderate to low
18	Self-managing teams perform better in realizing change than traditionally managed teams	can neither confirm nor reject	high to low

* Quality of research evidence was high when fair process alone was evaluated, but low when combined with organizational change

† Minimal because construct of culture lacks agreed upon definition for this multidimensional phenomenon, limiting quality of systematic comparison

§ Minimal support as measured (emphasis the authors') because no meta-analyses or systematic reviews met the inclusion criteria

© 2023 Paul Gibbons and Tricia Kennedy

Figure IX.3: Organizational change axioms from the book *Reconsidering Change Management* (2017). Part of the analysis Steven ten Have and his authors performed for their 2017 book was to first identify the 18 most common organizational change axioms, only then did they dive into the scientific literature to examine any likelihood of truth.

Since *Reconsidering Change Management* is the most exhaustive systematic review of organizational change management axioms of which we are aware, we took their results one step further and plotted each axiom on a graph with the two dimensions used by ten Have and colleagues in their analysis (see Figure IX.4).

Some axioms were found to have been subjected to sufficient investigation and at high enough quality to warrant believing its truth or falsehood (i.e., top half of the graph). For example, that goal setting combined with feedback is a powerful change leader tool (axiom 15) seems almost certainly true (see top-right quadrant or quadrant 1); whereas that a transformational leadership style is more effective than a transactional one when managing change (axiom 5) is almost certainly false (see top-left quadrant or quadrant 2).

Other axioms were found to have been subjected to either insufficient investigation or only with weaker quality research (and some simply lacked enough conceptual clarity to make a determination), so we have less certainty about their truth or falsehood (i.e., the bottom half of the graph). For example, the importance of change process fairness (axiom 12) appears likely true (see bottom-right quadrant or quadrant 4); whereas the need to defuse change resistance (axiom 11) appears likely false (see bottom-left quadrant or quadrant 3).

Before moving on, pick two or three of your favorite change concepts. Do they appear on this graph? If so, in which quadrant? If not, where do you imagine they might be?

Let us be open. Some notions, such as participation and the importance of culture, are dear to us as practitioners. We treat the work of ten Have and colleagues as a cautionary tale—to pay attention to contextual features that may lead toward greater participation or to do further research on when and how culture matters most. (Further, participation has ethical merit—people should be informed or consulted about matters material to their livelihoods.)

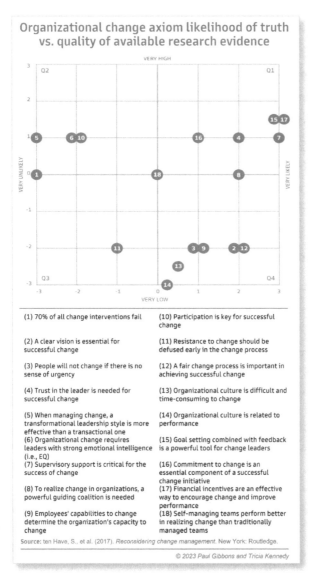

Organizational change axiom likelihood of truth vs. quality of available research evidence

(1) 70% of all change interventions fail

(2) A clear vision is essential for successful change

(3) People will not change if there is no sense of urgency

(4) Trust in the leader is needed for successful change

(5) When managing change, a transformational leadership style is more effective than a transactional one

(6) Organizational change requires leaders with strong emotional intelligence (i.e., EQ)

(7) Supervisory support is critical for the success of change

(8) To realize change in organizations, a powerful guiding coalition is needed

(9) Employees' capabilities to change determine the organization's capacity to change

(10) Participation is key for successful change

(11) Resistance to change should be defused early in the change process

(12) A fair change process is important in achieving successful change

(13) Organizational culture is difficult and time-consuming to change

(14) Organizational culture is related to performance

(15) Goal setting combined with feedback is a powerful tool for change leaders

(16) Commitment to change is an essential component of a successful change initiative

(17) Financial incentives are an effective way to encourage change and improve performance

(18) Self-managing teams perform better in realizing change than traditionally managed teams

Source: ten Have, S., et al. (2017). *Reconsidering change management.* New York: Routledge.

© 2023 Paul Gibbons and Tricia Kennedy

Figure IX.4: Organizational change axiom likelihood of truth vs. quality of available research evidence. While scientific literature is only one of four components that make up evidence-based practice (EBP), it can be the most overwhelming one. Luckily Steven ten Have and his co-authors put 18 common organizational change axioms to the test for in their 2017 book *Reconsidering Change Management.*

Cohort studies—Why *Good to Great* is not so great

"The basic message of Built to Last and other similar books is that good managerial practices can be identified and that good practices will be rewarded by good results. Both messages are overstated. Knowing the importance of luck, you should be particularly suspicious when highly consistent patterns emerge from the comparison of successful and less successful firms. In the presence of randomness, regular patterns can only be mirages."

DANIEL KAHNEMAN (NOBEL PRIZE WINNER IN ECONOMICS)

As we move down the spectrum on the quantitative half of diagram IX.2, we run into a popular (but oft abused) research method—the cohort study.

Cohort studies appear near the middle of Figure IX.2, meaning these designs do not seek to establish mathematical relationships between variables (i.e., cause and effect or correlation). Yet they feature in three of the top-ten best-selling business books of all time: *Good to Great*[72], *Built to Last*[73], and *In Search of Excellence*[74]. Studies such as these are prevalent in business and (usually) so poorly designed that they furnish terrible quality evidence. To illustrate the difference between a strong cohort study and a poorly designed one, consider an example from medicine.

In medical literature, there are examples of well-designed, well-executed cohort studies. Two such studies are the Nurses' Health Study and the Harvard Health Study (also called the Grant and Glueck study). Both studied large groups of people, their behaviors, and their health outcomes over long periods (75 years in the Harvard study). The Nurses' Health Study observed 280,000 nurses. Over such long time periods and with such robust sample sizes, important health insights were gleaned.[75] By comparison, organizational-research cohort studies frequently use small sample sizes and weak methods.

The cohort study designs used in the three business books above use the opposite of robust cohort study design—picking companies they thought were excellent, then hunting around for commonalities. For example, splitting research subjects into predetermined groups based on the variables under study is the antithesis of the random sampling favored by most researchers—random sampling is one of the techniques that allow study findings to be generalized beyond just the study's subjects. In doing so, the guru researcher has already drawn some conclusions (for example, that Wang Labs—who? —is a great company). The researchers also have variables they are looking to support and variables they aren't. In science, this is called "drawing the graph, then plotting the data." In other words, it is going in the wrong direction, starting with a conclusion, and then seeking evidence to support it.

Not only do some conclusions drawn in these three books look questionable after the passage of time (e.g., some of the companies deemed "great" either no longer exist or have run into legal trouble, including Wells Fargo, Wang Labs, and Circuit City), but also their conclusions are dubious because preselecting so-called great companies to include in the cohort under study makes the researchers highly susceptible to **the halo effect.**

The halo effect is another cognitive bias (first coined by psychologist Edward Thorndike, but most well-known from a 2007 book of the same name by Phil Rosenzweig)—where an existing, subjective, and positive impression about something irrationally expands to encompass its other aspects (e.g., a person, a company, a brand, a product). For example, Tricia's favorite brand of yogurt is Oikos Triple Zero (it is delicious and has no added sugar or artificial sweeteners!); the halo effect takes hold when she then irrationally projects her positive impression of this yummy product further to a general, positive impression of the company itself (e.g., assuming, for instance, that Oikos is a good company that is well run and has ethical practices).

Unsurprisingly, the halo effect also often shows up in organizational change studies. One commonly aired finding from a self-declared leader in the field of organizational change asserts that because a cohort of "successful change programs" used proactively managed change, therefore, this action **leads to** successful organizational change. However, another thought experiment raises doubt. If a change project is deemed successful, are people likely to say the change leadership and support were awful? Unlikely. Conversely, if a project hits the skids, are people likely to say the change leadership and support were exemplary?

Another example of false conclusions drawn from poorly executed, pseudoscientific cohort studies is generation theories—that generations share characteristics and values distinctly different from other generations, such as Boomers, Gen-X, Gen-Y, Millennials, and Gen-Z. While it is trivially true that a 65-year-old may behave differently than an 18-year-old, most research attributes these differences to life stage, not generation. One literature review firmly dumpsters generation theory, noting that:

> "[T]here is little empirical evidence that generations exist, that people can be reliably classified into generational groups, and, importantly, that there are demonstrable differences between such groups that manifest and affect various work-related processes."[76]

Qualitative research methods

"By combining multiple observers, theories, methods, and data sources, [researchers] can hope to overcome the intrinsic bias that comes from single-methods, single-observer, and single-theory studies."

NORMAN K. DENZIN (AMERICAN SOCIOLOGIST)

Moving down the research design spectrum in Figure IX.2, research designs become less about statistical relationships between a number of variables and become more descriptive and exploratory. The purpose shifts, accordingly, to more about understanding both people's experiences and the characteristics and complexities of an idea, theory, or construct.

The stories and narratives of qualitative research deepen our understanding of people, behavior, and the world, providing insight into how people **create meaning** from their experiences, how meaning informs choices, and how choices shape a system.

Well designed and performed, qualitative research is also rigorous, with systematic sampling and data collection. Qualitative research data varies widely, consisting of historical documents, structured interviews, behavioral observations of individuals or groups in action, among others. Data collection often takes place in "the field" (real-world settings) but can also occur in lab-like settings (think of a typical focus group).

With qualitative research designs, we get more meaning, more depth, and more in-context understanding, but we get less information about relationships between specific variables and less ability to generalize findings to another context. If our goal is to produce change in a system, understanding narratives and context may be more valuable than a rigorously established relationship between two variables, in some cases.

While arguably somewhat slanted toward qualitative methods, Figure IX.5 is a solid take on a high-level comparison across quantitative, qualitative, and mixed method traditions, and illustrates those traditions complementing each other to progress knowledge broadly and deeply (adapted slightly from a table by Michael Patton).

Scientific research quality criteria across traditions

Criteria	Quantitative	Qualitative	Mixed Methods
Aspiration	Empirical generalizations across time and space	In-depth, holistic, contextually sensitive understanding of phenomena	Integrating in-depth understanding with broader generalizations
Science philosophy roots	Positivism and logical positivism, scientific empiricism and realism	Social constructivism, phenomenology, hermeneutics, Verstehen tradition	Pragmatism
Inquiry approach	Hypothetical-deductive inquiry: Specifying independent and dependent variables to test causal hypotheses	Naturalistic inquiry: Entering real-world settings to observe, interact, and understand what emerges	Sequential inquiry: Qualitative inquiry for exploration followed by quantitative inquiry for verification and generalization
Data collection	Quantitative data through valid and reliable experiments, tests, surveys, and statistical indicators	Qualitative data through fieldwork, such as observations, action research, and in-depth interviewing	Combining quantitative and qualitative data
Researcher stance	Objective, independent, detached, value free	Engaged, acknowledged subjectivity, value laden, reflexive	Neutral, adaptable in accordance with nature of the inquiry
Conceptual approach	Operationalize (quantify) variables; concept of interest doesn't exist until it can be measured	Open-ended inquiry into sensitizing concepts to find out what people mean them, and how they use them	Measure what can be statistically and explore additional understanding and meaning qualitatively
Natural variation approach	Control variables through experimentation with carefully designed treatment and control group comparisons	Study and document diversity and natural variation; minimize control to study how things unfold in the real world	Design flexibility dependent on nature of research question
Sampling strategy	Random, probabilistic samples to achieve representativeness and high internal validity	Strategic case selection and purposeful sampling of rich information for in-depth study and to document diversity	Multiple and combined sampling approaches depending on nature of the inquiry
Analysis and comparisons	Deductive analysis: Use standardized instruments to measure central tendencies and variation statistically; test hypotheses derived from theory	Inductive analysis: look for themes and patterns across cases; theory emerges from cases studied	Compare statistical results with qualitative patterns
Criticism of the others	Qualitative data are "soft," ambiguous, too susceptible to researcher bias; designs can't establish causality; samples too small for generalization	Important things can't be reduced to standardized instruments; quantitative data only scratch the surface of human experience; experimental designs are too rigid and controlling	Both quantitative and qualitative approaches have strengths and weaknesses; need to mix methods to overcome weaknesses of each (critical multiplism, Shadish, 1993)

Source: Patton, M. Q. (2014). *Qualitative research & evaluation methods* (4th ed.). Thousand Oaks, CA: Sage
© 2023 Paul Gibbons and Tricia Kennedy

Figure IX.5: Scientific research quality criteria across traditions. Although quantitative and qualitative traditions have different premises, all well done research adheres to certain quality criteria; it is when the two traditions are combined that breadth and depth of knowledge progresses.

Consulting firm research—Case studies, benchmarking, and surveys

"If I had asked customers what they wanted, they would have said faster horses."

HENRY FORD [PERHAPS APOCRYPHAL]

Case studies and benchmarking

A **case study** is one of many qualitative research methods, or designs. An elegant, well designed and executed case study examines a real-life "case" in-depth to help understand certain phenomenon within their context, say a project. Case studies do not study relationships between variables or control for any confounding factors, so we can't reliably generalize its conclusions beyond their context. That is, their findings cannot straightforwardly be exported (extrapolated) to other businesses.

Consulting firms often suggest that they have found such magical ingredients in their sales material. The consulting case study, experience statement, or "proof point" are sales tools that consist of stories about how their firm's methods succeeded in one client (ergo, we can implement them in your business with the promise of similar successful results). These are not the rigorous, robust case studies of formal research that use this qualitative design. Consulting firms take creative license with this method and then use the same name to enhance the study's credibility (again, marketing and sales tools, not rigorous, formal research).

Although **benchmarking** attempts comparison across contexts (unlike case studies) of performance indicators, metrics, processes, and the like, the **lack of generalizability applies equally to both methods**. Benchmarking studies are a core product of consulting firms, intended to both promote their genius and sell more of their services. These studies extend the notion that the best firms have a special sauce, and that this sauce can be copied and pasted into other companies conferring similar results on the emulator.

However, even if you believe Goldman Sachs' culture is a cause of (thus predicts) its success as an investment bank, "cultural DNA" cannot be simply and unproblematically copied and pasted from one company to another because culture is highly contextual (i.e., it is an emergent quality of complex systems). Yet, this is exactly what many business publications, consultants, and gurus would lead us to believe: Not only is there a secret ingredient to high-performing companies, but you too can obtain similar high performance simply by adopting said special ingredient (which, of course, can only be done by hiring the genius consulting firm).

The premise that "what we did over there will also work over here" isn't true. Moreover, consulting firms are apt to gloss up such stories. We have seen truly awful projects written up as glowing successes (they are promotional tools, after all).

Moreover and in harsh caricature, benchmarking surveys are like driving a car by looking in the rear-view mirror—had Elon Musk surveyed the banking, auto, and space industries, we would not have PayPal, Teslas, Starlink, or Falcon 9 rockets.

Unsurprisingly, in all research and with all designs it matters who conducts it, who publishes its findings, and the intentions behind conducting the study. Suspicion is warranted for any case studies and benchmarking studies (and other studies) by firms to sell services. On the other hand, a rigorously conducted case study lets the chips fall where they may (again, follow the evidence where it leads) can be of great value. One such example is MIT's case study of the BP Deepwater Horizon disaster, retold in *The Science of Organizational Change*, that found a myriad of cognitive biases played a role in the trillion-dollar mishap.

Surveys

Surveys are somewhat unique given their sheer range and variety, and for this reason are **probably more easily understood as a data collection method than a research design.** They can be quantitative or qualitative, and more often a little of both (i.e., mixed methods). Degree of sophistication and intended use are **all over the map**, from your everyday user-generated social media poll to the robust linear-regression analysis of formal research. This breadth, then, further stipulates a distinction between the rigorous, systematic formal research variety (which starts with review of the existing academic literature) and the sales and marketing variety (which take creative methodological license)—the same distinction we saw with case studies.

Figure IX.6 displays a table of data classification types and their appropriate measurement levels for central tendency and dispersion—provided not only because it is conceptually important for both survey users and survey-based evidence consumers, but also because it helps illustrate how easily surveys can blur lines between quantitative and qualitative traditions and are most often mixed methods. (Figure IX.6 excludes the kind of qualitative data that comes from open-ended survey questions, which usually uses an emergent-theme technique for analysis.)

Data Classification Type		Central Tendency Measure	Dispersion Measure	Data Type Definition	Data Type Example
Categorical (qualitative)	Nominal	Mode	Range	List of categories to which objects can be classified and have no meaningful rank order among classifications.	When a participant is given the fixed-choice option of hair color with choices of blonde, brown, red, or black; where one color is not considered "better" or "of higher rank" than the other.
	Ordinal	Median or mode	Interquartile range	Measurement scale that assigns values to objects based on their ranking with respect to one another, or a meaningful order among the values, and have imprecise differences between consecutive values.	When a doctor uses a scale of 1 to 10 to measure improvement in some condition, from "0" (no improvement) to "10" (disappearance of condition), where a score of "4" is certainly "better" or "of higher rank" than a score of "2"; but the improvement from "2" to "4" does not imply it is twice as good.
Continuous (quantitative)	Interval	Mean, median, or mode	Standard deviation	Measurement scale in which a certain distance along the scale means the same thing no matter where on the scale you are, but where "0" on the scale does not represent the absence of the thing being measured.	Fahrenheit and Celsius temperature scales, where Celsius has a temperature of 0 but it is an arbitrary measure with an equivalent of -32 in Fahrenheit. You cannot talk of a "lack of temperature" with these measurements.
	Ratio	Mean, median, or mode	Standard deviation	Measurement scale in which a certain distance along the scale means the same thing no matter where on the scale you are, but where "0" on the scale represents the absence of the thing being measured.	Kelvin temperature scale because it has an absolute zero and where a temperature of 300 Kelvin on such a scale implies twice as much as a temperature of 150 Kelvin.

Data classification types and measurement levels

Figure IX.6: Data classification types and measurement levels. Proper data classification and alignment to measurement levels for central tendency and dispersion are not only conceptually important for both survey users and survey-based evidence consumers, but also help illustrate how easily surveys can blur lines between quantitative and qualitative traditions and are most often mixed methods.

Moreover, surveys and survey-based evidence are inescapable, the stuff of everyday life. This prevalence extends to business contexts; they are used extensively by consulting firms and specialist survey firms (e.g., Gallup and Nielsen), especially in their research publications—and even used by the occasional change practitioner.

Despite this incredible range and variety, there is **one constant to all surveys: People** (i.e., only people respond to surveys)—and as we have seen, people are fallible.

A survey might find that (say) 40% of people are considering switching jobs, and it might uncover factors people "say" they weigh, such as pay and learning opportunities. However interesting that may be, without a controlled experiment you can't predict with any certainty which factors people truly weighed. In another example, 90% of people say they consider the environment important when choosing a new car. Post purchase, only 35% had.[77] A broad swathe of research evidence reveals that **people are wildly inaccurate when self-reporting behavior**, both before (intention) and after (constructive memory and recall), and not just for job hunting and car purchases.

In caricature, surveys are mere aggregates of opinion. In seriousness, this means **surveys can only ever measure one thing: Self-perception** (e.g., beliefs, opinions, and thoughts), and only the ones respondents are willing to admit.

Positively, self-perception measures can be of value, such as offering business leaders insights into what employees, competitors, and customers are thinking about. These surveys might reveal something like 58% of CEOs said that work-life balance is a top priority. (We made that up. No CEO ever said that.) A change practitioner might try to learn more about what affected stakeholders believe (or "say" they believe) about an organizational change. (Only using a validated tool like the Organizational Change Recipients Belief Scale, of course. No change professional would just make up their own survey, right?)

But even in situations like these, where it is only self-perceptions from which insights are sought, **survey evidence is still chock full of weaknesses**—large spoonfuls of salt are to be taken with survey evidence.

On one hand, survey creators (who write the questions or statements) might be untrained, inept, or even have an agenda. Research evidence not only reveals people tend to accept survey questions and statements as presented (i.e., **acquiescence bias**), but how they are written (e.g., tone, register, and subtext of word and phrase choices) are also subject to priming effects, directing thoughts in a certain direction, as well as other cognitive biases.

On the other hand, **survey respondents (who answer the questions) aren't always truthful** (intentionally) or simply don't really know what they feel and think (unintentionally untrue). Research evidence indicates a slew of reasons why survey responses—and all evidence based on self-report data— are largely unreliable:

- People tend to avoid the most extreme response options and answers (i.e., **central tendency bias**),
- People want to portray themselves or their organizations in a positive manner (i.e., **social desirability bias**),
- People tend to respond in a way they think the "asker" wants to hear (e.g., **social legitimacy and retaliation concerns**),
- People tend to construct beliefs retrospectively, often from unrelated and disconnected details, into overly simplistic narratives (i.e., **narrative fallacy**), and
- People are also simply unwilling to admit certain things (e.g., **privacy concerns and discomfort**).

Lastly, or a third hand if you will, survey findings (and again, all evidence based on self-report data) are unlikely to be **representative**—or degree of confidence that the aggregate of collected self-perceptions accurately reflect the larger group of people whose opinions are of interest. Even when the group of interest is relatively small (e.g., a single department), rigorous countermeasure procedures are used (e.g., random sampling), and/or response rates are sufficiently high, the threat of **sampling bias** (i.e., tendency for a resultant sample of responses to be non-representative) only diminishes, it is never eliminated.

Once again, this is because of people's complexity, we tend to **self-select** as survey respondents. For instance, by either

- Not responding (e.g., they are completely checked out or disengaged, too busy to bother, or simply don't care) or
- Exhibiting a propensity to respond (e.g., they are an always-respond overachiever, have an axe to grind, or have strong feelings, positive or negative, about a topic).

Research from consulting firms and specialist firms would improve immeasurably if it relied less on aggregate opinions and more on mixed methods research designs, methodological rigor, and academic literature from psychology, neuroscience, behavioral economics, sociology, social psychology, and other relevant disciplines.

Consulting firm "research evidence" on organizational change

Consulting firms sometimes publish research studies showing how, for example, organizational change is linked to performance or how MBTI use increases team performance. We cringe every time we see such "studies" because they are usually poorly conducted and land a long way from producing conclusions that a practitioner can take to the bank. Just a few common flaws are:

- Research relies on (e.g., assumes the accuracy of) debunked models, especially if the model is a core component of their service offerings.
- Research tries to understand organizational change in terms of a universal, individual change experience (especially if they assume a fixed, linear set of stages).
- Attempts at universality muffle individual experience and reactions to change (a core component of psychology) and the context of change (a core component of sociology).
- Assumes that complex, individual experiences are easily and usefully aggregated to explain group experience.

- Social phenomena are excluded, especially when discussing group-level impacts, blending individualized reactions such as performance reviews and job roles with systemic factors such as processes and systems.
- Survey and assessment results rely heavily on leadership, top-down inputs rather than data collected from the affected stake-holders themselves.
- Assumes the predictability of individual behavior over time while ignoring the emergent and evolving nature of individuals, social groupings, and organizations as complex systems.

Consulting firm research on organizational change is worth questioning, especially the premises from where they start, the assumptions they make about how change works, and the interests served by their conclusions.

Conclusion—Certainty and evidence

"When there is repetition and accumulation of evidence that points in the same direction, then there is rational basis for believing it to be true even if we must always hold out the possibility that some future evidence may later overthrow it."[78]

LEE MCINTYRE (PHILOSOPHER OF SCIENCE)

One cognitive trap with evidence of any kind is that it provides false assurances of certainty. Neither the centuries of climate science researchers who predict a much warmer climate nor the layperson who uses the evidence of a winter storm as proof that Earth isn't warming can be absolutely certain of their conclusions.

Historically, all swans seen in Europe had been white; the evidence that swans were white was uniform. The expression "unlikely as a black swan" was even used to refer to impossibility. Then, the story goes, Dutch explorers in late 17th-century Australia found a black swan. Even if all the evidence you have seen to date points in a single direction, there is always the possibility that new evidence emerges to overturn the old. Humans should remain humble and skeptical about what they know or think they know, and equally open to new evidence as it emerges.

Still, humans like to be sure of themselves. Certainty provides a measure of psychological comfort in a chaotic world. We also expect certainty from public figures more than we should. TED talkers, politicians, and media pundits don't get where they are by speaking in nuances, caveats, and probabilities. U.S. President Harry Truman, fed up with his economists' nuanced, equivocal arguments (on the one hand this, on the other hand, that) once exclaimed, "someone find me a one-handed economist!"

Philosopher Isaiah Berlin recapitulated an ancient Greek parable of the hedgehog and the fox: Hedgehogs describe the world through single, big, and certain ideas, while foxes talk about context, nuance, and complexity. In a complex world, we need more foxes, but we instead tend to vote, download, like, share, and subscribe to the views of hedgehogs—dogmatic, charismatic one-trick ponies.

Lack of certainty, we think, creates the exciting possibility of new knowledge. That mystery and possibility drives science and progress. But even science does not produce certainty. It accumulates and progresses toward clarity, sometimes called warrant, not certainty. Like Xeno's arrow, we get progressively closer but never quite arrive.

So, the better scientists tend to be careful with their word choice. And as we saw with the Dunning-Kruger effect, this makes experts less sure-sounding than laypeople. Researchers tend to use more uncertain expressions such as:

- The weight of evidence points toward...
- Based on the best current evidence...
- Research indicates...
- Our findings suggest...
- The abundance of evidence warrants...

In contrast, popular media and organizational gurus tend to use expressions with more certainty such as:

- A new study proves ...
- A new study confirms ...
- Research shows...
- Science says...

Critical-thinking radars (i.e., your BS detector) should light up bright red when overtly certain terms arise.

If you walk away from this chapter with nothing else, remember the takeaways in Figure IX.7.

Evidence takeaways
Certainty increases with replication and accumulation:, the more high - quality evidence you have, the higher likelihood it is true (i.e., warrant).
The two ends of the formal research design spectrum complement each other:, quantitative for narrow findings applied more widely, and qualitative for depth of understanding and meaning applied more narrowly.
All research designs, across the spectrum, involve tough choices around tradeoffs between strengths and weaknesses; and all can be performed either well or poorly.
Quantitative research evidence lends itself more readily to broad evaluation of truth, such as the universal application of models, constructs, and axioms.
Qualitative research evidence lends itself more readily to deeper understanding of meaning and sense making, or different lived experiences and the critical nature of context and social systems, such as how people and groups navigate, interpret, and behave within an organizational setting.

© 2023 Paul Gibbons and Tricia Kennedy

Figure IX.7: Evidence chapter takeaways. A scientific mindset embraces the idea of "warrant" instead of certainty and the idea of knowledge as cumulative and, thus, evolving and changing as more and more evidence emerges.

What comes next?

When heavyweight authorities make claims about an idea that feels intuitive, they can be hard to dislodge.

Next, we discuss the differences between actual neuroscience and neurobabble in change.

CHAPTER X

Neurobabble: Are brains magnificently adaptable or do they "hate change"?

A central, recurring theme in this book is whether useful generalizations can be made about change. Generalizations are useful because they allow transfer of knowledge from one situation to another: Generally, when a physician detects a fever, usually, there is infection or inflammation.

This book attempts to unpick such generalizations about change, to see whether they are broadly accurate as well as useful guides to action. As you have seen, the death-and-grief of change curves failed both tests—accuracy and utility.

The most common generalization is that change is, **by necessity**, difficult, painful, and hard. Some authors have even tried to ground the "change is painful" notion in neuroscience. In this chapter, we debunk that misuse of neuroscience. This leads to a discussion about the usefulness and pitfalls of neuroscience in guiding organizational change theory and practice.

Claim

Change is painful, not just emotionally or metaphorically, but neurobiologically according to authors David Rock and Jeffrey Schwartz—two credentialled neuroscientists. They say, "**change is pain. Organizational change is unexpectedly difficult because it provokes sensations of physiological discomfort.**"[79] Moreover, they add that the inevitable pain of change is a "hardwired" function of the human nervous system, and that "brains hate change."

Our brain circuitry, on their account, creates friction, sends error signals, experiences stress, and "hijacks the amygdala" when we encounter novel circumstances or are asked to do things differently. Does the claim have neuroscientific teeth? Or, as a generalization, is the idea that organizational change creates physiological pain nonsense?

Backstory

"Nothing is so painful to the human mind as a great and sudden change."

MARY SHELLEY (AUTHOR OF *FRANKENSTEIN*)

Folk wisdom would have us believe human nature is relatively fixed and attempts to change it are difficult: A leopard never changes its spots and you cannot teach an old dog new tricks. Two centuries ago, *Frankenstein*'s author Mary Shelley also suggested that change pains the mind. Machiavelli opined in the 15th century, "nothing is more difficult to plan, more doubtful of success, nor more dangerous to manage than the creation of a new system."

Behavioral science, in our century, suggests cognitive biases that may irrationally predispose us to the status quo. But can we leap to "change is pain" from these historical intuitions?

How can LIAR help us parse the "change is pain" claim?

LIAR and "change is pain"

"If the brain were so simple we could understand it, we would be so simple we could not."

EMERSON PUGH (PHYSICIST)

Intuition (I)

For myths to spread, they need to accord with **intuition** (the I in LIAR). Everyone has had difficulty with **some** personal change or other. Friends, family, and colleagues have struggled with **some** changes, **some** of the time. Around us, we see political change create social upheavals and we see public health and climate crises create drama and conflict, where given the abundance of scientific evidence supporting the subject matter behind them, there ought not to be much. And we see organizational changes, especially those poorly managed, that clobber employee experience.

Neuroscience, we now hear, backs our intuitions up. Whew! There is a satisfying "click" when our intuition and new inputs accord.

The critical thinker double-checks their intuition knowing that our minds are susceptible to **priming** and other biases. When we encounter the idea that brains hate change, priming guides our memory toward painful examples, like the breakup, the unfamiliar new school, or pulling up stakes and moving to a new city.

One cognitive bias, the **positive-negative asymmetry effect**, makes this worse. The psychological effects of negative events tend to outweigh those of positive events. Memory, so far as we understand it, remembers events with most emotional salience, and it **remembers the bad more easily than the good**.[80]

Critical thinking is wary of how seductive **confirmation bias** is and uses logic to avoid its allure, as well as knowing **availability bias** means we overweight what is more memorable—the painful stuff.

In the Spotting BS chapter (Chapter XII), we suggest a critical thinking test—are there counter examples? Critical thinking guides us to look for memories of counterexamples that **disprove** intuition, for examples where change was graceful, exciting, and welcome. When confirmation bias has been tickled, you might ask: Can I think of organizational or personal examples where change was not painful?

Paul recalls getting his first laptop, walking into his first job, and being thrown into the deep end of managing his first consulting project. Tricia remembers the agony of starting over after moving to a new city, again and again from childhood through adulthood, but loved every minute of the move to start university for undergraduate studies.

In February 2020, very few of us had worn a mask every day. By March 2020, in an instant, such things became nearly automatic. Wearing a mask might be an unpleasant change, they are uncomfortable, but was doing so painful? Did our *hippocampi* scream in agony? There were disruptions to our lives in 2020 that were difficult, but the mask-wearing change, we suggest, was handled without psychological pain and with much good grace. (Yes, yes, masks became a political hot button in a few countries, but we argue the mask wearing itself rarely involved psychological or physiological pain.)

And while you might disagree with our (unresearched) intuitions about masks and pain, you can still likely come up with counterexamples of a significant change that was not painful.

Logic (L)

A critical thinker notices the use of metaphor and questions whether the metaphor is apt. As we saw earlier, this is particularly important in politics as politicians are skilled at emotive metaphor: Is there a "tsunami" of immigrants "flooding" our country? Do we need to "take our country back?" From whom? How did "they" take it from us? Where did they put it when they took it?

Business gurus are also adept at emotive metaphor—that is how they become gurus. "Brains hate change" is a metaphor because brains, as entities, do not "hate" anything. The brain itself feels no pain—there are no **nociceptors** in neural tissue (there are in the scalp, of course).

"Hate" is a narrative and narratives are "added" to physiological sensations as a sense-making tool. The physiological experience of a roller-coaster ride is similar in a person who finds it thrilling (one narrative) and a person who is scared to death (a different narrative).

While this may seem hair-splitty, it matters because we have **considerable power over narratives**, but considerably less over neurochemistry. While certain parts of the brain are activated when shown an image of a jilting ex-lover, those same parts (the putamen and insular cortex) share "circuitry" (another metaphor) with the "love circuit."[81] When "triggered" (another metaphor), we can create a hate narrative or another (say forgiveness or gratitude).

To believe that stimuli (e.g., ex-lovers or organizational change) necessitates a certain reaction is not only disempowering, but also irrational—human responses are mercurial and individual.

Another logical flaw in "brains hate change" is the giant leap from "some" to "all" (perhaps the greatest absurdity of the brains-hate-change claim). It is simply **not universally true**. How about getting married? How about finishing university and starting that first big job? How about the birth of a child? Job changes and career changes are often exciting and engaging. If the claim is not universally true, then why do we so easily accept such a facile generalization as true about organizational change?

It might be boring to hear: The mind **sometimes** treats **some** unwelcome organizational changes as a stressor. But that may be as general as we can be. (As we see below, weak generalizations prevent us from asking the important questions.)

Authority (A)

To the intuition that makes brains hate change seem plausible, we add some heavyweight **authority**—Jeffrey Schwartz is a psychiatrist at UCLA's David Geffen School of Medicine and David Rock, his co-author, is a best-selling author of multiple books about brains and work. As change experts, we must be alert to **how much the umbrella of authority protects a broad and general claim** such as "brains hate change." It is easy to be seduced, to be lulled into thinking that narrow expertise allows broad pronouncements. We must also be alive to the temptation for highly credentialled people to sensationalize their findings. In Schwartz's case, the sensational title of his 2002 book—*The Mind* *and the Brain: Neuroplasticity and the Power of Mental Force*—is far sexier than his peer-reviewed "Caudate glucose metabolic rate changes with both drug and behavior therapy for obsessive-compulsive disorder." Notice the specificity of the claim in the peer-reviewed journal.

Rock has done tremendous work bringing neuroscientific concepts to the attention of the business world, but as we see below, the rush to apply neurobiology to macro-level concepts such as organizational change means there is more sizzle than steak in such claims.

Research evidence (R)

When testing claims with the R tester, or research evidence, two key questions arise (again): Is the research **robust and replicated**? More importantly, does the research design and quality, even if robust, warrant **transferability** from "the lab" to the context in which we wish to use them? In the case of brains hate change, the answers are mostly and absolutely not.

One argument is that **change is stressful,** and we do know that stressors trigger certain areas of the brain: Stressors trigger the HPA (hypothalamic-pituitary-adrenal) axis, which produces a hormone known as ACTH (adrenocorticotropic hormone, if you must ask), which triggers the release of cortisol. We also know that a stress response diminishes higher cognitive functions and is injurious to long-term health with prolonged exposure. This is the great survival mechanism when faced with the proverbial lion: Fight, flight, or freeze. But is this survival instinct transferable to all stress reactions and contexts? How many lions do we encounter during a working day? How much stress is equivalent to potentially being a lion's next meal? Must our sophisticated cognitive apparatus be "hijacked" by workplace lions? Even schoolchildren today are taught that their amygdala's get hijacked for any feeling of discomfort. Is it accurate, or even useful, to equate all stress and discomfort to the variety that threatens our existence (i.e., the lion variety)? Hardly.

Notice that we have jumped from talking about change to talking about stress—as if they were the exact same thing. Is change a stressor? Even if it is, is it like other extreme stressors, such as car accidents or harsh life events (or the lion)? And even if it is like other extreme stressors (neurobiologically), can we use this insight to modify organizations and design change interventions?

Furthermore, we know that some areas of the brain deal with routine and habitual functions (the basal ganglia), and that novelty requires at least some engagement of other areas (higher cortical areas). Some researchers claim that the engagement of higher cortical functions (rather than the areas of the brain that handle routine), in some regards, is also an unpleasant experience. Changing habits requires attentional effort and taxes working memory more than comfortable, routine, and predictable activity. Additional effort may overtax the prefrontal cortex (PFC) which is involved in metacognition, impulse control, planning, and strategy.

But is effort the same as pain, discomfort, and stress? If taxing working memory and the prefrontal cortex "hurts," why do people play chess and poker or do crosswords?

Most "research" on brains hate change goes like this—using facts about brain structures to extrapolate conclusions about change (see sidebar on neurobabble).

Neurobabble versus neuroscience—Ask yourself which one

Currently it is en vogue to couch well-known concepts with the prefix "neuro"—neuro-change, neuro-leadership, neuro-success, neuro-coaching, neuro-entrepreneurship, and more. Does attaching a neuro prefix to a management theory increase its validity? Or is this trend getting ahead of the evidence? It sounds science-y, but we can talk about working memory, attention, and arousal without relying on brain biology.

The reaction of octane with oxygen is fundamental to the internal combustion engine, yet no book on becoming a successful Formula One driver is likely to include this chemical equation. Knowing where the camshaft resides is unlikely to help a driver navigate the chicanes at 250 kilometers per hour.

Our fellow mythbuster Alex Boulting calls this "brain over-claim"—taking results from experimental lab conditions, such fMRI studies, and extrapolating these to complex social phenomena (e.g., learning, trust, psychological safety).

Some self-styled neuro-coaches (who shall remain nameless) talk pure nonsense. For example, "by understanding the brain science behind commitment, coaches and managers can develop interventions that target the anterior cingulate cortex (ACC) to reach the amygdala." Targeting anatomical structures sounds awfully clever, but they could have just said: Impulses must be interrupted to form new habits. The fancy prefix and big words don't add much to the message.

We leave the reader with the question: Does knowing the amygdala has a role in emotion management or oxytocin produces feelings of closeness help improve leadership (as many popularizers would have us believe)? Is our neuro-coach above adding any value with the word salad? Would a couple in therapy benefit from discussing hormone and neurotransmitter levels?

In what is today, we believe, is the best book on neuroscience and change, *Neuroscience for Organizational Change*[82], the author makes her claim the same way: Change creates uncertainty, and uncertainty and ambiguity provoke neurophysiological patterns, ergo "brains hate change." As you can see, the conclusion depends upon all change provoking uncertainty. Some do and some do not. If all uncertainty was painful, there would be no such thing as a nice surprise.

Brains, like bodies, respond to changes in external stimuli (otherwise they wouldn't be brains). However, if you are interested in macro-level and complex social phenomena such as learning and organizational change, is it interesting which parts of the brain responds to different stimuli? Authors Scott Lilienfeld and Sally Satel sum it up in *Brainwashed: The Subjective Appeal of Mindless Neuroscience* as, "these mappings are oversimplifications. **Most of the brain is zoned for mixed use.**"[83]

Brain-scan images (see an example in Figure X.1) now adorn many a leadership guru talk—they look fancy.

Look here, that purple bit, the hippocampus, is activated, ergo....

However, as the late philosopher Jerry Fodor quipped, "If the mind happens in space at all, it happens somewhere north of the neck. **What exactly turns on knowing how far north?**"[84] Do we care, in our case, how "far north" organizational change happens in the brain?

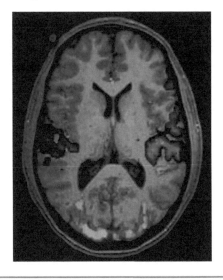

Example fMRI brain scan

© 2023 Paul Gibbons and Tricia Kennedy

Figure X.1: Example fMRI brain scan. Knowing which anatomical regions stimuli activate has advanced understanding. Yet each "lit up" area may contain a billion or more neurons, and complex mental processes typically involve many such billion-neuron areas. Also, a single anatomical structure, say the amygdala, may be involved in hundreds of macro-processes (and not just threat responses).

For example, seeing amygdala activation does not mean the subject is experiencing fear—the amygdala is also involved in positive emotions. When change and leadership experts refer to the amygdala as the fear center, they are telling two white lies: Many brain areas are involved in a fear response and the amygdala is involved in many different emotions, not just fear.

Other neuroscientists and philosophers share this view. Neuroscientist William Uttal (author of *The New Phrenology: On the Localization of Cognitive Processes in the Brain*) sums it up as, "fMRI is as distant as the galvanic skin response or pulse rate is from cognitive processes."[85]

Costs and consequences

"Frightened of change? But what can exist without it? What's closer to nature's heart? Can you take a hot bath and leave the firewood as it was? Eat food without transforming it? Can any vital process take place without something being changed? It's just the same with you."

MARCUS AURELIUS (MEDITATIONS)

The idea that change is pain has implications for other myths in this book, such as change resistance, unfreeze-change-refreeze, and creating a sense of urgency. It has become a premise, an axiom, and a foundational truth on which change theory and practice sit. Change is painful, therefore there will be resistance; change is painful, therefore leaders must create a sense of urgency; change is painful, so organizations must be "unfrozen." This logic is a shaky foundation on which to build knowledge.

What are some of the painful costs of thinking this way?

Self-fulfilling prophecy?

There is an apocryphal story that when a toddler takes a tumble, if parents keep their composure, the child is less likely to cry. In other words, our expectations as parents that the fall hurts tilt the child's response one way or another.

Words create worlds, so as practitioners, if our focus is on resistance and brains hating change then this is the mental model you will create for others and yourself—it may become a self-fulfilling prophecy. When a change professional enters a client or program, their expectations (that it will be painful) help create and reinforce that notion. Does this expectation, rather than reality, guide our approach?

Neuro-talk is a distraction from real issues

Could **thinking about neurotransmitters and hormones and brain anatomy may be harmful**, not helpful in organizational change? Does introducing such abstractions (e.g., dorsolateral prefrontal cortex or GABA receptors) prevent leaders from dealing with disengaged workers or damaged trust?

Imagine a couple in marriage counseling.

"Honey, when you forget our anniversary, my 5-HT receptors become saturated and my *nucleus accumbens* can't regulate my reward centers."

"Yes, dear, but my glutamate receptors in my *substantia nigra* can't bear it when you don't do the dishes."

As in organizational change, macro-level factors such as trust, empathy, respect, listening, history, and love do the work of healing— not neurobiological abstractions.

A narrow and dim view of human adaptability

When we endorse the brains-hate-change mantra, we are also priming people to be less tolerant of uncertainty and creating a dim view of human adaptability. Such narratives may be self-fulfilling and may misguide policy. For example, if we understand human behavior in strictly terms of carrots and sticks, we will design organizations with carrots and sticks in mind and lose any benefits of intrinsic motivation. If we are to make broad generalizations about change that are only loosely tied, if at all, to research evidence, we should at least consider whether they are empowering or disempowering.

Another way of looking at change is that routines are dull, and new ways of doing things are exhilarating. Humans are a species that loves to learn and are incredible at adaptation—it is what we do substantially better than other mammals. Good learners embrace that "clunky" feeling when trying something for the first time. We seek out novelty, emotional uncertainty, and suspense for entertainment. Rather than our brains hating change aren't our brains also built for excitement, surprise, and curiosity?

We also risk brushing over nuances of how people really learn and change in social environments and potentially make our people less resilient and our organizations less agile when we perpetuate the brains-hate-change myth.

Alternatives and conclusions

The 21st century may well be the century of the brain, where our knowledge multiplies the way genome knowledge did after the 1944 discovery that DNA was the carrier of genetic information. (Think how far we have come in just 70 years!) We speculate that within decades the tragedy of degenerative diseases of the brain and spinal cord injury may leave us the way that killer diseases like Polio and Smallpox did a few decades ago.

The neuroscience "project" is to connect the biology of the brain to mind and behavior—crudely, sensations, thoughts, feelings, and actions. Some applications, such as neuropharmacology, are examples of this success—by changing the chemistry of the brain (through drugs), we can affect mind and behavior (e.g., depression, addiction, ADHD). It is also worthwhile to note that just because a pharmacological treatment exists, especially psychopharmacology treatments, does not mean we know how or why it works. Again, the brain is mostly still a mystery that neurobabble oversimplifies.

In change, by understanding the brain's "circuitry" better, perhaps we can intervene more accurately. For designing interventions "with the brain in mind," it is still early days. There are some good ideas floating about labeled neuroscience but don't depend on neuroscience to be useful. For example, David Rock's SCARF (i.e., status, certainty, autonomy, relatedness, and fairness) model is a useful way of understanding responses to threats at work. However, to use it, you don't need to understand the neurobiology on which it is (very loosely) built. Similarly, Rock's AGES (i.e., attention, generation, emotion, and spacing) model is a useful rubric for thinking about human learning and perception. Similarly, you don't have to understand neurobiology to use it.

Another helpful rubric: The more neuroscientific a concept (that is to say, the more it refers to the biology and chemistry of the brain), the less useful it is likely to be as an organizational change a concept.

The wrong end of the telescope

When change is **essentially, generally, or always** hard, the change professional is tasked with easing the journey of followers and affected stakeholders—to make the essentially, inevitably difficult thing (the change) easier. With this mindset, our **focus is on the**

change recipients (the people affected and their reactions), **not the change itself**—and not on executive decisions about what is to change and how change is to happen.

The biggest cost of facile generalizations about change, such as "brains hate change," is that they allow us to evade the important questions:

- Which kinds of change are hardest? Why are they hard? What can leaders do about that?
- In which contexts is change easiest? Under which circumstances is change joyful and easy?
- Which psychological predispositions make change easier or harder?
- Which organizational considerations make change easy and welcome, and which make it harder?
- How much responsibility for a reaction to change lies with the individual, and how much with the organization?

Those are better questions and, most importantly, they can guide how change experts intervene.

What comes next?

Next, we dive briefly into a few meta myths that are tricky to test empirically, yet they inform a great deal of organizational change knowledge and practice.

CHAPTER XI

Change meta myths

Some myths don't fall neatly into well-defined constructs that are easily evaluated (as we saw with DABDA). Some are metaphors, some are heuristics, some are meta-models, and some are deeply held assumptions about organizations and change.

In this chapter, we look at two of these:

- Communication changes behavior and
- Organizations are static and must be unfrozen before changing.

Communication changes behavior

Nobody walks around saying communication changes behavior. It is a deeply held assumption, a cultural norm baked-in so profoundly that it does not appear to bear examination. Most leaders and change experts enact the assumption in their day-to-day, in-use mental models about how behavior change happens in organizations.

In the academic discipline Public Understanding of Science, this false notion is called the **information-deficit model**. That is, providing citizens with enough information about a scientific topic, such as climate change or vaccination, changes behavior. This supposition proves false, both in society and in business organizations. While we would like everyone's behavior to change with the communication of new information, it happens unreliably.

Consider how skill building is typically tackled (say, time-management skills). Paul has taught these skills extensively at major business schools and at Fortune 100 companies. Attendees learn the concepts, processes, and practices of time management during two- and three-day courses.

By some estimates, 80% of managers have taken some kind of time management training. Yet, survey findings by consultants at Acuity suggest 82% of managers do not have a time management system, 25% of people just deal with what comes up, and only 12% schedule tasks in their calendar or diary in advance (a recommended practice). Training, our default behavioral change method, falls flat in this instance.

Adoption of new technology systems provides another problem example (say, a knowledge management application). One client launched such a application at great cost and with great fanfare. They threw the kitchen sink at communication: Emails, posters, workshops, training sessions, town halls, leadership videos, Slack channels, and employee surveys. Behavior didn't change much and the application quickly fell into disuse. Again, even exhaustive, multi-channel, and excellent quality communication failed to make a dent in behaviors.

Another client example involves a high-flying tech unicorn (HFTU) wanting to create a "coaching" culture. The business case was robust: By instilling a coaching culture among leaders at all levels, the performance potential of every employee would "level up." The theory's math worked for this context, employees became

1% more effective every week, and an employee would be more than 66% more effective by year-end. Further, internal research suggested frequently giving employees supportive attention would effectively promote engagement and alignment with organizational goals. So, the HFTU rolled out a "Coaching for Excellence" culture-change program. In mandatory training sessions, leaders were taught speed-coaching skills, or how to deliver performance improvement in fifteen minutes. Standards were set, and leaders were expected to spend fifteen minutes coaching their reports weekly. Metrics were created and added to leaders' goals, the program was sponsored top-down, and the CEO made a series of videos that were shared broadly. The communications team used Slack and email fulsomely. Leaders thought it was a good idea, they were "bought in." Everybody had the skills. Staff were hungry for it. But few leaders followed through with action, they didn't do it. Despite superlative communication and stellar skill training, behavior did not change.

If communication doesn't work, what does?

Behavioral sciences (economics, sociology, psychology, and others) offer some solutions. A communication-only approach faces a problem called the **intention-action gap**—the gap (sometimes chasm) between what people think and what they do. Communication can alter the former, but most change methods in organizations leave it there: Here is the change, isn't the vision inspiring? Have at it and good luck. Even when leaders are at their most persuasive and inspirational or skills courses at their most potent, this gap remains.

Behavioral sciences also provide not only insights but techniques to change behavior (otherwise, they would be no better than communication-only approaches). Some of these techniques include choice architecture, nudges, cognitive-behavioral therapy, systemic-focused therapy, trying behaviors first, and behaviorally tuned communications such as MINDSPACE.

Example experiments demonstrate behavioral-science improvements over communications-only approaches:

- Altering a **default setting** on driver's license applications by just changing a single word for the organ donor option, from opt-in to opt-out, almost triples the percentage of people who elect to donate organs in the event of death.
- Sending a letter to domestic energy users comparing them with their neighbors' usage decreases energy use by 7% (for the cost of a postage stamp!). (Yes, this is a communication, but **behaviorally designed** – another chapter for another book.)
- Deploying behavioral-science techniques was almost three times as effective as education in increasing savings rates.

Considering how much effort leaders put into changing behavior with little-to-no results, behavioral science technique results almost feel like black magic.

Much behavioral science research is focused on marketing, or consumer behavior (as Clyde told Bonnie, that is where the money is). However, governments around the world are experimenting with behavioral science techniques in areas such as wellness, public policy, public health, and sustainability. What has happened much less is using behavioral science techniques in organizational change, culture change, operations, and leadership—or at least it is only beginning to scratch the surface.

A common leadership whine is: But I told them to do it—a familiar refrain when traditional change management techniques don't change behaviors. Our experience demonstrates that even when leaders tell them (over and over again) and very skillfully, behaviors change is rarely forthcoming.

It seems fair to think of change communications as necessary but insufficient for organizational change, people do need to be aware something exists and understand expectations of them, but this is more of an organizational change precursor than a strategy. Developing behavioral science use cases from marketing and public policy for organizational change and consulting has potential to transform the profession.

Organizations are static

Much organizational change writing portrays organizations as rigid, static entities punctuated by programmatic change (large, formally defined change projects). The logic continues that if organizations are static, some sort of disruption (such as a sense of urgency or crisis to unfreeze the status quo) is required. (Moreover, organizations are populated by change-resistant humans who feel pain when change happens around them.) This is a naïve view.

Change is the stuff of all life and life doesn't exist without change. As Heraclitus said a few thousand years ago, "you cannot step in the same river twice, for the river is never the same, nor is the man."

The same is true of organizations. Like biological life, including human beings, organizations are open, complex systems. They are open to their environment, which means if the environment changes more rapidly than the responsive capabilities of the organization, the "tectonic sheer" can destroy it. Not only are they open to their environment, but they are also not passive actors—their "outputs" change the environment (e.g., new products).

Organizations (again like all biological life) respond to external changes through complex, dynamic internal systems. Every day there are new strategies, hires, customers, technologies, and policies. Hundreds of change initiatives may be scattered across business functions—from eight-figure technology implementations to rolling out major new policies. Organizational changes can come from the top down, but also bottom up, such as the use of 21st-century communications methods or when people at "the bottom" are empowered to innovate and initiate changes.

Yes, in some ways and some of the time organizations are stuck. They have repeating habits and routines whether or not these serve the business or its employees. There is rigidity galore in unspoken norms, loyalties, and power structures, as well as policies, processes, and workflows. Sometimes this is called bureaucracy (although this is a misuse of the term), and long-time IBMers call it the "blue goo."

General statements about organizational dynamics are not easy to make, but this does not stop people from frequently doing so. Consultant white papers often proclaim the rhetoric of constant change, yet the same consultants also sometimes run into the brick wall of the blue goo (i.e., organizational rigidities). It helps to understand that **stuck features of an organization evolved for a reason, rational or not, and often in response to their environment changing around them. Delving into these reasons is often a key to effecting change.**

Organizational agility is the argument that organizations can respond more quickly to changes in their environment with dynamic development approaches, strategies, policies, people, and culture. Paul advanced the concept in 2013 suggesting that more agile organizations would require less change management "firefighting"—the so-called anti-fragile organization.

While agile, dynamic, responsive organizations still seem a reasonable ideal, sometimes the converse is also true (though far less popular): Organizational change sometimes needs to introduce stability when an organization's features are overly chaotic, random, unreliable, or too reactive to the external environment. (But what consultant ever sold a project promising to make an organization more rigid?)

As with other myths in this book, the organizations are static or frozen myth is not only unhelpful, but also wrong and has (mis) informed decades of change theory and practice.

And because organizations are static, they must be "unfrozen"

From the myth of static organizations comes the notion that change is episodic and interrupts organizations that are otherwise in a state of equilibrium. According to Lewin, therefore, the first step in changing an organization is to "unfreeze" it. His three-step change model surfaces during the late 1940s and at the end of his life.

A famous passage from the three paragraphs that mention unfreezing and refreezing towards the end of his long manuscript:

> "[A] successful change includes therefore three aspects: Unfreezing (if necessary) the present level L1, moving to the new level L2, and freezing group life on the new level."[86]

The three-step unfreeze model has foundational significance in academic change study. It is taught and talked about not as a historical artifact or merely a breakthrough step along the road to more sophisticated, contemporary models—the way we might about the four elements (air, water, earth, and fire) as naïve precursors to the periodic table of 118 elements. Instead, unfreeze-change-refreeze is taught and talked about as a fixed and proven way to understand change in organizations, which has withstood the test of time (recall the myth of timeless truths).

Moreover, unfreeze-change-refreeze is a prescriptive model, not a descriptive model. That is, it is general instruction on how planned change should be achieved, not just a description of how unplanned change happens. Our emphasis on the word "general" means that the model is not situational, contextual, or specific to only some types of change in some types of organizations; instead, it is a prescription for all planned change.

From this aspect of Lewin's work grew hundreds of n-step change models—from Kotter's eight steps to Hiatt's ADKAR, from Tichy's three-act model to Kanter's Ten Commandments, and from Theory U to Beer's six steps. Owing much to Lewin, the nascent organizational development (OD) discipline picked it up and ran. Some of the discipline's biggest names, including Beckhard, Schein, Burke, Trist, Bamforth, Weisbord, McGregor, Argyris, and Bennis, jumped on the bandwagon.

But does this ice metaphor hold water? Are organizations ever frozen? Do organizations need to unfreeze before they can change? Does change become a planned journey with a clear beginning and end?

Figure XI.1 illustrates some of the change models that have Lewin's unfreeze-change-refreeze at their foundation.

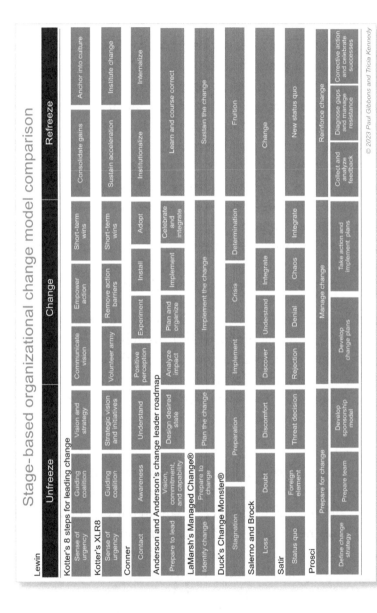

Stage-based organizational change model comparison

© 2023 Paul Gibbons and Tricia Kennedy

Figure XI.1: Stage-based organizational change model comparison. The intellectual roots of Lewin's ideas about freezing and unfreezing to achieve change not only run both deep and wide, but also rest on highly questionable premises. As we see time and again, a big, famous name can carry bad ideas far.

Unfreezing the unfreeze-change-refreeze model

Lewin might be rolling over in his grave. Unfreeze-change-refreeze appears only toward the end of his first "Frontiers of Group Dynamics" article, appearing almost as an afterthought and in only three short paragraphs—and the **only time in Lewin's nearly 40-year career that he mentions the idea**. This uber-scholar and groundbreaking scientist published no book, no peer-reviewed article, and no empirical research on unfreeze-change-refreeze. There are three ways to interpret this fact: The idea is like the intellectual toenail clippings from someone of Lewin's intellectual stature that strangely went on to sow the seeds of an entire profession, Lewin didn't view the notion as worth pursuing further, or it is a brilliant and timeless truth, that was left unexplored before Lewin died (as its proponents sometimes claim).

If we read Lewin's work more carefully, which few academics in the organizational development (OD) discipline seem to have taken the trouble, we see that Lewin did not think of organizations as frozen. In his first Frontiers article, Lewin maintains that "change and constancy are relative concepts; group life is never without change, merely differences in the amount and type of change exist."

Intuition runs both ways. It makes shallow sense that an organization might need to be shaken up or unfrozen before changing, such as through an artificial crisis. Yet in our experience with clients, we have never seen a workplace frozen, in any sense of the word. Among hundreds of metaphors from which to choose, "frozen" isn't on our list. We have no idea how many change practitioners take unfreeze-change-refreeze seriously but are willing to bet 100% of them were taught this model during their education. Furthermore, among our community of practitioners, the ones we engage with, only a few try to operationalize the freezing metaphor in their client work—as in, we need to first unfreeze (or other, similar word).

One of those few who do use this model maintains, "its simplicity helps people get a better understanding of change management as a whole without getting lost in a lot of industry jargon or complicated steps." The need to break things down into explainable chunks for clients is real and understandable, but we doubt doing so via unfreeze-change-refreeze advances anyone's understanding of complex organizational dynamics.

As with change curves, linear and n-step change models feel highly intuitive. In contrast, we know that change is messy, iterative, and emergent. We do our clients disservice when we frame change as simple, sequential, and linear. That is not how organizations work. That is also not how projects work.

To paraphrase centuries of war theorists, **no plan survives first contact with the organization**. Major change programs are often planned well in advance of execution. Sometimes that detailed planning finds its way into consulting contracts. However, as soon as we intervene in an organization its context starts to shift—like Heraclitus' river, the organization is no longer the same and continues to evolve. Change plans, contracts, and project goals built upon a premise that the organization is static, quickly become outdated (even at first real contact). Agile approaches are a vast improvement because the short-sprint structure allows frequent re-evaluation of priorities, however agile methods in big projects are often housed inside static, waterfall-style program structures. Those latter structures lack the necessary flexibility, contrary to what is baked into senior executives' strategic goals, roadmaps, and mindsets (e.g., the project must be delivered this quarter).

Business schools still teach organizational change in traditional ways: Static businesses punctuated by highly structured and episodic change, orchestrated top-down, and often supported by consultants with fixed legal contracts who try to influence resistant stakeholders with information-deficit tactics.

Change doesn't always have to be hard, but when you approach it this way, it is harder than it needs to be.

What comes next?

Wanna-be experts have ways of making big claims that are highly persuasive. Among their techniques are charisma, misused metaphor, exaggeration, and overgeneralization.

Next, we offer 10 questions to help see through BS, both in change and in life.

CHAPTER XII

Spotting BS in change (and in life)

*"When an honest man speaks, he says only
what he believes to be true; and for the liar, it is
correspondingly indispensable that he considers
his statements to be false. The bullshitter does not
care whether the things he says describe reality
correctly. He just picks them out, or makes them up,
to suit his purpose."*[87]

HARRY G. FRANKFURT (*ON BULLSHIT*, 2005)

Consultants and business school professors are skillful storytellers:
I've used this with bajillions of clients to enormous success. They
are masters at drawing attention to their expensive ideas. To garner
attention, their ideas must be easily intelligible, simple as possible,
intuitive to understand, and visually attractive (what realtors call
curb appeal or Paul's IBM colleagues call "third-grade simple").

This communication practice may be effective, but it also leads to
grand oversimplification and overblown change claims.

Rigor, complexity, context, and nuance are traded for their aesthetic on PowerPoint slides. Because of their story-telling and narrative nature, change ideas are difficult to test side-by-side: It is hard to empirically compare eight steps, four boxes, five-level pyramids, six-stage processes, and 7Ss. We end up with an intellectual free-for-all that allows bullshit to prosper and propagate.

This chapter offers 10 questions (see Figure XII.1) to sharpen your BS radar—or help you decide whether something encountered (or used today) might be bullshit. These 10 questions are loosely based on astrophysicist Carl Sagan's Baloney Detection Kit.

10 questions for detecting BS
1. Is the language hyperbolic?
2. Is the metaphor sloppy?
3. Does terminology have multiple meanings? Is it being used correctly?
4. Is the claim always true?
5. Does the claim a use broad generalizations, stereotypes, and/or black-and-white thinking?
6. Are there counterexamples?
7. Is the framework or model exhaustive?
8. Is a causal claim justified? Could the reverse be true?
9. Is the cited research relevant to the claim?
10. Do visuals accurately represent the data and reality?
© 2023 Paul Gibbons and Tricia Kennedy

Figure XII.1: Ten questions for detecting BS. Answering a combination of these questions when evaluating a claim or piece of evidence helps more quickly identify nonsense (ahem, bullshit).

Is the language hyperbolic?

Here come the adjectives: **Groundbreaking. Exponential. Radical. Transformative.**

Consultants are partly salespeople, which risks their rhetoric being more propaganda than truth. Change consultants have the unenviable job of pitching their services to clients dismissive or ignorant of change principles. (Or, in big consulting firms, pitching their services to technology partners who reckon their expertise is sufficient.)

These days it seems nothing just grows, it grows "exponentially." Every project is a "transformation," whether it catalyzes change (or not). Things aren't important, they are "game changers." Ideas are no longer new, they are "paradigm-shifting."

Few things in the real world, including the business world, grow exponentially. A workforce scaled at 50% a month (that is, exponentially) would hire 50 people in January and 4,324 people in December. Apple's revenue from the initial iPhone launch qualifies as exponential growth as do some viral phenomena and fads. However, few change effects are literally exponential—the overuse of that term is an example of linguistic puffery.

The word "transformation" entered the organizational change discourse in the 1990s. No longer interested in mere organizational change, it had to be transformational to qualify as valuable. But what makes a business change transformational? Does it have to affect the entire organization? Must it involve a dramatic change in strategy or business structure? A chrysalis changing into a butterfly could be called a transformation, as could a stem cell changing into a neuron—but what in the business world resembles these transformations? Arguably, Covid-19 effected a work transformation: 73% of knowledge workers switched to remote work literally overnight. However, truly transformational shifts of this kind are generational in frequency.

Beware of organizational change writing using hyperbole. It is a complex, and sometimes difficult, discipline—we don't get to make hyperbolic claims if we want to track anywhere near reality.

Is the metaphor sloppy?

"Mind your metaphors. Metaphors help structure complex realities, but we must make sure that the metaphors we use track reality."

PAUL GIBBONS

"**Culture eats strategy for breakfast**." A catchy aphorism (if only we could come up with one as catchy). Let's parse this nice sounding, but sloppy metaphor.

Culture does not literally eat anything, let alone breakfast. What does the phrase mean? There are two possible interpretations: Culture is **more important** than strategy or culture **causes strategy**.

To say culture is more important than strategy is like saying eating is more important than breathing—both are important, and you can't have one without the other. Culture without supporting strategy is directionless; strategy without aligned culture is likely to fail. Competitive advantage requires robust connectivity between strategy and culture. Can you imagine a fantastic workplace culture (e.g., values-driven, nurturing, purpose-driven) at a directionless or strategically inept company? We can.

The second culture-eating-strategy option implies that **culture causes** or pre-determines strategy. It may be true that leaders' values inform strategic decisions, but are they the single most-important factor in strategy (i.e., are they so important that nothing else contributes to a company's strategy)?

Alibaba and Amazon have very different corporate cultures, yet their retailing strategies are similar. Different cultures do coexist with the same strategy, and thus, culture cannot "cause" strategy. It is daft to suggest that the U.S. Environmental Protection Agency's (EPA) strategy mirrors that of the U.S. Internal Revenue Service (IRS) simply because of any cultural similarities that result from being big federal-government agencies.

Arguably, culture was neglected by strategists and technologists in days gone by. Given that context, perhaps the culture-eating-strategy catchphrase was historically an intentional exaggeration to draw attention to culture's neglect as an important factor in company performance. We doubt any successful executive today is deluded enough to think culture does not matter.

Does the term mean anything? Anything specific? Is it being used correctly?

"You keep using that word. I do not think it means what you think it means."

INIGO MONTOYA

Business folk, including organizational change professionals, tend to misuse words (intentionally or unintentionally, who knows). One guru-blogger defines organizational culture as, "a positive work environment." Oops, that is a facet of organizational climate not culture. Similarly, one major-consulting firm partner defined organizational culture as values and norms. Oops, again, values and norms are only one component (among many) of culture. Another common refrain is that culture is "unwritten rules for the way we do things around here." Not wrong, per se, but an oversimplification too general to be very useful on its own.

Beware of hyperbole, buzzwords, jargon, and how words are used. Often the words are being used to mean something different than their actual definition; often they are words with many different meanings and thus are intended to obfuscate (what does leadership mean, anyway?). Ask yourself: What precisely do they mean by the term? Are they using the term correctly?

Is the claim always true?

Creating a sense of urgency is the first of John Kotter's eponymous eight steps for leading change. Chapter VIII asked whether it is **always** the case that urgency is a required first step toward organizational change. We went further, worrying that urgency is a harmful notion with has toxic effects on change efforts, climate, culture, and workers.

Leaders Eat Last is a 2014 best-selling business book by Simon Sinek. It is outstandingly clever and without doubt you can't think of examples where it should have been true, or examples where you wish a leader had eaten last. However, a contrary maxim in change is **before trying to change others to first start with yourself.** You might focus on changing your own behavior in merited ways and focus on areas in which you need to grow, and work to overcome your own limitations. When the oxygen masks descend on an airplane, the flight attendants unilaterally instruct putting on your own first, before others. But "leaders eat first" is a crap book title.

Does the claim use generalizations, stereotypes, or black-and-white thinking?

"There are two kinds of people in the world. People who believe the BS that there are two kinds of people in the world, and people who don't."

ATTRIBUTED TO ROBERT BENCHLEY (20TH-CENTURY JOURNALIST)

Evolution of the organizational change field has been an ongoing attempt to universally generalize how people and businesses change, every single time. However, most broad generalizations ignore context and diversity, and are often stereotypes and over-simplifications. Paul recalls a $1,000-an-hour executive coach recently opining that "women are too emotional to run companies." Clearly, some generalizations manage not only to be false stereotypes, but also toxic.

Other generalizations may be harmless, yet still based on bad science. As we saw earlier, results of value surveys often appear in articles with generalizations such as Millennials value learning and growth whereas boomers value financial security, or that people in their 60s and 70s who live on savings and pensions worry less than Millennials about learning new skills (except perhaps shuffleboard).

Black-and-white thinking (also called binary thinking because things are either black or white) is a source of mental distress and sometimes a symptom of mental disorder. It also frequently finds its way organizational change: People are either "onboard" or "resisting," a leader is either "bought-in" or "against." In any organizational change, people's feelings are nuanced and multifaceted. People may like some aspects and hate others, or they may be ambivalent and undecided, among other possibilities.

Don't fall into the insidious trap of characterizing people with all-or-nothing, black-and-white labels. There is a lot of gray area when talking about people (and life), and more still when considering how people experience and respond to change. All that gray in the middle is what matters.

Are there counterexamples?

*"Every genuine test of a theory is an attempt to falsify it or to refute it. **Confirming evidence should not count** except when it is the result of a genuine test of the theory, and this means that it can be presented as a serious but unsuccessful attempt to falsify the theory."*[88] *[emphasis ours]*

KARL POPPER

When presented with an idea, humans naturally search their "mental databases" (memories) for examples that confirm it. A family of cognitive biases enables this (e.g., the anchoring effect and the confirmation bias).

Perhaps you read a horoscope that says Libras are peacemaking, tactful, and diplomatic. Scanning your mental database, you locate your Libra friend, Joan; she certainly fits the mold. Come to think of it, so does your Libra roommate, Jamal.

Identifying confirming examples of claims is much easier than exerting more effort to find counterexamples. For instance, according to the internet, Vladimir Putin and Heinrich Himmler are also Libras—seeming counterexamples to the peaceful and tactful Libras first considered.

If we think finding change difficult is "hardwired" or "brains hate change," confirmation bias again scans your mental database for confirmatory examples: Moving to a new town at age 12, losing a relative, or the last re-organization your company underwent. Confirmation bias nods vigorously: Yup, change is hard. In contrast, critical thinking leads to looking for counterexamples. Getting married, having a child, and graduating from college are among the most significant life changes people experience. Were those experiences hard? Did your brain hate them? While many people have heard of confirmation biases, less is written about **de-biasing** or minimizing biases. Seeking counterexamples to prove yourself wrong is one tactic to help de-bias thinking.

Figure XII.2 provides a lighter hearted sampling of organizational change myths, presented in the spirit of both David Letterman and the Internet age's propensity for list-icles—a seventh inning stretch or tea break, if you will, during our 10-question journey through bullshit detection.

Top-10 warning signs to keep looking when interviewing change professionals

1. We guarantee 100% adoption.

2. Be prepared to handle all folks going through an inevitable pit of despair, or death valley of change.

3. First, we need to create a sense of urgency or burning platform.

4. Our detailed communication plan will lead to commitment.

5. Behavior ultimately comes down to rewards and punishments, or carrots and sticks.

6. We shouldn't waste time getting to know the impacted stakeholders, managers can tell us how they think and feel.

7. Hearts and minds, it's all about hearts and minds.

8. They just need more training.

9. The most important thing is to deal with resistors and get them "with the program."

10. Let me show you a monkey video (or rodent video) that demonstrates how all people behave in similar situations.

© 2023 Paul Gibbons and Tricia Kennedy

Figure XII.2: Top-10 warning signs to keep looking when interviewing change professionals. Given the Internet age's propensity for list-icles, we couldn't resist providing our own *Change Myths* top-10 list.

Is the framework or model exhaustive?

"Essentially, all models are wrong, but some are useful."

GEORGE E.P. BOX (MATHEMATICIAN)

Box was of course correct: The map (trivially) isn't the territory. However, his statement is often used to justify a certain **epistemological nihilism**—"if all models are wrong, then I can pick and choose which ones I think are useful." But again, without evidence how do you know your wrong model is useful? (Your wrong map of Westeros won't get you to King's Landing.)

The change world is replete with models for how people change, how ready they are for change, and what leaders need to do to effect change. ADKAR is one, unfreeze-change-refreeze is another, and the plethora of so-called transformational change models are others. There are perhaps thousands of branded change models in existence covering the gamut of change theory. While an advisor to Deloitte Consulting, Paul researched **change readiness** and found dozens of competing models—are they all right? None of them?

In academia, there are research-based models of change: Two robust examples are the theory of planned behavior (TPB) and COM-B (i.e., capability, opportunity, motivation). These two models point to over a dozen factors to consider or levers to pull. In contrast, the ones made up by consultants and look better on a PowerPoint slide have only around three-to-six factors.

One oversimplified and incorrect model, ADKAR (awareness, desire, knowledge, ability, reinforcement), passes the simple elegance test, is popular, and is used by some companies, despite head-shaking disdain from human behavior experts. It is billed and used as a model of individual change to answer the question of what drives individual change (according to Prosci's website). (See sidebar for more on why we think ADKAR misses the mark.)

The worlds of human and organizational change are complex. Even college-level psychology students have a broader and more accurate view of individual change than many change practitioners, both of which can still only ever be partial. The business leader or change leader wants simplifications that allow them to act more easily. However, bad simplifications do not cover the bases and oversimplifications lead to errors.

As a simplification, is ADKAR better than nothing? That depends on how high the stakes. If you have had a heart attack and your two options are to change your behavior or die, it would be wise to employ an advisor who understands human behavior in depth. Likewise, if your time-sensitive transformation project has a $10-million budget, relying on ADKAR alone to help change employee behavior would be foolish.

That is not to say ADKAR doesn't get a few things right, simply that it is not enough to enable individual change in organizations on its own. Its focus on awareness, desire, knowledge, ability, and reinforcement neglects additional, powerful influences of individual and organization change, including systems and social dynamics.

Furthermore, using a popular but bad model risks inspiring more confidence than is warranted, given its overly simplistic and incomplete view of human change.

As an alternative to ADKAR, consider the scientifically developed and validated Organizational Change Recipients Belief Scale (OCRBS)[89] and/or Readiness for Organizational Change[90] scale.

Both are public domain (read, free!) survey tools that measure and support understanding of individual-level feelings, attitudes, and beliefs about a change among its affected stakeholders. Neither are what ADKAR claims—necessary and sufficient stages to individual change—but both do offer an evidence-based tool for your change toolbox to better understand what affected individuals think and feel. (Importantly, both survey affected individuals directly—straight from the horse's mouth, so to speak—as opposed to assessment tools completed by change practitioners or sponsors based on their own perceptions.)

Debunking Prosci's ADKAR model

College psychology students understand there are dozens of factors that may help or hinder individual change such as attention, planning, beliefs, identity, resilience, environmental cues, social norms, workplace climate, incentives, psychological safety, mindsets, values, and habits (to name just a few). Any one of these factors ADKAR excludes might be the lynchpin, without which a change is doomed.

For example, psychological safety is absent from ADKAR, whereas research evidence indicates that it affects people's willingness to try new behaviors, voice concerns, learn, and change.[91]

Some companies, such as Google, believe psychological safety is the single-most critical factor in enabling change. Only a deeper inquiry into behavioral antecedents (or drivers) will tell which factors you might be missing and they likely differ by context. If ADKAR is your primary tool, you risk missing the most important factors and mistakenly believing you are doing what is needed.

Sufficiency and necessity are two critical thinking tests used to assess whether a model is useful, asking: If I "do ADKAR," is it necessary or sufficient for behavioral change? The answers are no and no.

Think about a difficult personal change like losing weight or working fewer hours. If you struggled and/or failed to achieve those changes (as many people have) was it because you weren't aware (A)? Was it because you didn't desire (D)? Was it because you didn't have sufficient knowledge (K), ability (A), or reinforcement (R)? ADKAR doesn't seem sufficient.

Go further and question whether these elements are always necessary. Again, the answer is no, at least not always. Behavioral science provides thousands of research-backed examples of personal change that bypass ADKAR dimensions. ADKAR is neither sufficient, nor necessary, for organizational change.

Is a causal claim justified? Could the reverse be true?

Correlation is not causation. High crime neighborhoods may have a lot of police, but that does not mean police cause crime. Umbrellas and rain are highly correlated, but umbrellas do not cause rain, only that the two things occur together.

Our homeopathy friends swear its treatments cure ailments, but the **placebo effect** tells us they likely start feeling better after using it even if it provides no physiological benefits. (The placebo effect is especially relevant to homeopathy given homeopathy's underlying principles—in other words, its treatments dilute any active ingredient to the point of nonexistence, believing it is the spirit or essence of the no-longer-present active ingredient that heals.) The homeopathy pill and recovery are correlated, but colds and other viruses usually get better on their own. People often take pills when they feel terrible, but they also usually do other things in tandem like getting more rest and fluids; they also may have already started to recover simply due to time and the immune system in action (separate from any over-the-counter medication).

These examples, again, illustrate the **post-hoc ergo propter-hoc fallacy**: If it preceded it, then it must have caused it.

This fallacy's signature example is the job satisfaction and performance relationship from the industrial and organizational (I-O) psychology world. An intuitively attractive idea on which a considerable amount of money is spent investing in worker happiness, hoping for better performance. However, the relationship between happy workers and their productivity is largely correlational (not causal), and only a minimal one. Any correlation simply means the two variables move together, it provides no indication of causation, which means there is more to productivity than happy workers. Who knew?

Given it is only correlation, the relationship could also indicate the opposite: **Productive people are happier**. When your authors feel as if they have accomplished a great deal in a day, they lift that evening glass of wine a happier camper than on a day they accomplish less.

We also saw studies linking organizational change efforts to project success, giving the appearance of **correlation** but going further to imply causation. However, these findings are from **post-hoc**

surveys, and this research design suffers from limitations related to self-report, halo effects, and after-the-fact assessment. Again, what are people likely to say about a failed project? Probably not, "it failed, however, the organizational change management was awesome." Conversely, when a project is successful, the glow from the successful experience inclines people toward answering survey questions more positively (e.g., the change sponsorship on this project was effective).

Is the cited research relevant to the claim?

Organizational change writers rarely ground their rhetoric in basic research from psychology or its sibling disciplines in the human and behavioral sciences. When they do, we run into a transferability problem. We saw this with Kübler-Ross' DABDA as template for understanding how people respond to organizational changes transferred from the dying experience and we saw this with Yerkes and Dobson's experiments on rodents receiving electric shocks, and learning transferred to humans.

A great deal of the research evidence we evaluate and incorporate into our change work comes from different contexts and disciplines.

Research context and transferability are especially relevant to organizational change because, as a field or discipline, it is largely an amalgamation of different fields and disciplines, such as learning and development, leadership development, communication, psychology, sociology, behavioral economics, anthropology, and more. Large portions of change knowledge do not come from research designed to study organizational change.

Be wary of how research from one context applies to another context (or not), particularly when either the original or destination context is a complex social system.

Do visuals accurately represent the data and reality?

It is said that a picture is worth a thousand words. Images can also obfuscate the truth.

Visuals such as infographics, graphs, and models (along with the symbols they use) convey information that can be oversimplified, misleading, and distorting when presenting a claim or piece of evidence. Even innocent-looking symbols such as a plus (+), minus (-), or equals (=) tell a tale.

Figure XII.3 shows a well-known change "equation" purporting levers to overcome resistance. First and foremost, and as we saw earlier, resistance to change is a problematic way to frame organizational change. Second, is there any research evidence to support this equation?

For the sake of discussion, let's assume for a moment the visual is true (even though it is not). The symbols communicate that these three variables (e.g., dissatisfaction, vision, and first steps) in combination are **always greater than** any resistance. Is this model useful? Are there other factors beyond these three that might trigger a response (unhelpfully) called resistance? (Recall Figure VI.1, there are many.) How might these many other variables distort or alter the equation presented in the visual? Are the three variables in this visual necessary for change? **Do you have to be dissatisfied with the status quo to act differently?** Does only dissatisfaction drive great athletes to greater heights? (Not generally, a great performer can be delighted with a match performance, but still see opportunity for growth.)

Tricia remembers being perfectly satisfied with a car she owned (even paid off). Yet when an opportunity presented itself to buy a newer, nicer car at a discounted price, she jumped at it. Thus, dissatisfaction cannot always be a necessary factor for action or behavior change.

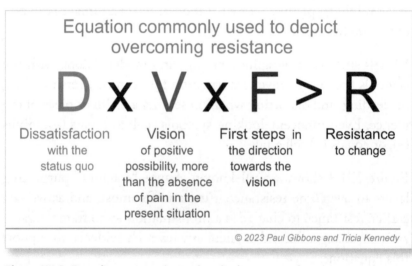

Equation commonly used to depict overcoming resistance

$$D \times V \times F > R$$

| Dissatisfaction with the status quo | Vision of positive possibility, more than the absence of pain in the present situation | First steps in the direction towards the vision | Resistance to change |

© 2023 Paul Gibbons and Tricia Kennedy

Figure XII.3: Equation commonly used to depict overcoming change resistance. The equation claims the combination of status-quo dissatisfaction, a positive vision of what's possible, and action towards the vision is always greater (or stronger) than any change resistance. It is an oversimplification of not only the complexity of human behavior, but also the complex social dynamics that influence organizational behavior. (Source unknown.)

Figure XII.4 shows a purported relationship between time and degree of support for change from a pioneer and founding father in organizational change and his colleague[92]. The straight line going up from left to right is the classic illustration for a perfect, positive correlation. But is a positive correlation between time and degree of support for change supported by research evidence? Not that we have found. Also, does this straight line accurately depict how change happens in organizations or are their reversals, dips, backtracking, and different paths for different folks?

Then there are the stages laid out on top of the correlation graph. Do all folks experiencing change progress through these sequential stages? We have seen that people don't work this way; they are complex organisms. Again, awareness and understanding are depicted as the necessary factors to reach change commitment; but we know information in the form of communication is insufficient for commitment and behavior change.

Further, there is evidence that people may adopt a change without initially liking it and then come to like it after trying it. New skills frequently work that way—kids rarely pick up the cello and immediately love it. Instead, progress is made before learning to like it. Sometimes people understand a change and immediately like it, but once they adopt it find things to dislike (like in the honeymoon period of a relationship).

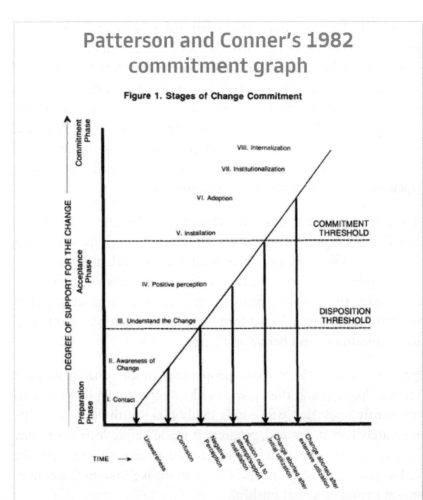

Figure XII.4: Patterson and Conner's 1982 commitment graph. The straight line angling up from bottom-left to top-right in this graph tells us there is a perfect, positive correlation between the two variables (which are time on the x-axis and degree of change support on the y-axis). Even assuming intervention to address the stated goals along the line (I to VIII), this premise raises a red flag.

You don't have to be an expert in symbolism to be wary of and double-check messages conveyed by visuals that depict them. You also don't have to be a mathematician to be wary of and double-check messages conveyed by visuals that include mathematical lines and curves.

Critical thinking suggests a little time to dig deeper and evaluate messages communicated by visuals (e.g., symbols, graphs, infographics) for potentially misleading, oversimplified, or distorted claims—sometimes just a quick Google or Wikipedia search can help get you on the right path.

Leveraging these 10 bullshit-detector questions offers a quick-and-easy way to critically examine claims encountered every day, improving the ability to decide if you should buy what is being sold.

What comes next?

Organizational change, as commonly described, is stressful and necessarily challenging, but humans also often change enthusiastically and gracefully. Adaptability is a hallmark of our species.

The final chapter summarizes key, recurring themes, makes a case for the notion of "change is hard" as self-fulfilling prophecy, and lays out a vision for a critical thinking and evidence-based future.

CHAPTER XIII

Conclusion: The future of organizational change

"Lately it occurs to me: What a long, strange trip it's been."

ROBERT C. HUNTER (AMERICAN LYRICIST)

Several themes weave their way throughout *Change Myths* and steer organizational change toward a future grounded in critical thinking and evidence-based practice:

- Useful and accurate change generalizations do not exist because people and organizations are diverse.
- Likewise, people do not fit tidily into broad categories or types.
- Beliefs form, propagate, and stick independent of their veracity.
- All people (even experts) are fallible and "predictably irrational."
- Information disorder exacerbates humans' natural irrationality.
- Logic and scientific research evidence help combat irrationality.
- Systems theory and complexity science inform human behavior.

We knit these themes together beginning where we started: All change is hard.

Talk about change so it doesn't hurt

"Biologically, physiologically, we are not so different from each other; historically, as narratives—we are each of us unique."

OLIVER SACKS (BRITISH NEUROLOGIST AND WRITER)

Rock and Schwartz would have us believe that change is pain because it triggers the same neural pathways and brain structures as physiological and psychological pain (a biological argument about change we hope was successfully refuted). As we saw, this generalization is too simplistic to reflect individual difference and diversity and it also reinforces a dismal, inaccurate, and self-fulfilling view of human adaptability.

Orthodoxy that all change entails negative reactions is self-fulfilling—we get what we expect the same way we observe that which confirms our beliefs. If expecting constancy (falsely), for instance, change always shows up as an unpleasant surprise.

Yet life is all change and adaptation. It is inevitable at every level, from molecules to organs, from organisms to ecosystems, and from human beings to organizations. Given this inevitability, is anyone well served by change orthodoxy's myopic focus on negative, self-fulfilling narratives? A lesson might be learned from Buddhist philosophy, where stability is an illusion and ongoing change is not part of life, it is life.

Most people are laid off or fired at least once in their careers. Re-organizations of some kind happen regularly in big companies. New technology introductions feel constant. Technological advances replace human workers. Change happens and most of it is out of our control. We won't like or agree with all of it. Some of it will be hard.

In contrast, we see people and organizations change with great grace. Take the most disruptive worldwide change since World War II as an example: 2020's COVID epidemic. Tens of millions of workers pivoted on a dime to remote work and organizations provided the flexibility and tools to make it possible. Urban lifestyles were upended: Streets, gyms, bars, and restaurants were empty. Governments instituted policies intended to slow the virus' spread. Vaccine researchers went to work, collaborating across borders and companies, delivering a vaccine in 14 months (when vaccine development historically averages 10-15 years). Though 7-million deaths are a tragedy, public health experts believe that human and institutional adaptability allowed us to dodge a deadlier bullet.

Figure XIII.1: London's busiest shopping street during COVID pandemic lockdowns (2020). People are quite capable of being incredibly adaptable, which flies in the face of many preconceived notions about human behavior, and organizational change axioms we hold on to so tightly. (Yes, even old dogs really can and do learn new tricks.)

Consequences of the all-change-is-hard paradigm

"Primum non nocere [first, do no harm]."

HIPPOCRATES (*OF THE EPIDEMICS*, 400 BCE)

Are there harmful consequences to the all-change-is-hard premise? Yes, and we think those significant.

First, from the beliefs that change is hard and that people resist change follow the idea that organizations and people must be un-frozen, and an effective means of doing so is use of power, some-times fear (urgency), and sometimes carrots and sticks. We've seen substantial unintended consequences of managing change this way. In this regard, all change is hard introduces a **self-fulfilling prophecy**. The means we use to enable change makes it harder than it need be by forcing change through.

Second, the all-change-is-hard notion allows those in charge to **evade responsibility** when change does get hard. (People are struggling? Well, all change is hard, so of course.) Notice how leader behavior, decision making, and strategy matter less in this fatalistic worldview. The telescope, to reuse an earlier analogy, points the wrong way—not toward "how could we, as leaders, have orchestrated this change cor-rectly?" Blame for the negative experience lands on the people being changed and the inevitability that it will be hard.

As change professionals, we have all been pulled in late to put out "change fires." Rare is the leader who wonders: Do I have the capability and expertise to lead change? Does my team? Have we the right expertise in change strategy? What part of the change burden, if there must be one, can **we** shoulder? If we consider the lives and experiences of our workers and weigh them fully, what is the right way to get this change done?

We tend to hear, "let's not revisit ancient history, let's focus on the future." (Heaven forbid there might be lessons to learn). History without lessons learned is doomed to repeat itself. Our view is that change leaders need to "eat first." Before attempting to change their people, they might look, for example, at what skills they need to build.

Finally, all change is hard ignores how change affects people dif-ferently. We manage change with that generalization in mind, whereas there may be people who feel quite differently. To treat someone who may be struggling the same as someone who is excited and engaged risks poor communications disconnected from the diversity of human experience.

When educators and professionals (of any flavor) teach change as an exception rather than the rule, an outlier rather than a day-to-day part of life, and teach that it is unavoidably painful, they do a great disservice to those whom they serve.

Transcend the biological narrative

"Words are loaded pistols."

JEAN-PAUL SARTRE (FRENCH PHILOSOPHER)

More important than our current rudimentary understanding of brain structures and chemistry is the power of narratives in driving human experience. Instead of clinging onto negative narratives (i.e., change is always hard, painful, and requires some force), change orthodoxy has an opportunity to reframe its narratives to talk about change in a more positive, empowering, and scientifically more accurate way.

Individuals may not have control over every change that comes their way, but people do have some control over how they frame their narratives. Meaning-making and sense-making are human superpowers that are bigger than their biological responses. Encouraging and reframing more positive narratives is not to say the answer is an overly Pollyanna-ish attitude, stiff-upper-lip Stoicism, or even grin-and-bear-it positivity—these examples strike us as false positivity and dishonest. Yet, there is power in honest reframing, reimagining, and redesigning meaning through narrative.

As change professionals responsible for facilitating and guiding organizations and stakeholders through changes, we can not only do a better job appreciating and empathizing with the diversity of individuals and their change reactions—positive, negative, and in-between—but also leveraging that deeper empathy and appreciation to craft and empower honest and helpful narratives.

"Predictably irrational" and crooked timber

"Out of the crooked timber of humanity, no straight thing was ever made."

IMMANUEL KANT (ENLIGHTENMENT PHILOSOPHER)

Humans are storytellers. The narratives we tell ourselves, share with others, consume, and internalize exert influence over our beliefs, mindsets, and worldviews, as well as our behaviors and lived experiences. Stories are not only easy to remember and retell but are also powerful sense-making and meaning-making mechanisms. Words, stories, analogies, and metaphors provide vivid descriptions, shared understanding, and are powerful instruments of communication and persuasion.

People are also fallible and irrational (more than most are comfortable admitting). All people are susceptible to hundreds of cognitive biases along with mental shortcuts like heuristics. Most of the time these biases and heuristics work quite effectively and efficiently, demonstrating human's incredible adaptive capacity. But In situations where they fail, we run into trouble.

Not even experts are immune to cognitive biases. Indeed, experts (along with celebrity thought leaders, influencers, and gurus) might be **more** susceptible to certain biases if their identity and sense-of-self are tied to "being an expert" and/or they have commercial interests in their expertise area or celebrity. For instance, confirmation bias and illusory superiority, even Dunning-Kruger effects when venturing beyond their expertise area. (See Figure XIII.2 for list of biases in *Change Myths*.)

Further complicating both human fallibility (generally) and experts' susceptibility to self-deception (more specifically) is the Internet age's rise in **information disorder** (see Appendix B).

Today's world of information overload means not only easier, faster access to more information and a democratization of content production than at any other point in human history (yay), but also fewer quality gates (boo). In other words, there is a quality free-for-all from low barriers to creating, sharing, publishing, distributing, and promoting information.

Anyone with an opinion and a keyboard can present themselves as an authority, and if charismatic and persistent enough can gain an audience regardless of truth or correctness. Audience leads to more authority, which leads to more audience, in an amplifying cycle. Since any Kieran, Celeste, or Hugo can contribute to the information glut, our ability to rely on intuition (I) and authority (A) for knowledge are taxed and their pitfalls more pronounced. **Popularity becomes a proxy for expertise and commercial success becomes a proxy for validity.**

Cognitive biases in *Change Myths*

Bias Name	Bias Description
Acquiescence bias	When you participate in a data collection activity (e.g., survey questionnaire, poll), you tend to agree with statements as presented.
Anchoring effect	When you identify a reference point (anchor) in advance of a decision, your decision becomes irrationally bound to and influenced relative to the reference point (i.e., your decision would be different without any anchor and different with another anchor).
Availability bias	The easier you can bring something to mind, the more likely you are to erroneously connect it to a conclusion or judgment, and also to overestimate its occurrence or likelihood to occur.
Backfire effect	When you become more convinced of a belief or set of beliefs if confronted with evidence that conflicts with those beliefs (a manifestation of confirmation bias).
Barnum-Forer effect	When you assign high-accuracy ratings to a description of your personality because you believe it was personalized just for you, even though it is so vague it could apply to almost anyone. Also, when you are more likely to accept negative feedback if you believe it is personalized and you believe the person giving it to you is a high-status professional.
Central tendency bias	When you participate in a data collection activity (e.g., survey questionnaire, poll), you tend to avoid the most recent extreme responses.
Confirmation bias	When you look for, interpret, and more easily recall information that confirms your pre-existing beliefs, while also ignoring, dismissing, or avoiding information that contradicts your pre-existing beliefs. Tendency is stronger when related to a deeply-held belief, an emotionally-charged topic, or an outcome you want and hope for or will benefit you.
Dunning-Kruger effect	(A form of illusory superiority.) When you have an inflated view of your knowledge or ability, along with inflated confidence in your knowledge or ability, for topic or activity of which you actually have low levels of knowledge or ability. Whereas people with higher levels of actual knowledge or ability in a topic or activity tend to express less confidence.
Endowment effect	When you assign an inflated value to and an aversion to losing an object because you own or posses it (even if only for a few minutes).
Familiarity bias	When you irrationally favor the familiar over the novel, and also when a familiar situation triggers you to revert your state of mind or behaviors to the situation.
Halo effect	When you have a positive impression of one part of something (e.g., person, product, company) and irrationally project that positive impression to that things' other parts (e.g., from a product to the company that makes it, from an attractive person's looks to their character).
Illusory superiority	When you overestimate your own qualities and abilities compared to others.
Narrative fallacy	When you retrospectively make up an overly simplistic cause-and-effect explanation for an event based on random and unrelated details, especially for rare and unpredictable events.
Placebo effect	When you unknowingly use an inert or ineffective treatment (e.g., sugar pill that you believe is medication) that then exhibits results simply because you believed it would.
Positive-negative asymmetry effect	When negative events imprint quicker, effects you more (psychologically), and are easier to remember than positive or neutral events, even compared to equally salient positive events.
Post-hoc ergo propter-hoc fallacy	When you make up or assume a causal relationship to the first of two sequential events, simply based on their order of occurrence, and without considering any other possible factors.
Priming effect	When you unknowingly process a stimulus (target stimulus) in relation to a stimulus you were exposed to shortly before (priming stimulus).
Reactance	When you feel like your choices or behaviors are being unduly restricted due to something else (such as rules, regulations, or another person).
Sampling bias	When you participate in a data collection activity (e.g., survey questionnaire, polls), a tendency for a subset of all participants to not represent the defined population under study.
Self-serving bias	When you irrationally perceive yourself in an overly favorable manner, and when you're distort your self-perceptions to protect your self-esteem.
Social desirability bias	When you participate in a data collection activity (e.g., survey questionnaire, polls), you tend to respond in a way that tries to portray yourself (or your organization) in a favorable light.
Status-quo bias	When you emotionally and irrationally prefer the current state of affairs and even avoid actions that might alter it. Also, when you use your current state of affairs as a reference point, or baseline, from which any deviation is seen as a gain or loss.

Figure XIII.2: Cognitive biases in *Change Myths*. There are hundreds of cognitive biases, which are either learned or inherited mental shortcuts. The ones in *Change Myths* only scratch the surface.

Combat irrationality with evidence

"Many highly intelligent people are poor thinkers. Many people of average intelligence are skilled thinkers. The power of a car is separate from the way the car is driven."

EDWARD DE BONO (MALTESE PHYSICIAN, PSYCHOLOGIST, INVENTOR, AND AUTHOR)

People also turn to **evidence, in all its flavors**, to inform their stories and narratives and to help make sense of and navigate the world around them. But each evidence flavor has its own shortcomings (i.e., strengths and weaknesses) and no single evidence flavor tells a complete story on its own.

We saw both **intuition and authority (I and A from LIAR)** are valuable sources of knowledge, but on their own they often lead us astray. Mental shortcuts (trusting our gut, trusting in authority) are useful, but their efficiencies may be overwhelmed in a more complex world characterized by information disorder.

Logic and scientific research evidence (L and R from LIAR) are powerhouses of rationality. Especially since the Age of Enlightenment, logic and research evidence provide effective countermeasures to cognitive frailty and information disorder's challenges. They come to our rescue in situations where our biases fail. That is, if we leverage them.

Recall Kahneman's wisdom that, "an unbiased appreciation of uncertainty is a cornerstone of rationality." Certainty comes in degrees and only formal logic provides "proof." We learned that we are better served in both life and change by the scientific term "warrant" (i.e., an abundance of high-quality research evidence warranting belief) than the words proof or certainty.

In addition to the LIA sources of knowledge, each with their own strengths and weaknesses, there are sub-flavors of research evidence (R in LIAR), which are different approaches to research called research designs. As with all LIAR components, each research design alone tells only part of the story and critical thinkers need to understand their tradeoffs, strengths, and weaknesses. Research designs span a spectrum between quantitative (more predictive) and qualitative (more descriptive). **Only together and with mixed methods do research findings progress knowledge by contributing their evidence sub-flavors at different levels of breadth and depth** (e.g., from cause-and-effect at the quantitative pole to personal narratives at the qualitative pole).

We saw that a scientific attitude (to use the title of McIntyre's book) and the ability to parse contradictions across LIAR's components leads to **one of the 21st century's most essential skills: Critical thinking**. As Grant reminds us, critical thinking combines "weighing the strongest evidence more heavily" with "recognizing your own biases and giving serious consideration to facts that contradict your hopes and beliefs."

Look backward to leap forward

"In solving a problem of this sort, the grand thing is to be able to reason backwards. This is a very useful accomplishment, and a very easy one, but people do not practice it much."

SIR ARTHUR CONAN DOYLE (*A STUDY IN SCARLET*, 1887)

Organizational change orthodoxy to date appears a long, expensive, and mostly fruitless quest for broad, general models that accurately and usefully represent a universal template for how people change (all of which bear the mark of its predominantly negative narrative). For example:

- From change as loss that causes grief to change as physical pain,
- From change as dominance and fear (stamping out opposition) to change as carrots and sticks, and
- From change as a slog through sequential n-steps (e.g., three, eight) to change as one-way information (often just adding to today's overwhelming deluge of information).

The resultant cannon of change ideas and models may be intuitively attractive, but they perpetuate the negative narrative, fall prey to a wide range of cognitive biases, and pigeonhole people into broad, inaccurate, and unhelpful categories. (In other words, they are myths.)

Furthermore, despite robust, cumulative evidence to the contrary, faulty beliefs about people and organizations from a mostly bygone era still persist (generally), and still form part of change orthodoxy's foundation and axioms (specifically). For example:

- People are inherently lazy, complacent, and self-centered (Theory X),
- All leaders are born to lead, or they are born with special traits and superpowers that pre-determine their destiny (great-man leadership), and
- Organizations exist in a general state of equilibrium and prefer to maintain their status quo.

Perhaps these dated, faulty beliefs persevere because biases lead us to **seek (even crave or demand) tidy stories, patterns, and categories, as well as broad generalizations, simplifications, and certainty (even when these things are illusory).**

Perhaps these dated, faulty beliefs persevere because, like all great lies, they have some truth to them. Research evidence warrants belief that personality traits, which we are born with, account for a small percentage of leadership effectiveness (at least when using the empirically developed Big Five trait taxonomy). Classic and operant conditioning's evidence base warrants belief that carrots and sticks tell part of the human behavior story (but far from the whole story). And that both individual differences and lived experience matter (or have their own role to play) in human behavior and change is not only almost uncontested but also robustly supported by its body of knowledge (just not solely, as change orthodoxy suggests).

Whatever the many, interrelated reasons for how the change world got to where it is today, it finds itself at an intellectual crossroads.

At an intellectual crossroads

"There is always a level of generality at which any two things can be said to be essentially the same, and always a level of particularity at which they can be distinguished."

MICHAEL SCRIVEN (PHILOSOPHER)

At first blush, organizational change's intellectual history appears to follow what Kuhn called a "normal" pattern of scientific investigation, when knowledge builds incrementally on past ideas. Some of these past ideas take the form of axioms. As we saw, many change axioms are myths and only some useful and valid. It is time, we believe, to stop building change knowledge on shaky foundations.

Kuhn's history of science may show the way. According to his opus, *The Nature of Scientific Revolutions*[93], the overbearing weight of disconfirming evidence, unanswerable questions, and paradoxes (what he collectively called "anomalies") interrupts incremental progress, straining the normal order to crisis. Crisis pushes the discipline's science and practitioner community into a new phase (Kuhn called "revolutionary"). Bluntly, falsified axioms are tossed into the intellectual trash heap to follow research evidence where it leads, eventually putting the discipline back onto a new-normal science path with its new paradigms.

As a discipline, organizational change currently exhibits all three anomalies. For example:

- Myths in this book are all examples of **disconfirming evidence** for persistent, faulty beliefs,
- Constraints from a focus on negative narratives and a single, universal template for how individuals experience change raise many **unanswerable questions**, and
- Enormous investments in worker engagement programs, **paradoxically**, have not budged reported engagement rates.

Has organizational change reached an intellectual crisis point as described by Kuhn?

Follow the lead

"I knew I should have taken that left turn at Albuquerque!"

BUGS BUNNY

To shed light on the intellectual conundrum in which the change world finds itself, consider how organizational change's knowledge state compares to psychology's trajectory—a sibling discipline that overlaps with organizational change.

Like organizational change, psychology's early intellectual history was full of attempts to categorize and simplify the diversity and complexity of humankind (mind and behavior) into simplified, universal templates. We saw change-relevant examples from psychology such as DABDA, personality typing, binary resistance, and learning styles.

Psychology took this path because it had a **relatively immature empirical research profile and rudimentary understanding of the phenomena with which it is concerned**, especially in comparison to natural science's knowledge sophistication and rapid progress at the time. Psychology was a young discipline, just a baby, compared to the natural sciences. Its fragmented tradition of mostly discrete theoretical orientations (e.g., psychoanalysis, behaviorism) with their own foundational premises was more ideological than scientific and reflected its youth. As philosopher of science Michael Scriven reminds us, "ideology is to research what Marx suggested the economic factor was to politics and what Freud took sex to be for psychology."[94]

Psychology shifted gears early in the early 21st century by formally adopting evidence-based practice and principles[95], putting itself on a path toward a more integrated, less ideological discipline built on empiricism and scientific research evidence.

Organizational change finds itself at a similar intellectual crossroads to psychology, who provides a role model to follow.

In pursuit of an evidence-based future

"The future is already here; it is just unevenly distributed."

WILLIAM GIBSON (SCIENCE-FICTION WRITER)

Taking our own advice to follow the strongest evidence where it leads, a handful of critical lessons surface to point organizational change toward an evidence-based future.

Follow the evidence

"Human beings are social creatures. We are social not just in the trivial sense that we like company, and not just in the obvious sense that we each depend on others. We are social in a more elemental way: simply to exist as a normal human being requires interaction with other people."

ATUL GAWANDE (SURGEON AND JOURNALIST)

First and foremost, **following evidence doesn't happen without critical thinking**—that essential 21st-century skill. It is integral to evidence-based practice because it empowers the parsing and weighting of evidence in all its flavors and combinations.

Second, evidence suggests there are **real, harmful consequences (albeit mostly unintentional) to both organizations and workers** that result from change orthodoxy's ingrained but faulty and inaccurate axioms. Where organizations experience economic waste from misguided beliefs and advisory, they also evade responsibility and scrutiny for change and often abuse their dominance. Workers expected to adopt changes, usually dictated from above, carry a disproportionate weight due to axioms' false and myopic focus on individual "experiences." Simply, workers are held responsible for things out of their control, while organizations and their leaders are relieved of their own responsibility.

To say orthodoxy's false axioms result in a myopic focus on the individual change "experience" is not to say interventions focus on each affected individual, one at a time, and is not to say change professionals don't "group" affected stakeholders. Certainly communications target audience groups, training courses teach learner groups, and affected individuals are grouped into practical categories (e.g., geographic location, organizational affiliation, managers and non-managers). Yet, aggregations of individual-level phenomena into groupings, audiences, and categories are distinct from phenomena that result from the dynamic contextual interactions, connections, and relationships of social and systemic phenomena. (See the individual "experience" sidebar.)

The individual "experience"

"No man is an island, entire of itself; every man is a piece of the continent, a part of the main."

JOHN DONNE (16TH-CENTURY ENGLISH POET AND CLERIC)

How a person "experiences" something (such as an organizational change) is highly individualized. People interpret their interactions with the world through a unique blend of beliefs, schemas and heuristics, perspectives, learned biases, past experiences, narratives, and more.

This unique, individualized interpretation is a combination of individual-level phenomena. Examples of individual-level phenomena include:

- Skills (e.g., Lakshmi is able perform tasks in the new application whereas Dikembe is not),
- Feelings (e.g., "I don't desire this change" or "I am bought-in to this change"),
- Attitudes (e.g., "my company needs this change to stay competitive" or "my managers and/or supervisor don't appear to want this change"),
- Beliefs (e.g., "this change encroaches on my autonomy" or "this change is consistent with my personal values"), and
- Thought processes (e.g., "I wonder if my job might be at risk with this change" or "perhaps this change comes with opportunity to expand my skillset").

But as in life and organizational change, this latent, individualized experience does not tell the whole story of a person's mind and behavior because it is not fixed and does not form or evolve in a vacuum. It emerges from ongoing, dynamic connections and interactions between individual-level phenomena combined with social-level and systemic-level phenomena.

"Never underestimate the power of the social environment [situation]."

ERYLENE PIPER-MANDY (SOCIAL PSYCHOLOGIST)

Where the individual experience is a unique interpretation of the world we navigate, social- and systemic-level phenomena are the world around us—or the ever-evolving and changing context that feeds and shapes individualized experiences.

As with people's natural irrationality, the power of contextual influences on an individual's experience might be uncomfortable (especially in predominantly Western "rugged individualistic" cultures). None the less, evidence warrants belief in their strength as an influence on mind and behavior.

Social-level phenomena are contextual factors from connections and interactions with other people and groups. For example, power dynamics alter how a person experiences and responds to the world when comparing a social situation where they are a group leader (say, board director at a charity) to one where they are not (say, a staff-augmentation contractor role at work).

A few more change-relevant examples of social phenomena include:
- People's attitudes and feelings differ by situation,
- In-group and out-group dynamics in varying situations,
- Leader-follower dynamics (e.g., manager and supervisor unspoken expectations), and
- Situations trigger habitual feelings and behaviors.

Systemic-level phenomena are contextual factors from connections and interactions with systems (which are similar to social phenomena but less focused on groups of people). For example, performance metrics alter how a person experiences and responds to the world when comparing reward or punishment for departmental or business unit competition (say, a zero-sum competition for budget) to collaboration (say, strategic priority budgeting).

A few more change-relevant examples of system-level or systemic phenomena include:

- Performance metrics that reward individual accomplishments when team-based emergent qualities provide desired results,
- Subcultures coexist and are nested within a larger organizational culture (sometimes conflicting), and
- Processes and workflows drive actions (sometimes forcing workarounds), and
- The built-in hierarchal properties of organizational designs, processes, and culture.

For the purposes organizational change—or evaluating and intervening to influence attitudes, beliefs, and behavior in a work setting—evidence indicates all three phenomena levels are intertwined, or inseparable, and deserving of equal attention in how the discipline conceptualizes its work.

Third, evidence also points to the **contextual of social and systemic phenomena as equally, if not more, important than an individual's change experience**. Absent the contextual (of social and systemic phenomena), we only have an inadequate and partial story of human thought processes and behavior relevant to change—and the illusion that these are fixed and static. For instance, another bedrock insight from Kuhn's opus is that since research is performed by fallible humans, its reasoning and evidence should be understood within the context of its time—recall Schein's evolution from brainwashing prisoners to his helping philosophy of process consulting. Despite a natural inclination to separate ourselves (e.g., in-groups and out-groups), understanding change and behavior require understanding context.

Orthodoxy's narrow focus on the individual and a universal experience is not only harmful to organizations and workers, but it also **obscures from the change discipline the important nature of context and situation,** along with its implications for knowledge and practice. Where the evidence clearly indicates the inseparable, interconnected, and dynamic nature of individual experiences within their context, the change profession seems to have a blind spot that conceals a more holistic, useful conceptualization of organizational change.

Fourth and furthermore, evidence reveals that **complexity science and systems thinking inform human minds and behaviors** because organizations, groups, and people display emergent properties of nested, complex systems. Like Heraclitus' river, complex systems are constantly in motion and evolving, interacting with and adapting to their environment, and behavior is not explained by deconstruction of its parts. To understand the river also requires crossing traditional disciplinary boundaries because its complex ecosystem is vast—the water itself, creatures that live in its waters, creatures that rely on it to survive, its physical landscape, its climate, and more. It is humbling. Predictability and causality are hard to pin down, even more so than in simple and complicated systems. (See Figure XIII.3 for illustration and examples of organizations, groups, and people as nested complex systems.)

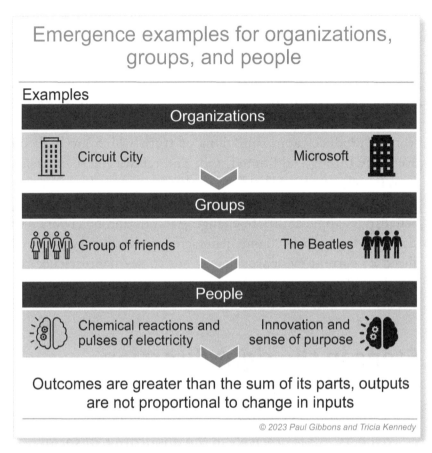

Figure XIII.3: Emergence examples for organizations, groups, and people. Organizations, groupings of people, and people are nested complex systems and these examples illustrate how all three exhibit emergence.

It also illustrates the **inadequacy of orthodoxy's circumscribed and overly simplistic views of change.** Such as, a hard slog through sequential steps that represent a universal template, inordinate attention to an individual's change experience at the expense of its complex context, and predominantly one-way communication and training (often just adding to an overwhelming deluge of information). These axioms won't survive intact in an evidence-based future.

Finally, the application of **critical thinking to follow the strongest evidence where it leads is not about absolute certainty, age, or novelty**. It is an iterative process where evidence accumulates, building a basis for either warranted belief or the intellectual trash heap (and, as we saw, is always open to the direction of new evidence). As Leedy and Ormrod suggest research, "produces approximations of truth which are built on over time through additional study and replication to create an overall body of knowledge."[96] For instance, psychological safety is not a new idea but has a large body of evidence warranting belief in its applicability to changing minds and behaviors. We also saw that claims about neuroscience and change are well ahead of current evidence; that is not to say neuroscience research evidence cannot inform change theory and practice in the future, it just isn't there yet.

Steps in the right direction

"Complexity theory seems to be of particular importance in relation to management in all its aspects.... It is precisely in the application of social sciences that we find innovation and open-minded thinking."

DAVID BYRNE AND GILL CALLAGHAN (SOCIOLOGISTS)

As a professional discipline and subject of formal research, organizational **change is not without hope**. Its future direction is guided by the lead of related disciplines (e.g., psychology, systems thinking) and the evidence itself (e.g., lessons above).

Hopeful glimmers crop up with a closer examination of change's history and full scope. There are already peripheral exceptions to orthodoxy's traditional-but-faulty paradigmatic emphases (i.e., always hard, universal template, individual experience without context) that point in the same direction as the current evidence.

First, while the critical **nature of situation and context** (or social and systemic phenomena) to change orthodoxy is obscured, it is not wholly absent. For instance, change leadership and sponsorship are integral components of organizational change, albeit frequently deployed as a one-off means to influence individual change experiences. None the less, leadership is a social phenomenon inseparable from followers. As leadership expert Gordy Curphy often says, "leadership is a team sport."

Moreover, retrospectives of Lewin's life and work establish that not only did he never explore or research his unfreeze-change-refreeze idea[97], but also that his work focused on change's contextual and complex nature, driven by his life mission to enable social change. This foundational change paradigm is lifted posthumously by his followers from a single, brief mention written just before Lewin's sudden death, who then hoisted it onto the nascent discipline's mantle in Lewin's name, without evidence supporting its validity.[98] Oops!

Second, neither is the **nature of complex systems** wholly absent from organizational change (again, only obscured by and peripheral to orthodoxy). For instance, recognition that organizational culture, along with its nested subcultures, affects change outcomes is often found among change professionals and researchers—culture is an emergent property of complex systems.

Moreover, evidence from the sibling disciple of learning and development indicates learning outcomes are highly sensitive to the predictability of learning's context—context sensitivity is also a property of complex systems. In other words, traditional learning techniques that emphasize repetition (e.g., practice and experience) only improve learning outcomes when the context is highly predictable. Conversely, these same techniques hamper learning outcomes in less predictable contexts, where learning techniques that emphasize the trial-and-error of experimentation improve learning outcomes.[99]

Vision for change's future

"Science has explored the microcosms and the macrocosms; we have a good sense of the lay of the land. The great unexplored frontier is complexity."

HEINZ PAGELS (AMERICAN PHYSICIST)

Like the human condition in full transcends brain chemistry explanations to understand people's minds and behaviors, especially with science's currently rudimentary understanding of the brain: Organizational change in full transcends individual-experience explanations to understand it, especially when further limited by orthodoxy's faulty paradigms.

The future of organizational change reveals itself when critical thinking lights the path to following the evidence where it leads. The tocsin has sounded, and time appears ripe for the change world to make a Kuhnian turn onto a revolutionary path toward an evidence-based future, guided by a cross-disciplinary roadmap with complexity science as its north star.

Parting words and an invitation to gather

"A thick tree grows from a tiny seed. A tall building arises from a mound of earth. A journey of a thousand miles starts with one step."

LAOZI (ANCIENT CHINESE PHILOSOPHER AND POET)

Taking our cue from philosopher of science Karl Popper's admonition that "science must begin with myths, and the criticism of myths"—we set out not only to put these eight change myths through the rigors of LIAR's lens, but also to:

- Generate new change insights,
- Counter misinformation (and provide tools to help you do the same),
- Pique curiosity,
- Advocate evidence-based practice (EBP) as the future for organizational change, and
- Promote critical thinking as an essential life skill.

We hope these goals were accomplished.

We did not to set out to claim ultimate authority over organizational change and its theories, practices, and models (like a hypothetical supreme court). The future direction of organizational change as an evidence-based discipline depends on its larger community embracing myth busting, well beyond these eight, to lead the way forward.

More intellectual debate and discussion, as a community and collective, are necessary to achieve this book's vision for the future of organizational change. To enable such debate and in the spirit of Latour's wisdom to be "one who offers arenas in which to gather," we invite you to **join the Evidence-Based Change Forum on LinkedIn** (https://www.linkedin.com/groups/12208516).

APPENDIX A

Organizational change management axioms

"Science is not an end in itself but merely a means toward an end."

TEN HAVE ET AL. (*RECONSIDERING CHANGE MANAGEMENT*, 2017)

Reconsidering Change Management covers 18 organizational change axioms culled from popular change writing and then weighed by ten Have and colleagues against formal research evidence on the topics. These are plotted by their likelihood to be an axiomatic truth in Figure XIV.1.

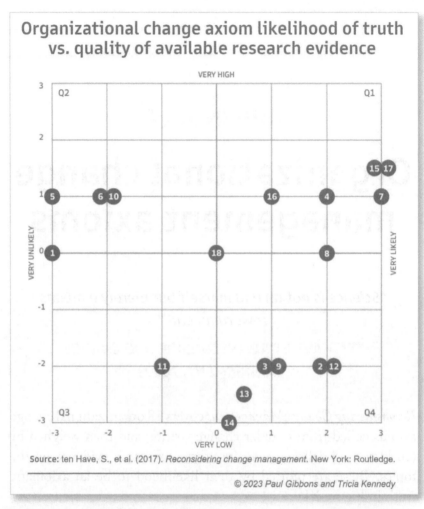

Figure XIV.1: Organizational change axiom likelihood of truth vs. quality of available research evidence. While scientific literature is only one of four components that make up evidence-based practice (EBP), it can be the most overwhelming one. Luckily Steven ten Have and his co-authors put 18 common organizational change axioms to the test for in their 2017 book *Reconsidering Change Management*.

Top half of graph

Very high-to-moderate quality evidence available; in other words, there is more certainty for the conclusion.

Quadrant 1

Likely to be true (in order of strength of conclusion).

- Axiom 17—Financial incentives are an effective way to encourage change and improve performance.
- Axiom 15—Goal setting combined with feedback is a powerful tool for change leaders.
- Axiom 7—Supervisory support is critical for the success of change.
- Axiom 4—Trust in the leader is needed for successful change.
- Axiom 16—Commitment to change is an essential component of a successful change initiative.
- Axiom 8—To realize change in organizations, a powerful guiding coalition is needed.

Quadrant 2

Unlikely to be true (in order of strength of conclusion).

- Axiom 5—When managing change, a transformational leadership style is more effective than a transactional one.
- Axiom 6—Organizational change requires leaders with strong emotional intelligence (EI or EQ).
- Axiom 10—Participation is key for successful change.
- Axiom 1—70% of all change interventions fail.

Data point in the center

There is not enough evidence to say with any certainty one way or another; in other words, we simply don't know if this is true or untrue.

- Axiom 18—Self-managing teams perform better in realizing change than traditionally managed teams.

Bottom half of graph

Low-to-poor quality evidence available; in other words, there is less certainty for either conclusion, likelihood to be true or false.

Quadrant 3

Probably untrue but more and better evidence is needed to increase certainty (in order of strength of conclusion).

- Axiom 11—Resistance to change should be defused early on in the change process.

Quadrant 4

Might be true but more and better evidence is needed to increase certainty (in order of strength of conclusion).

- Axiom 12—A fair change process is important in achieving successful change.
- Axiom 2—A clear vision is essential for successful change.
- Axiom 9—Employees' capability to change determines the organization's capacity to change.

- Axiom 3—People will not change without a sense of urgency.
- Axiom 13—Organizational culture is difficult and time consuming to change.
- Axiom 14—Organizational culture is related to performance.

Information disorder: A primer

[APPENDIX EXTRACTED FROM PAUL'S UNPUBLISHED MANUSCRIPT TRUTH WARS.]

"The idea that the 'common man' should evaluate truth for themselves, using reason and evidence, is new and perhaps the most liberating and important historical transformation in human consciousness. This radical idea upended the stranglehold that kings and priests had on truth before the Enlightenment and ushered in the scientific revolution, the notion of equal rights for all humans, and the democratic revolutions of the 18th century."

PAUL GIBBONS (*TRUTH WARS* MANUSCRIPT)

In the mid-2010s and three decades into the Internet age, professionals from information theory, media studies, political theory, and philosophy began to observe growth of a novel phenomenon.

This phenomenon, which includes more familiar terms such as fake news and post-truth, would soon be called information disorder.

When the term was coined in 2016, much more information was reaching us digitally, people began to consume news predominantly from social media, and there was a diversification of alternative information sources—think miracle-bleach cures. The theory posits that the information base upon which we make decisions in all our life roles (e.g., voters, citizens, consumers, parents) has been corrupted. Information disorder is defined narrowly by some experts in terms of the speaker (institutional or personal). By this definition, there are three categories:

1. **Disinformation** is sharing false content with intent to harm,
2. **Misinformation** is sharing content without realizing it is false, and
3. **Malinformation** is sharing information loosely tied to facts but with intent to harm.

We define information disorder more broadly. Not just as a condition of the speaker (their truthfulness and intent), but as a systemic, cognitive, technological, and cultural phenomenon that affects the transmission and the reception of information, and the outcomes and decisions that result.

A macabre example

"A wealth of information creates a poverty of attention."

HERBERT SIMON (NOBEL PRIZE WINNER IN ECONOMICS)

Take the Comet Pizzeria shooting of 2016. Shooter Edgar Welch believed former Secretary of State Clinton and her "cabal" were running a paedophile ring in the basement of the Washington D.C. pizzeria. He travelled 368 miles to the restaurant with his AR-15, opened fire, and was arrested. Thankfully no lives were lost.

Information disorder affected each step in Welch's decision:

- How did receive the information? (Alternative, fake news transmitted through technology.)
- Why did he believe it was true? (Cultural and network effects, and cognitive frailty.)
- From where, even if he believed it, did he get the license to act? (Cultural norms around violence.)

The misinformation, the "data" if you will, is but a tiny slice of what was causal in this event. Welch believed something extraordinary and false. He believed it so strongly because the existence of this sex-slave ring was accepted as a firm truth in his online communities. His knowledge was cultural, not just personal.

He got his information from the Internet—which at its noblest should make humans more informed and more connected to one another. The truth is more complex.

The information Welch relied upon hits an organic information processor that makes systematic errors in cognition (i.e., the brain). If we were to imagine a perfectly rational and disciplined researcher, a truth seeker in Welch, his critical thinking and investigative skills might have unearthed the actual truth or shed enough doubt to dissuade him from violence.

Sketching boundaries

"We have terrible cultural habits when it comes to information. In short, we spend far too much time interrogating and disputing what we disagree with and far too little time trying to triple-check things we agree with."

PAUL GIBBONS (*TRUTH WARS* MANUSCRIPT)

Nobody is likely to kill anybody over organizational change, but information disorder, defined broadly as we do, affects our information world and our world as change professionals. Without presenting a flawed and necessarily simplified infographic, here is a rough sketch of the problem's dimensions:

- The **quantity of information** we receive has grown exponentially. Information scientists estimate that we collectively receive several zettabytes (that is 21 zeros) of digital information per day, or 175 newspapers per person per day. While matter moves approximately at the same speed as in 1923 (think oil tankers), information travels roughly a trillion times faster (think analogue radio to digitally compressed video files).

- Sources of information have **diversified and democratized.** That sounds good, even ideal, but anyone with a keyboard and enough marketing flair can become an authority.

- Moreover, most people get their news first from social media—and most of what you see on social media is shared by connections. There is no longer a passive consumer and an active producer—each of us is an **information "prosumer."** Few have the editorial, research, and fact-checking skills of an experienced journalist.

- The information we receive is **algorithmically filtered.** Items with the most clicks get even more attention—a viral phenomenon. However, "clicks" are largely emotional responses. Particularly in politics, the most salacious content gets the most clicks. (On LinkedIn, the most feel-good content gets the most clicks.) As Guardian editor Katherine Viner puts it, "publishers that are funded by algorithmic ads are locked in a race to the bottom in pursuit of any audience they can find—desperately binge-publishing without checking facts, pushing out the most shrill and most extreme stories to boost clicks."

- Humans are **cognitively and attentionally challenged**. Cognitively, our biases lean us toward "like" where we already believe and digging into what we suspect to be false (see 22 such biases in Figure XIII.2). Attentionally, each of us has fewer hours than we would like and almost none of us have the hours to fact-check every social media post.

- What passes for "good" content is **culturally determined.** Our culture, click-addicted, and forever doom-scrolling, values readability, brevity, salience, and emotions. Another culture—in an alien world—might value reasoned, fact-laden argument. Moreover, we think in tribes—what we believe is socially determined.

- **Post-truth** was the Word of the Year in 2016. As philosopher Frankfurt reminded us in chapter XII, the truth-teller has a commitment to the truth, the liar a commitment to falsehood, the post-truth (bullshitter) cares about neither truth nor falsehood.

- What counts as authority is manipulated by **corporate misinformation** campaigns. For example, in 2020, 11 million people died from smoking-related illnesses and there were 1.1-billion smokers worldwide. Yet a causal link between smoking and heart disease and cancer was established in the 1960s. (Imagine something else on the shelves of the grocery stores that killed just a dozen people, never mind millions. Quiz: There is another substance as harmful as tobacco in grocery stores, prizes for guessing what it is.)

- In a less direct way, **popularity and commercial success become proxies for validity.** The marketing and commercial presence of MBTI, for example, lends truthfulness to its claims (how could something everybody uses be false?).

- The media, the **Fourth Estate,** at its most noble, intermediates between the complexity of the world and the citizen. Historically, or at least ideally, the job of the news was to inform, not inflame or entertain. However, boundaries are blurring resulting in edu-tainment, info-tainment, and adver-torials. Traditional media, arguably the most committed to truthful accounts must compete for clicks, advertisers, and eyeballs with salacious, polarized media. This affects specialized press, such as in organizational change, where dull stories and books on myths with nuanced conclusions and alpha coefficients compete with pat, trivial, oversimplistic, and easily understandable content.

Most important "war" of our age?

In an ideal world, we would get the real truth about products we consume, choices we make, and people we vote for. As individuals we tend to lie when it suits us. Corporations and politicians have something to sell. The media need viewers, clicks, and subscribers. Our information processing system is flawed. The truths we get are increasingly corrupted, and when these corrupted truths meet our limited cognitive abilities and cognitive weaknesses, we make choices based on half-truths or outright lies.

We buy that product that claims to make us richer, thinner, happier. We vote for people who are (often) feeding us nonsense. This world is characterized by a glut of information and a scarcity of facts—some of this is life threatening. Thirty years ago, there were "tobacco wars" as big tobacco spent tens of billions to persuade us that smoking was not harmful (despite science that had been around for 50 years and conclusive for decades). Today that war (on you) is fought on many fronts. Is vaccination essential for the health of children (or does it cause autism)? Is sugar the new tobacco, as harmful to public health and subject to the same kind of disinformation campaign? Are GMOs dangerous? Is gluten bad for you? Is fluoridated drinking water harmful or necessary? Do homeopathy and acupuncture work? Does big pharma manipulate drug trials to their benefit and our detriment? Do over-the-counter medicines work? Is low-fat or low carb really low, and does it matter?

Money can't buy happiness, but it can buy truth. In the information age, information is a powerful weapon. In our complex world, in which we are inundated by low-quality information, we need to worry. How much influence does big money have on our perception of facts and reality? How much of the money spent to influence us is either in our interests, harmless puffery, or contrary to our interests? We pride ourselves on our liberty, our freedom to make important decisions that affect our lives. Yet, if our beliefs are constantly muddied by powerful interests, how free are we? Should we worry about climate "research" paid for by fossil fuel companies, celebrity doctors peddling pseudoscience, consumer protection policies written by corporate lobbyists, and falsely marketed health products that cost lives?

REFERENCES

Alshehhi, K., & Zawbaa, S. (2021). Employee retention prediction in corporate organizations using machine learning methods. *Academy of Entrepreneurship*, March.

Ariely, D. (2010). *Predictably irrational: the hidden forces that shape our decisions*. New York: Harper Perennial.

Armenakis, A. A., Bernerth, J. B., Pitts, J., & Walker, H. J. (2007). Organizational change recipients' beliefs scale: development of an assessment instrument. *The Journal of Applied Behavioral Science*, *43*(4), 481-505.

Bonanno, G. A., Wortman, C. B., Lehman, D. R., Tweed, R. G., Haring, M., Sonnega, J., Carr, D., & Nesse, R. M. (2002). Resilience to loss and chronic grief: a prospective study from preloss to 18-months postloss. *Journal of Personality and Social Psychology*, *83*(5), 1150-1164.

Briner, R. (2018). Do personality types have a place in HR? *HR Magazine*, Nov, retrieved from https://www.hrmagazine.co.uk/content/features/do-personality-typing-tools-have-a-place-in-hr

Burnes, B. (2004). Kurt Lewin and the planned approach to change: a re-appraisal. *Journal of Management Studies*, *41*(6), 977-1002.

Byrne, B., & Callaghan, G. (2014). *Complexity theory and the social sciences*. New York: Routledge.

The Center for Complicated Grief at Columbia University, retrieved Sept. 2022 from www.prolongedgrief.columbia.edu

Coch, L., & French, J.R.P. (1948). Overcoming resistance to change. *Human Relations*, *1*(4), 512-532.

Coffield, F. (2004). *Learning styles and pedagogy in post–16 learning: a systematic and critical review.* London: Learning and Skills Research Centre.

Collins, J. C. (2001). *Good to great, why some companies make the leap and others don't.* New York: HarperBusiness.

Collins, J. C., & Porras, J. I. (1994). *Built to last: successful habits of visionary companies.* New York: HarperBusiness Essentials.

Conner, D. R. (1992). *Managing at the speed of change: how resilient managers succeed and prosper where others fail.* New York: Random House.

Conte, J. M., & Landy, F. J. (2019). *Work in the 21st century: an introduction to industrial and organizational psychology* (6th ed.). Hoboken, NJ: Wiley.

Covey, S. R. (1989). *The 7 habits of highly effective people: powerful lessons in personal change.* New York: Free Press.

Crowley, K. (2022). Exxon's exodus: employees have finally had enough of its toxic culture. *Bloomberg Businessweek*, retrieved from https://www.bloomberg.com/news/features/2022-10-13/exxon-xom-jobs-exodus-brings-scrutiny-to-corporate-culture

Cummings, S., Bridgman, T., & Brown, K. G. (2016). Unfreezing change as three steps: rethinking Kurt Lewin's legacy for change management. *Human Relations, 69*(1), 33-60.

Curry, L. (1990). A critique of the research on learning styles. *Educational Leadership, 48*(2), 50-56.

Dembo, M. H., & Howard, K. (2007). Advice about the use of learning styles: a major myth in education. *Journal of College Reading and Learning, 37*(2).

Dent, E. B., & Goldberg, S. G. (1999). Challenging resistance to change. *The Journal of Applied Behavioral Science, 35*(1), 25-41.

Digman, J. M. (1990). Personality structure: emergence of the Five-Factor Model. *Annual Review of Psychology, 41*, 417-440.

Elrod, P. D., & Tippett, D. D. (2002). The "death valley" of change. *Journal of Organizational Change Management, 15*(3), 273-291.

Emre, M. (2018). *The personality brokers: the strange history of Myers–Briggs and the birth of personality testing.* New York: Doubleday.

Epstein, D. (2019). *Range: why generalists triumph in a specialized world.* New York: Riverhead Books.

Falk, A. (2008). *Anti-semitism: a history and psychoanalysis of contemporary hatred.* Westport, CT: Praeger, 110–111.

Fodor, J. (2009). Diary. *London Review of Books, 21*(19), 68-69.

Frankfurt, H. G. (2005). *On bullshit.* Princeton, NJ: Princeton University Press.

Frazier, M. L., Fainshmidt, S., Klinger, R. L., Pezeshkan, A., & Vracheva, V. (2017). Psychological safety: a meta-analytic review and extension. *Personnel Psychology, 70,* 113-165.

Frost, P. J., & Egri, C. P. (1994). The shamanic perspective on organizational change and development. *Journal of Organizational Change Management,* Feb.

Furey, W. (2020). The stubborn myth of "learning styles" —state teacher-license prep materials peddle a debunked theory. *Education Next, 20*(3), 8-12.

Galen, F. (1869). *Hereditary genius.* London: Macmillan Publishers.

Gardner, W., & Martinko, M. (1996). Using the Myers-Briggs Type Indicator to study managers: a literature review and research agenda. *Journal of Management, 22*(1).

Gibbons, P. (2019). *Impact: 21st century change management, behavioral science, digital transformation, and the future of work.* Denver, CO: Phronesis Media.

Gibbons, P. (2019). *The science of organizational change: how leaders set strategy, change behavior, and create an agile culture.* Denver, CO: Phronesis Media.

Gibbons, P., & Barrett, S. (2018). How to spot quackery! Chiropractic, vitamins, chelation, homeopathy, and other health frauds. *Think Bigger, Think Better* podcast, April.

Gibbons, P., & Lilienfeld, S. (2018). Learning styles, neurobabble, and other psychological myths. *Think Bigger, Think Better* podcast, March.

Grant, A. (2014). Five myths about introverts and extroverts at work. *Government Executive*, retrieved from https://www.govexec.com/management/2014/02/5-myths-about-introverts-and-extroverts-work/79055/

Hanley, S. (2008). Autolist study shows environmental concerns have little impact on car buying decisions. *Clean Technica*, retrieved from https://cleantechnica.com/2018/09/10/autolist-study-shows-environmental-concerns-have-little-impact-on-car-buying-decisions/

Heath, C., & Heath, D. (2010). *Switch: how to change things when change is hard*. New York: Currency.

Hogarth, R. (2001). *Educating intuition*. Chicago, IL: University of Chicago Press.

Holt, D. T., Armenakis, A. A., Field, H. S., & Harris, S. G. (2007). Readiness for organizational change: the systematic development of a scale. *The Journal of Applied Behavioral Science, 43*(2), 232-255.

Hughes, M. (2011). Do 70 percent of all organizational change initiatives really fail? *Journal of Change Management, 11*(4), 451-464.

Husmann, V. et al. (2018). Another nail in the coffin for learning styles? Disparities among undergraduate anatomy students' study strategies, class performance, and reported VARK learning styles. *Anatomical Sciences Education, 12*(1).

Janusz, M. L., & Czapinski, G. P. (1992). Positive-negative asymmetry or when the heart needs a reason. *European Journal of Social Psychology, 22*(5), 425-434.

Judge, T. A., Bono, J. E., Ilies, R., & Gerhardt, M. W. (2002). Personality and leadership: a qualitative and quantitative review. *Journal of Applied Psychology, 87*, 765-780.

Kahneman, D. (2011). *Thinking, fast and slow*. New York: Farrar, Strauss, and Giroux.

Kahneman, D., & Klein, G. (2009). Conditions for intuitive expertise: a failure to disagree. *American Psychologist, 64*(6), 515-526.

Konnikova, M. (2020). *The biggest bluff: how I learned to pay attention, master myself, and win*. New York: Penguin Books.

Konnikova, M. (2016). *The confidence game: why we fall for it...every time*. New York: Penguin Books.

Kotter, J. P. (2008). *A sense of urgency*. Boston, MA: Harvard Business School Press.

Kotter, J. P. (1996). *Leading change*. Boston, MA: Harvard Business School Press.

Kuhn, T. S. (2012). *The structure of scientific revolutions* (4th ed.). Chicago: University of Chicago Press.

Lafuente-Lafuente, C., Leitao, C., Kilani, I., Kacher, Z., Engels, C., Canouï-Poitrine, F., & Belmin, J. (2019). Knowledge and use of evidence-based medicine in daily practice by health professionals: a cross-sectional survey. *BMJ Open, 9*(3), e025224.

Leedy, P. D., & Ormrod, J. E. (2013). *Practical research: planning and design* (10th ed.). Upper Saddle River, NJ: Pearson Education.

Lepore, J. (2014). The disruption machine: what the gospel of innovation gets wrong. *The New Yorker, Annals of Enterprise, 6*(23). Retrieved from https://www.newyorker.com/magazine/2014/06/23/the-disruption-machine

Levant, R. F. (2005). *Report of the 2005 presidential task force on evidence-based practice*. American Psychological Association (APA), 2005 Presidential Task Force.

Lewin, K. (1951) *Field theory in social science: selected theoretical papers* (ed. Cartwright D). New York: Harper & Row.

Lewin, K. (1947). Frontiers in group dynamics II: channels of group life; social planning and action research. *Human Relations*, *1*(2), 143-153.

Lewin, K. (1947). Frontiers in group dynamics: concept, method, and reality in social science; social equilibria and social change. *Human Relations*, *1*(1), 5-41.

Lilienfeld. S. O., Lynn, S. J., Ruscio, J., & Beyersyein, B. L. (2010). *50 great myths of popular psychology*. Malden, MA: Wiley-Blackwell.

Lovegrove, H. (2015). *The change manager's handbook*. London: Linchpin Books.

Mawson, A. R., Day, B. D., Bhuiyan, A. R., & Jacob, B. (2017). Pilot comparative study on the health of vaccinated and unvaccinated 6- to 12-year-old U.S. children. *Journal of Translational Science*, *3*(3), 1-12.

McCrae, R. R., Terraciano, A., & 79 members of the Personality Profiles of Culture Project (2005). Personality profiles of cultures: aggregate personality traits. *Journal of Personality and Social Psychology*, *89*, 407-425.

McCrae, R. R., & Costa, P. T. Jr. (1987). Validation of the Five-Factor Model of personality across instruments and observers. *Journal of Personality and Social Psychology*, *52*, 81-90.

McIntyre, L. (2021). *How to talk to a science denier*. Cambridge, MA: The MIT Press.

McIntyre, L. (2019). *Philosophy of science: a contemporary introduction*. New York: Routledge.

Melchert, T. P. (2007). Strengthening the scientific foundations of professional psychology: time for the next steps. *Professional Psychology: Research and Practice*, *38*(1), 34-43.

Menninger, W. W. (1975). *The meaning of morale: a Peace Corps model. Business and Society in Change*. New York: American Telephone and Telegraph Co.

The Myers-Briggs Company. Retrieved from https://www.themyers-briggs.com

Nikula, U., Jurvanen, C., Gotel, O., & Gause, D.C. (2010). Empirical validation of the classic change curve on a software technology change project. *Information and Software Technology, 52,* 680-696.

Paschler, H., McDaniel, M., Rohrer, D., & Bjork, R. (2008). Learning styles: concepts and evidence. *Psychological Science in the Public Interest, 9*(3), 105-119.

Patterson, R.W., & Conner, D.R. (1982). Building commitment to organizational change. *Training and Development Journal, 36*(4), 18-30.

Patton, M. Q. (2014). *Qualitative research & evaluation methods: integrating theory and practice* (4th ed.). Thousand Oaks, CA: Sage.

Perlman, D., & Takacs, G. J. (1990). The ten stages of change. *Nursing Management, 21*(4), 33.

Peters, T. J., & Waterman, R. H (1983) *In search of excellence: lessons from Americas best-run companies.* New York: HarperBusiness Essentials.

Pfeffer, J. (2022). *Seven rules of power: surprising—but true—on how to get things done and advance your career.* Dallas, TX: Matt Holt.

Pittenger, D. J. (2005). Cautionary comments regarding the Myers-Briggs Type Indicator. *Consulting Psychology Journal: Practice and Research, 57*(3), 210-221.

Pittenger, D. J. (1993). Measuring the MBTI and coming up short. *Journal of Career Planning and Employment,* Jan.

Popper, K. (1957). *Science: conjectures and refutations.* British Philosophy Mid-century, Mace.

Porter, J., & Jick, H. (1980). Addiction rare in patients treated with narcotics. *New England Journal of Medicine, 302*(2), 123.

Prosci (2020). *Best practices in change management* (11th ed.). Fort Collins, CO: Prosci Inc.

Rawson, K., Stahovich, T. F., & Mayer, R. E. (2017). Homework and achievement: using smartpen technology to find the connection. *Journal of Educational Psychology, 109*(2), 208-219.

Robson, D. (2008). Hate circuit discovered in brain. *New Scientist*. Retrieved from https://www.newscientist.com/article/dn15060-hate-circuit-discovered-in-brain/

Rock, D. (2009). Managing with the brain in mind. *Strategy+Business*, *56*.

Rock, D., & Page, L. J. (2009). *Coaching with the brain in mind: foundations for practice*. Hoboken, NJ: Wiley & Sons, Inc.

Rock, D., & Schwartz, J. (2006). The neuroscience of leadership. *Strategy+Business*, *43*.

Rozenblit, L., & Keil, F. (2002). The misunderstood limits of folk science: an illusion of explanatory depth. *Cognitive Science*, *26*(5), 521-562.

Rosenzweig, P. M. (2007). *The halo effect…and the eight other business delusions that deceive managers*. New York: Free Press

Rubin, A., & Bellamy, J. (2012). *Practitioner's guide to using research for evidence-based practice* (2nd ed.). Hoboken, NJ: John Wiley & Sons.

Rubin, A. (2008). *Practitioner's guide to using research for evidence-based practice* (1st ed.). Hoboken, NJ: John Wiley & Sons, Inc.

Rudolph, C. W., Rauvola, R. S., Costanza, D. P., & Zacher, H. (2021). Generations and generational differences: debunking myths in organizational science and practice and paving new paths forward. *Journal of Business Psychology*, *36*(6), 945-967.

Sarayreh, B. H., Khudair, H., & Barakat, E. A. (2013). Comparative study: the Kurt Lewin of change management. *International Journal of Computer and Information Technology*, *2*(4), 626-629.

Satel, S., & Lilienthal S. (2013). *Brainwashed: the subjective appeal of mindless neuroscience*. New York: Basic Books, 12.

Scarlett, H. (2019). *Neuroscience for organizational change* (2nd ed.). Kogan Page, retrieved from https://www.perlego.com/book/1589966/neuroscience-for-organizational-change-an-evidencebased-practical-guide-to-managing-change-pdf

Schein, E. (2005). From brainwashing to organization therapy, a conceptual and empirical journey in search of systemic health and a general model of change dynamics: a drama in five acts. *Organizational Studies, 27*(2), 287-301.

Schein, E. (1961). *Coercive persuasion: a socio-psychological analysis of the "brainwashing" of American civilian prisoners by the Chinese Communists.* New York: W.W. Norton.

Schmidt, F. L., & Hunter, J. E. (1998). The validity and utility of selection methods in personnel psychology: practical and theoretical implications of 85 years of research findings. *Psychological Bulletin, 124*(2), 262–274.

Scriven, M. (1972). *Objectivity and subjectivity in educational research.* In L. G. Thomas (Ed.), Philosophical redirection of educational research: the seventy-first yearbook of the national society for the study of education (pp. 94–142). Chicago, IL: University of Chicago Press.

Senge, P. (1990). *The fifth discipline: the art and practice of the learning organization.* New York: Random House.

Seth, A. (2021). *Being you: a new science of consciousness.* New York: Dutton (an imprint of Penguin Random House LLC).

Shermer, M. (2008). Five fallacies of grief: debunking psychological stages. *Scientific American,* https://www.scientificamerican.com/article/five-fallacies-of-grief/

Stroebe M., Schut H., & Boerner K. (2017). Cautioning health-care professionals. *Omega (Westport), 74*(4), 455-473.

ten Have, S., ten Have, W., Huijsmans, A., & Otto, M. (2017). *Reconsidering change management: applying evidence-based insights to change management practice.* New York: Routledge.

Thebault, R. (2019). Three French executives were convicted in the suicides of their workers. *The Washington Post,* retrieved from https://www.washingtonpost.com/world/2019/12/20/three-french-executives-were-convicted-suicides-their-workers/

Tuckman, B., & Jensen, M. (1977). Stages of small-group development revisited. *Group & Organization Management, 2*(4), 419-427.

Tuckman, B. (1965). Developmental sequence in small groups. *Psychological Bulletin, 63*(6), 384-99.

United States government. (2020). Wells Fargo agrees to pay $3 billion to resolve criminal and civil investigations into sales practices involving the opening of millions of accounts without customer authorization. *Department of Justice, Office of Public Affairs*, retrieved from https://www.justice.gov/opa/pr/wells-fargo-agrees-pay-3-billion-resolve-criminal-and-civil-investigations-sales-practices

Uttal, W. (2003). *The new phrenology: the limits of localizing cognitive processes in the brain.* Cambridge: MIT Press.

Vaillant, G. E. (2012). *Triumphs of experience: the men of the Harvard grant study.* Cambridge, MA: Belknap Press (an Imprint of Harvard University Press).

Wardle, C., & Derakhshan, H. (2017). *Information disorder: toward an interdisciplinary framework for research and policy making.* Council of Europe, retrieved from https://shorensteincenter.org/information-disorder-framework-for-research-and-policymaking/

Wilkinson, D. (nd). Is the change curve a myth? *Oxford Review*, retrieved from https://oxford-review.com/is-the-change-curve-real/

ENDNOTES

1 Shermer, M. (2008). Five fallacies of grief: debunking psychological stages. *Scientific American*, https://www.scientificamerican.com/article/five-fallacies-of-grief/

2 Gibbons, P. (2019). *The science of organizational change: how leaders set strategy, change behavior, and create an agile culture*. Denver, CO: Phronesis Media.

3 LIAR is based on the work of philosopher Jenny Duke-Yonge at Macquarie University.

4 The Center for Complicated Grief at Columbia University, retrieved Sept. 2022 from www.prolongedgrief.columbia.edu

5 Bonanno, G. A., Wortman, C. B., Lehman, D. R., Tweed, R. G., Haring, M., Sonnega, J., Carr, D., & Nesse, R. M. (2002). Resilience to loss and chronic grief: a prospective study from preloss to 18-months postloss. *Journal of Personality and Social Psychology*, *83*(5), 1150-1164.

6 Stroebe M., Schut H., & Boerner K. (2017). Cautioning health-care professionals. *Omega (Westport)*, *74*(4), 455-473.

7 **Full disclosure:** Tricia is an Oxford Review member, and both appreciates and values David's work, although she does feel he missed the mark on change curves. (See https://Oxford-Review.com for more information and https://Oxford-Review.net for the members' community.)

8 Wilkinson, D. (nd). Is the change curve a myth? *Oxford Review*, retrieved from https://oxford-review.com/is-the-change-curve-real/

9 Menninger, W. W. (1975). The meaning of morale: a Peace Corps model. *Business and Society in Change*. New York: American Telephone and Telegraph Co.

10 Perlman, D., & Takacs, G. J. (1990). The ten stages of change. *Nursing Management*, *21*(4), 33.

11 Elrod, P. D., & Tippett, D. D. (2002). The "death valley" of change. *Journal of Organizational Change Management*, *15*(3), 273-291.

12 Nikula, U., Jurvanen, C., Gotel, O., & Gause, D.C. (2010). Empirical validation of the classic change curve on a software technology change project. *Information and Software Technology*, *52*, 680-696.

13 Frost, P. J., & Egri, C. P. (1994). The shamanic perspective on organizational change and development. *Journal of Organizational Change Management*, Feb.

14 Lepore, J. (2014). The disruption machine: what the gospel of innovation gets wrong. *The New Yorker*, *Annals of Enterprise*, *6*(23). Retrieved from https://www.newyorker.com/magazine/2014/06/23/the-disruption-machine

15 Rozenblit, L., & Keil, F. (2002). The misunderstood limits of folk science: an illusion of explanatory depth. *Cognitive Science*, *26*(5), 521-562.

16 Kahneman, D. (2011). *Thinking, fast and slow*. New York: Farrar, Strauss, and Giroux.

17 Hughes, M. (2011). Do 70 percent of all organizational change initiatives really fail? *Journal of Change Management*, *11*(4), 451-464.

18 McIntyre, L. (2021). *How to talk to a science denier*. Cambridge, MA: The MIT Press.

19 Mawson, A. R., Day, B. D., Bhuiyan, A. R., & Jacob, B. (2017). Pilot comparative study on the health of vaccinated and unvaccinated 6- to 12-year-old U.S. children. *Journal of Translational Science*, *3*(3), 1-12.

20 Porter, J., & Jick, H. (1980). Addiction rare in patients treated with narcotics. *New England Journal of Medicine*, *302*(2), 123.

21 Lovegrove, H. (2015). *The change manager's handbook*. London: Linchpin Books.

22 The Myers-Briggs Company. Retrieved from https://www.themyersbriggs.com

23 Insights Discovery®. Retrieved from https://www.insights.com/

24 Emre, M. (2018). *The personality brokers: the strange history of Myers-Briggs and the birth of personality testing*. New York: Doubleday.

25 Galen, F. (1869). *Hereditary genius*. London: Macmillan Publishers.

26 Falk, A. (2008). *Anti-semitism: a history and psychoanalysis of contemporary hatred*. Westport, CT: Praeger.

27 Konnikova, M. (2016). *The confidence game: why we fall for it…every time*. New York: Penguin Books.

28 Briner, R. (2018). Do personality types have a place in HR? *HR Magazine*, Nov, retrieved from https://www.hrmagazine.co.uk/content/features/do-personality-typing-tools-have-a-place-in-hr

29 Grant, A. (2014). Five myths about introverts and extroverts at work. *Government Executive*, retrieved from https://www.govexec.com/management/2014/02/5-myths-about-introverts-and-extroverts-work/79055/

30 **See:** Digman, J. M. (1990). Personality structure: emergence of the Five-Factor Model. *Annual Review of Psychology, 41*, 417-440.

McCrae, R. R., & Costa, P. T. Jr. (1987). Validation of the Five-Factor Model of personality across instruments and observers. *Journal of Personality and Social Psychology, 52*, 81-90.

McCrae, R. R., Terraciano, A., & 79 members of the Personality Profiles of Culture Project (2005). Personality profiles of cultures: aggregate personality traits. *Journal of Personality and Social Psychology, 89*, 407-425.

31 Conte, J. M., & Landy, F. J. (2019). *Work in the 21st century: an introduction to industrial and organizational psychology* (6th ed.). Hoboken, NJ: Wiley.

32 Pittenger, D. J. (1993). Measuring the MBTI and coming up short. *Journal of Career Planning and Employment*, Jan.

33 Pittenger, D. J. (2005). Cautionary comments regarding the Myers-Briggs Type Indicator. *Consulting Psychology Journal: Practice and Research, 57*(3), 210-221.

34 Schmidt, F. L., & Hunter, J. E. (1998). The validity and utility of selection methods in personnel psychology: practical and theoretical implications of 85 years of research findings. *Psychological Bulletin, 124*(2), 262–274.

35 Gardner, W., & Martinko, M. (1996). Using the Myers-Briggs Type Indicator to study managers: a literature review and research agenda. *Journal of Management, 22*(1).

36 Judge, T. A., Bono, J. E., Ilies, R., & Gerhardt, M. W. (2002). Personality and leadership: a qualitative and quantitative review. *Journal of Applied Psychology, 87*, 765-780.

37 **See:** Tuckman, B. (1965). Developmental sequence in small groups. *Psychological Bulletin, 63*(6), 384-99.

   Tuckman, B., & Jensen, M. (1977). Stages of small-group development revisited. *Group & Organization Management, 2*(4), 419-427.

38 Ariely, D. (2010). *Predictably irrational: the hidden forces that shape our decisions.* New York: Harper Perennial.

39 Alshehhi, K., & Zawbaa, S. (2021). Employee retention prediction in corporate organizations using machine learning methods. *Academy of Entrepreneurship*, March.

40 **See**: Pfeffer, J. (2022). *Seven rules of power: surprising—but true—on how to get things done and advance your career.* Dallas, TX: Matt Holt.

41 Dunning-Kruger effect is contested, but the balance of current evidence weighs in its favor.

42 Lafuente-Lafuente, C., Leitao, C., Kilani, I., Kacher, Z., Engels, C., Canouï-Poitrine, F., & Belmin, J. (2019). Knowledge and use of evidence-based medicine in daily practice by health professionals: a cross-sectional survey. *BMJ Open, 9*(3), e025224.

43 Coch, L., & French, J.R.P. (1948). Overcoming resistance to change. *Human Relations, 1*(4), 512-532.

44 Byrne, B., & Callaghan, G. (2014). *Complexity theory and the social sciences.* New York: Routledge.

45 Dent, E. B., & Goldberg, S. G. (1999). Challenging resistance to change. *The Journal of Applied Behavioral Science, 35*(1), 25-41.

46 ten Have, S., ten Have, W., Huijsmans, A., & Otto, M. (2017). *Reconsidering change management: applying evidence-based insights to change management practice.* New York: Routledge.

47 Senge, P. (1990). *The fifth discipline: the art and practice of the learning organization.* New York: Random House.

48 Furey, W. (2020). The stubborn myth of "learning styles"—state teacher-license prep materials peddle a debunked theory. *Education Next, 20*(3), 8-12.

49 Lilienfeld. S. O., Lynn, S. J., Ruscio, J., & Beyersyein, B. L. (2010). *50 great myths of popular psychology.* Malden, MA: Wiley-Blackwell.

50 Paschler, H., McDaniel, M., Rohrer, D., & Bjork, R. (2008). Learning styles: concepts and evidence. *Psychological Science in the Public Interest, 9*(3), 105-119.

51 Rawson, K., Stahovich, T. F., & Mayer, R. E. (2017). Homework and achievement: using smartpen technology to find the connection. *Journal of Educational Psychology, 109*(2), 208-219.

52 Coffield, F. (2004). *Learning styles and pedagogy in post-16 learning: a systematic and critical review.* London: Learning and Skills Research Centre.

53 Dembo, M. H., & Howard, K. (2007). Advice about the use of learning styles: a major myth in education. *Journal of College Reading and Learning, 37*(2).

54 Husmann, V. et al. (2018). Another nail in the coffin for learning styles? Disparities among undergraduate anatomy students' study strategies, class performance, and reported VARK learning styles. *Anatomical Sciences Education, 12*(1).

55 Idem.

56 Gibbons, P., & Lilienfeld, S. (2018). Learning styles, neurobabble, and other psychological myths. *Think Bigger, Think Better* podcast, March.

57 Heath, C., & Heath, D. (2010). *Switch: how to change things when change is hard.* New York: Currency.

58 Kotter, J. P. (1996). *Leading change.* Boston, MA: Harvard Business School Press.

59 Kotter, J. P. (2008). *A sense of urgency.* Boston, MA: Harvard Business School Press.

60 Conner, D. R. (1992). *Managing at the speed of change: how resilient managers succeed and prosper where others fail.* New York: Random House.

61 Schein, E. (2005). From brainwashing to organization therapy, a conceptual and empirical journey in search of systemic health and a general model of change dynamics: a drama in five acts. *Organizational Studies, 27*(2), 287-301.

62 Sarayreh, B. H., Khudair, H., & Barakat, E. A. (2013). Comparative study: the Kurt Lewin of change management. *International Journal of Computer and Information Technology, 2*(4), 626-629.

63 Schein, E. (1961). *Coercive persuasion: a socio-psychological analysis of the "brainwashing" of American civilian prisoners by the Chinese Communists.* New York: W.W. Norton.

64 ten Have, S., ten Have, W., Huijsmans, A., & Otto, M. (2017). *Reconsidering change management: applying evidence-based insights to change management practice.* New York: Routledge

65 Crowley, K. (2022). Exxon's exodus: employees have finally had enough of its toxic culture. *Bloomberg Businessweek*, retrieved from https://www. bloomberg.com/news/features/2022-10-13/exxon-xom-jobs-exodus-brings-scrutiny-to-corporate-culture

66 United States government. (2020). Wells Fargo agrees to pay $3 billion to resolve criminal and civil investigations into sales practices involving the opening of millions of accounts without customer authorization. *Department of Justice, Office of Public Affairs*, retrieved from https:// www.justice.gov/opa/pr/wells-fargo-agrees-pay-3-billion-resolve-criminal-and-civil-investigations-sales-practices

67 Thebault, R. (2019). Three French executives were convicted in the suicides of their workers. *The Washington Post*, retrieved from https:// www.washingtonpost.com/world/2019/12/20/three-french-executives-were-convicted-suicides-their-workers/

68 Covey, S. R. (1989). *The 7 habits of highly effective people: powerful lessons in personal change.* New York: Free Press.

69 Gibbons, P., & Barrett, S. (2018). How to spot quackery! Chiropractic, vitamins, chelation, homeopathy, and other health frauds. *Think Bigger, Think Better* podcast, April.

70 **See:** Center for Evidence-Based Management (CEBMa). Retrieved from https://cebma.org

Rubin, A., & Bellamy, J. (2012). *Practitioner's guide to using research for evidence-based practice* (2nd ed.). Hoboken, NJ: John Wiley & Sons.

Rubin, A. (2008). *Practitioner's guide to using research for evidence-based practice* (1st ed.). Hoboken, NJ: John Wiley & Sons, Inc.

71   Patton, M. Q. (2014). *Qualitative research & evaluation methods: integrating theory and practice* (4th ed.). Thousand Oaks, CA: Sage.

72   Collins, J. C. (2001). *Good to great: why some companies make the leap and others don't.* New York: HarperBusiness.

73   Collins, J. C., & Porras, J. I. (1994). *Built to last: successful habits of visionary companies.* New York: HarperBusiness Essentials.

74   Peters, T. J., & Waterman, R. H (1983) *In search of excellence: lessons from Americas best-run companies.* New York: HarperBusiness Essentials.

75   Vaillant, G. E. (2012). *Triumphs of experience: the men of the Harvard grant study.* Cambridge, MA: Belknap Press (an Imprint of Harvard University Press).

76   Rudolph, C. W., Rauvola, R. S., Costanza, D. P., & Zacher, H. (2021). Generations and generational differences: debunking myths in organizational science and practice and paving new paths forward. *Journal of Business Psychology, 36*(6), 945-967.

77   Hanley, S. (2008). Autolist study shows environmental concerns have little impact on car buying decisions. *Clean Technica,* retrieved from https://cleantechnica.com/2018/09/10/autolist-study-shows-environmental-concerns-have-little-impact-on-car-buying-decisions/

78   McIntyre, L. (2019). *Philosophy of science: a contemporary introduction.* New York: Routledge.

79   Rock, D. (2009). Managing with the brain in mind. *Strategy+Business, 56.*

80   **See:** Janusz, M. L., & Czapinski, G. P. (1992). Positive-negative asymmetry or when the heart needs a reason. *European Journal of Social Psychology, 22*(5), 425-434.

81   Robson, D. (2008). Hate circuit discovered in brain. *New Scientist,* retrieved from https://www.newscientist.com/article/dn15060-hate-circuit-discovered-in-brain/

82   Scarlett, H. (2019). *Neuroscience for organizational change* (2nd ed.). Kogan Page, retrieved from https://www.perlego.com/book/1589966/neuroscience-for-organizational-change-an-evidencebased-practical-guide-to-managing-change-pdf

83   Satel, S., & Lilienthal S. (2013). *Brainwashed: the subjective appeal of mindless neuroscience.* New York: Basic Books.

84 Fodor, J. (2009). Diary. *London Review of Books, 21*(19), 68-69.

85 Uttal, W. (2003). *The new phrenology: the limits of localizing cognitive processes in the brain.* Cambridge: MIT Press.

86 Lewin, K. (1947). Frontiers in group dynamics: concept, method, and reality in social science, social equilibria and social change. *Human Relations, 1*(1), 5-41.

87 Frankfurt, H. G. (2005). *On bullshit.* Princeton, NJ: Princeton University Press.

88 Popper, K. (1957). *Science: conjectures and refutations.* British Philosophy Mid-century, Mace.

89 Armenakis, A. A., Bernerth, J. B., Pitts, J., & Walker, H. J. (2007). Organizational change recipients' beliefs scale: development of an assessment instrument. *The Journal of Applied Behavioral Science, 43*(4), 481-505.

90 Holt, D. T., Armenakis, A. A., Field, H. S., & Harris, S. G. (2007). Readiness for organizational change: the systematic development of a scale. *The Journal of Applied Behavioral Science, 43*(2), 232-255.

91 Frazier, M. L., Fainshmidt, S., Klinger, R. L., Pezeshkan, A., & Vracheva, V. (2017). Psychological safety: a meta-analytic review and extension. *Personnel Psychology, 70,* 113-165.

92 Patterson, R.W., & Conner, D.R. (1982). Building commitment to organizational change. *Training and Development Journal, 36*(4), 18-30.

93 Kuhn, T. S. (2012). The structure of scientific revolutions (4th ed.). Chicago: University of Chicago Press.

94 Scriven, M. (1972). Objectivity and subjectivity in educational research. In L. G. Thomas (Ed.), Philosophical redirection of educational research: the seventy-first yearbook of the national society for the study of education (pp. 94–142). Chicago, IL: University of Chicago Press.

95 **See:** Melchert, T. P. (2007). Strengthening the scientific foundations of professional psychology: time for the next steps. *Professional Psychology: Research and Practice, 38*(1), 34-43.

Levant, R. F. (2005). Report of the 2005 presidential task force on evidence-based practice. *American Psychological Association (APA),* 2005 Presidential Task Force.

96　Leedy, P. D., & Ormrod, J. E. (2013). *Practical research: planning and design* (10th ed.). Upper Saddle River, NJ: Pearson Education.

97　**See:** Lewin, K. (1947). Frontiers in group dynamics: concept, method, and reality in social science, social equilibria and social change. *Human Relations, 1*(1), 5-41.

　　Lewin, K. (1951) *Field theory in social science: selected theoretical papers* (ed. Cartwright D). New York: Harper & Row.

98　**See**: Burnes, B. (2004). Kurt Lewin and the planned approach to change: a re-appraisal. *Journal of Management Studies, 41*(6), 977-1002.

　　Cummings, S., Bridgman, T., & Brown, K. G. (2016). Unfreezing change as three steps: rethinking Kurt Lewin's legacy for change management. *Human Relations, 69*(1), 33-60.

99　**See:** Epstein, D. (2019). *Range: why generalists triumph in a specialized world*. New York: Riverhead Books.

　　Hogarth, R. (2001). *Educating intuition*. Chicago, IL: University of Chicago Press.

　　Kahneman, D., & Klein, G. (2009). Conditions for intuitive expertise: a failure to disagree. *American Psychologist, 64*(6), 515-526.

Made in United States
Troutdale, OR
02/04/2024

17437885R00176